Wisdom for Parents

Wisdom for Parents

Key Ideas from Parent Educators

Edited by Certified Family Life Educators

Robert E. Keim, Ph.D., CFLE and

Arminta L. Jacobson, Ph.D., CFLE

Wisdom for Parents:
Key Ideas from Parent Educators

Edited by Robert E. Keim, Ph.D., CFLE and
Arminta L. Jacobson, Ph.D., CFLE

ISBN 978-1-897160-57-2

Publishers: de Sitter Publications, 2011, Robert E. Keim, 2017

Cover image:
Early morning fishing in autumn on a lake © geno sajko
www.fotolia.com

Cover and book design by de Sitter Publications
Chapter and page layout by: tanasigrafix.com

Ordering Information:
Order directly from the National Council on Family Relations online store: www.ncfr.org/store, click Shop NCFR's online Store, Publications. This benefits the fund raising goals of this book, helping the Certified Family Life Education program.

Printed in the United States of America

Table of Contents

Preface

What is one of the most important ideas about parenting–an idea that would benefit most parents? That is what this book is about. That question was answered by people who work with families, people who have studied the wisdom of parenting from scholars before them, people who care about you, your family, and your child or children. This book will share key parenting ideas by way of short articles or short descriptions in the last chapter.

During the last century, many approaches and theories have evolved, which you will discover more clearly in this book. It is filled with interesting, intriguing, insightful, and moving articles. In the last chapter, "Wisdom of the Ages," you will get a glimpse of key concepts of parenting as developed over the past eight or so decades.

Sometimes you will hear: "This book will give you all of the answers you will ever need!" No one should ever try to convince you that there is only one parenting book you will ever need or that there is one *best* parenting approach. This book **will be** a very helpful resource for you, but it is not the only parenting book you will ever need or want.

Unfortunately, some authors (not all, by any means) will infer or actually say that their approach is the one to use–when, in fact, it likely is not true. Such authors do a grave disservice to parents as well as other authors, theorists, and the broad parenting movement itself. Suggesting there is only one approach often leads to confusion for parents, causing them to think, "Whom can I believe? Why are there so many books out there on parenting when an author says I only need his/her book?" Or, parents might conclude: "The experts contradict each other, telling us different things to do, so why listen to them. We might just as well ignore them and do what common sense tells us!"–forgetting about Albert Einstein's observation, "common sense isn't too common."

Sometimes a given technique will work best with one problem or with a child with a particular temperament, or in some situations and not in others. Or, one parent may be drawn to one approach while another parent will not feel comfortable using it. Children are different, situations are different, parents are different, and approaches will differ. As parents we make a lot of choices about which method to use, sometimes trying a variety of ways before discovering which one works best–for us, for our child, in some particular situation. We hope that reading this book will provide you with more options for being a more effective parent.

An old proverb says, "*There's more than one way to skin a cat.*" Likewise, there usually are a number of ways to handle a given child-rearing problem. And so, in a way, we parent educators owe a collective apology to parents for some of the confusion they may have felt. It is our sincere hope that this book will help clarify some of this.

In terms of parenting programs offered in a community, there are many in which a parent can enroll. Honestly, over time, a parent likely would benefit by enrolling in several. Also, it is good to realize that most parenting programs and books all deal a little bit with some aspect of "communication skills." Our experience indicates that to significantly improve one's communication skills, more than a focus of just two or three sessions is needed. An actual parenting program of eight to ten sessions just focusing on communication skills would be best. An alternative to attending such a program would be to thoroughly read a book like Tom Gordon's, *P.E.T.: Parent Effectiveness Training* (mentioned later in this book), or Faber & Mazlish's book, *How to Talk so Kids will Listen and Listen so Kids will Talk.*

When Reading the Book:

You will find that many of the articles include references to various sources which might be of interest or helpful. Of course, some of the references are cited merely to provide support for what is being conveyed, making reference to research studies, evidence-based programs, or supporting theories.

Internet web sites often are listed for your use. Rather than meticulously trying to copy each letter of the address, or URL, you can merely Google an author's name and/or most of the title or words in the link and find the web site in that manner.

Read with Unhurried Reflection. We suggest that you read the articles with a reflective attitude, thinking of how the ideas might apply to your family or to your own actions. Try not to clutter your mind by reading too many articles during one sitting. For some articles, it might help to read the article again, after a day or so, reviewing the key ideas and gaining other impressions or ideas from its message. One researcher found that change comes best if we re-visit ideas in a couple of days and reinforce them by reading the ideas (or articles) again in about a week. Also, discussing an article in a book club, a parenting education group, or a college class would provide the perspectives of others and help you further reflect and apply what you have read.

Special Thanks to Michael H. Popkin

In 1984, within a year of the development of Michael Popkin's popular video based *Active Parenting* program (evolving now into Active Parenting Publishers, www.activeparenting.com), Popkin led a workshop which Co-Editor Keim attended. Impressed with Popkin's interpretation of the Adlerian approach (based essentially on the work of Rudolf Dreikurs, *Children: The challenge*, 1964), Keim began using Popkin's materials in his teaching, while also presenting other parenting approaches.

Of special note was Popkin's sharing of a humorous story of a fellow psychologist who had what he called his "Ten Ironclad Rules of Parenting." Then he had his own children and changed the name to "10 Guidelines for Parenting." "Now that my children are becoming teenagers," he said, "I'm thinking about changing it once again to 'Ten Helpful Hints.'"

This story, told by Michael Popkin, prompted Keim to develop his own "10." They were called the "10 Commandments for Parents" which he felt were important to share with most parents, although he realized that they might well have been titled: "10 Possible Ideas that Might Work Some of the Time with Some of Your Children; Good Luck!"

This concept of "key ideas," inspired by Popkin, is what led to the concept of this *wisdom* book. While attending a parent education focus group at an annual meeting of the National Council on Family Relations (NCFR), the idea of this book occurred. Very special thanks go to Michael Popkin for the results.

More on How this Book Came About

Slightly over 1,300 Certified Family Life Educators (CFLEs) were essentially asked this question: "What is your favorite, most important or unique *wisdom* or pet theme which you feel most parents should hear about regarding raising their children?" This book is the result of their responses, with spontaneous writings on topics they believe are very important for you to hear. The emphasis tends to be more upon character building, parent-child relationships, and guidance and discipline issues. Also, you will read some personal experience stories which convey the author's message, as well as several poems.

As mentioned earlier, there is a concluding, more comprehensive chapter on "Wisdom of the Ages," which includes parenting wisdom from writers and scholars spanning the past decades–wisdom that tends to not grow old, but still applies. You will find some unique and useful topics that have been "buried" over time in past writings. Some of the early articles in the book may allude to ideas you will read about in the last chapter; however, in it you will discover the roots of many of the childrearing approaches available today, under different names and different packaging. Granted, some of today's programs are seeking newer and more effective ways to convey these ideas to parents in different settings. So, upon reading the last chapter, you might begin to recognize the sources of some of the programs you encounter today. There are not too many brand new ideas today; often they are "discoveries" of the "wisdom of the ages."

We hope that you will read all of the articles in the spirit in which they were shared–*wisdom* that is spoken from the hearts of the authors, other men and women who happen to have focused their life's work on families and parenting issues. It is hoped that the articles help you in the task of raising your own children to become adults of whom you will be proud.

The CFLE authors are donating the proceeds of their writings to further the work of the CFLE program of the National Council of Family Relations.

A Note to College Teachers

This book, written to parents, may serve as a useful supplement for parent education, child development or marriage and family studies classes, providing helpful resources for students to use themselves or with parents. Students also may benefit from seeing the translation of theory and research into information for parents. Articles could serve well as a focus for group discussion on various topics. The first two items in the Appendix are guidelines to help facilitate group discussion.

Who Is a Certified Family Life Educator (CFLE)?

The National Council on Family Relations (NCFR) headquartered in Minneapolis, provides certification for the profession of family life education. Certification is awarded through completion of a CFLE-track of courses at one of over 120 NCFR approved academic programs,* or through the completion of the CFLE Exam. In order to receive Full Certification, work experience in family life education must be demonstrated.

The CFLE program encourages applications from professionals with preparation and experience in family education, including formal teaching, research/scholarship, community education, public information and education, curriculum and resource development, health care, military family support, and ministry. Certified Family Life Educators have a minimum of a bachelor's degree; many CLFEs have advanced degrees.

* For approved college programs, see: www.ncfr.org/cert/academic /programs/.

Choose a job you love, and you will never have to
work a day in your life.
– *Confucius*

About the Editors

Robert E. Keim, Ph.D. (Florida State University), CFLE Emeritus & Professor Emeritus, Northern Illinois University (NIU), taught at NIU for 28 years, while teaching a course on parent education for 21 years. Earlier careers included an accounting degree and becoming a C.P.A., receiving a M.Div. from the Pacific School of Religion, Berkeley, which included two full-time clinical internships: one at a large state mental hospital and one at a youth authority reception and evaluation center. He served briefly in California churches before seeking his doctorate in family science. He has been a student of the human behavior field for about 60 years and joined the National Council on Family Relations in 1966. During this time he also led various programs for couples and parents in over 100 settings and was certified in five evidenced-based parenting and family life related programs. He was Editor of the *Family Science Review* from 1993-1996 and has written numerous articles on family related issues and professional development. He has given over 200 professional and public presentations on parenting and family issues.

Arminta L. Jacobson, Ph.D. (Texas Woman's University), CFLE, CFCS, is a Professor at the University of North Texas and is the founder and director of the Center for Parent Education. She has directed an annual national, now international, conference on parent education since 1992. She has been a long-time member of the National Council on Family Relations and President of the Texas Council on Family Relations. Her areas of teaching, writing, and research include parent education and parent involvement in education. She is the co-author of the Parent Teacher Education Connection, composed of online parent involvement teacher training modules.

A Post Script by Keim: Gold Stars for Parents

For many years now, I have carried some Gold Star stickers in the side pocket of my datebook. The Gold Stars are for one purpose, to give them to a parent whom I see interacting or handling their child or children in a most loving, caring, patient, or thoughtful manner. The occasions occur in grocery stores, in restaurants, at airports, or wherever. When I observe such an event (often saying to myself, "WOW, that parent is really handling this situation well!") I do the following.

The parent is approached and I say to them in a friendly tone: "Trust me; I want to give you something. Would you please get out your billfold (or wallet)? I'm not going to steal it from you. I just want to give you something." As I'm saying that, I'm also start to getting my own datebook out of my side pocket and pulling out the sheet of Gold Stars. When the parent gets out their billfold (no one has ever refused), I ask them to open it up. Invariably, there is some open space on the inside covering of the wallet. I then say, "I want to put this Gold Star here, as a reminder to you of what a good parent you are," and we select a good place to put it. "It was very sweet (or 'a pleasure') to have just watched you and your child interact. You've been handling the situation so well (or 'It has been a delight to see you both.'). I wish you the very best," smiling at them during these last couple of sentences, as I center the star in the open space. And then we both move along with whatever we were doing.

If you ever have trouble finding some small sheets of Gold Stars, search the internet for "gold star stickers" or go to www.wisdomforparents.com and you'll see instructions for getting some. It will give you a joy to have an occasion to give one to a parent and see the grateful and pleased reaction. Don't do it for just every good parent behavior; wait for those "WOW" occasions.

No one can give you wisdom. You must discover it
for yourself, on the journey through life, which no
one can take for you.
– *Sun Bear*

Acknowledgements

Very special thanks is extended to Judy Carson. She has provided numerous, endless, and patient hours of very ["No, Bob, you just used 'very' in the previous sentence!" "Yep. Right! Okay,"] … 'immensely' helpful critiques and tireless copy editing sessions.

Thomas R. Chibucos, Ph.D., Bowling Green State University has our deep appreciation for his insightful counsel and encouragement at the outset and at numerous crucial points in the preparation of this book. Also, our thanks go to him for his review of the article, "The Spectrum of Light: Element of Truth in Each Idea," considering he was the co-editor the book, *Readings in Family Theory* (2005).

The ultimate publication of this book may not have occurred without the "intervening" assistance of David Knox, Ph.D., East Carolina University. At a crucial stage in our seeking publication, David brought his savvy to the fore, demonstrated by his own publishing of the 11th edition of a textbook, *Choices in Relationships: An Introduction to Marriage and the Family* (2012), of co-authoring *Behavioral Family Therapy: An Evidence Based Approach* (2009), and several other books. Besides helpful consul in the latter stages of this project, Knox connected us with the publisher, Shivu Ishwaran of de Sitter

Publications. Both David and Shivu have been most extremely helpful in bringing our book to parents and others who may be interested.

Scott W. Plunkett, Ph.D., Professor, Psychology, California State University, Northridge, being extensively conversant in the literature of parenting, has our deepest gratitude for his most thorough reading and immensely helpful feedback on the article, "Wisdom of the Ages."

Of special importance to the success of this book are those who gave numerous helpful hours of peer reviewing and sharing in the selection of articles to be used. The Editors' deep appreciation is extended to them. Of exceptional help were: Sharon M. Ballard, Ph.D., CFLE, East Carolina University, and Jerry Cook, Ph.D., CFLE, California State University, Sacramento. Also other reviewers who meaningfully assisted in the process were the following, most all of whom are CFLEs: Karen DeBord, Ph.D., Professor Emeritus, North Carolina State; JoAnn Engelbrecht, Ph.D., Texas Woman's University; Wm. Michael Fleming, Ph.D., Univ. of Northern Iowa; Cynthia Garrison, M.S., Practical Parent Education, Plano, TX; Deborah Barnes Gentry, Ed.D., Illinois State University; Kathleen R. Gilbert, Ph.D., Indiana University; H. Wallace Goddard, Ph.D., University of Arkansas; Laura Landry-Meyer, Ph.D., Bowling Green State University; Randall W. Leite, Ph.D., Ohio University; Sally Sommer Martin, Ph.D., University of Nevada, Reno; Wendy Middlemiss, Ph.D., University of North Texas; Judith A. Myers-Walls, Ph.D., Purdue University; M. Angela Nievar, Ph.D., University of North Texas; Cynthia H. Small, M.Ed., Family Dimensions, Inc., Carrollton, TX; and, James E. Van Horn, Professor Emeritus, Ph.D., The Pennsylvania State University.

Chapter I

Wisdom for Children of All Ages

We begin our articles with some topics which you may find helpful at various times during your family's life, regardless of the ages of your children. Some may be timelier for you to read now, others later on.

"I Gotta Be Me:" Each Child is Unique

Cynthia R. Garrison, M.S., CFLE
Certified Anger Management Specialist,
Owner/President CG Resources,
Allen, TX

"I Gotta Be Me." As parents, we hear this cry from our children on a regular basis. Have you heard it? The cry may be soft or heard from across the street. The cry may be subtle or may slap you in the face. Sometimes the cry is disguised and sometimes the child will tell you right out the desire. This cry is your child screaming: "Please let me be who I was designed to be." I believe our children are born with an innate combination of needs, desires and drive which I like to call "Beating to a Different Drum."

Each child is unique and special. Our job as parents is to help the child discover that personal design without imposing our own desires for the child too strongly, which may break the spirit of the child. This inherent part of your child's character can be shaped but not changed. This cry warrants special attention since it will show the parents the real child, and the joy will be overwhelming and the child's overall outcome will be ever positive once discovered.

Carl Rogers, a revered psychotherapist, says each person has a tendency to grow, to develop, and to realize his/her full potential. This is called the *Actualizing Tendency*, and simply stated says a tiger will never try to be a monkey or a rose will not strive to be a daisy. Children decide early on who they want to be and it is our job as parents to encourage them through this process.[1] It is the interaction with others which hamper that development. Sometimes parents don't even realize the damage they do when they disagree with a view of a child or try to make the child have desires which are not their own.

When we view the variations in expected behavior of our children in a negative way, we send the message "there is something wrong with you," when in fact the child may be trying to discover a new territory of ideas or creativity. When we as parents understand the need for this growth, we are able to give much attention to the encouragement and support to the child. As I work with parents daily, I hear many stories of just this occurrence.

One mother of a teenager stopped me after a presentation I had just completed to ask a question. She asked to make an appointment with me to talk about her son. After about 10 minutes into the session I noticed a common theme. Her son was trying to tell her he wanted to quit football to concentrate on other activities. Members of her family of origin had been huge football fans and she wanted her son to be a professional football player. She took inappropriate discipline techniques to drive her point across to her son. He began to fail at school, argue more with her and punch holes in the wall. He was naturally acting out. I asked her to let up on him about football during off season and see what happens. I also encourage her to try to find out the other activities he wanted to try. After two months, she showed up at my office unannounced, wanting to talk with me. She cried and cried. She was overjoyed because she said: "I have my son back." She discovered he wanted to join the debate team and play baseball. She also discovered a newfound positive relationship with her son. She found ways to let "him be him." (He later went on to receive a college scholarship to a private university in Louisiana in debate.)

When we actually listen and hear what our children say or do, we learn much more than if we are always doing the talking.[2] This story is not uncommon. We as parents want so much for our children and find ourselves pushing our children to change when in fact they cannot. Even in my own family we have unique children. My 12 year old daughter has worn boy's clothes for a couple of years now. She is very athletic and is more comfortable in such clothes. Every now and then my husband will make a comment about her wearing a dress or at least girl jeans. She of course looks at him as if he had two heads and smiles. I encourage him to let "her be her." I tell him she is the one who needs to be comfortable in her own skin. My 10 year old son has a complete different body temperature than I expected of any child. I no longer remind him to grab a jacket or hooded sweat shirt when going outside. He once said to me, "but mom, it will only get tied around my waist since I don't need it." What wise words from a 10 year old. Another such example comes from a book by Stephen W. Vannoy.[3] He noticed one day his daughter sliced up her orange to eat differently than he did. He wanted to tell her that his way produced just the right amount of juice from the fruit. Having the wisdom he did, he decided to compliment her on her creative way to eat an orange instead of asking her to slice it his way. While enjoying the movie "*Happy Feet*" with my children recently, I found myself thinking about the character who could not sing, but had a great talent to dance. He had to search far away from home to find others who accepted him as he was when his family and other penguins did not. Such small examples as these, yet such powerful statements we make to our children when we accept them for who they are meant to be. If parents continue to push to change the child, a conflict between experiences and the child's self-concept forms. This conflict within the child may cause other behavior and psychological problems in the future. Parents need to encourage growth of an activity or desire through validating the child's desire and supporting the child to reach goals the child has set.[4]

Many times different behaviors evoke varying reactions from parents. Some parents can become offended by a child trying new or different ways than the parent had originally tried to teach. Over the years I have come to realize, and research is showing,[1] when we as parents embrace the originality, creative, and unique attributes of our children, the children will show us a whole new non-judgmental world, where we don't always have to have the right answers or we don't always have to know everything. This type of realization brings about a more harmonious home and later a more harmonious world

References

[1] Rogers, Carl R. (1995). "What Understanding and Acceptance Mean to Me." *Journal of Humanistic Psychology 35 (4)*, 47-51.

[2] Young, Ed (2004). *The 10 Commandments of Parenting*. Chicago: Moody Publishers.

[3] Vannoy, Steven W. (1994). *The 10 greatest gifts I give my children*. NY: Simon & Schuster.

[4] Sharf, Richard S. (2000). *Theories of psychotherapy & counseling* (2nd ed.). SF: Brooks/Cole.

What Every Growing Person Needs:
Basic care, Stimulation, Guidance, Love and Affirmation

Lane H. Powell, Ph.D., CFLE
Consultant and Certified Family Life Educator
Lubbock, TX

Parenting advice in books and media programs can be confusing. Many of the sources offer a dizzying number of suggestions, advice, and precautions for anxious parents. Since most of us only go to the "school of our family of origin" (our parents) to learn how to parent, we also have seen modeled a variety of styles, reactions, and philosophies of parenting–some positive and many negative ones. There is certainly a need to get a clearer grounding of the principles of human development that are consistent over all circumstances and stages of life. These essential principles have been confirmed in my own life experience with children, adult relatives and grandparents.

Human development is the study of growth across the lifespan. Every person who is alive–young or old–is still capable of growth and needs to grow. It will not be in the same way or at the same rate for everyone, because growth is different for each person. It is more than just getting bigger. It also involves emotional and mental growth. Just as a growing plant needs soil, light and moisture, so the growing person has some essential requirements that allow growth to occur.

The four *essential needs* are: *basic needs, stimulation, guidance, and love and affirmation.* Each is important for the growing person, the child in the family as well as the parents.

Basic Needs. Over 60 years ago, Abraham Maslow proposed a *hierarchy of needs* in human development. [1] He arranged six categories of need into a pyramid of importance that he believed every human must satisfy in order to reach her/his full potential of self-actualization. The base of the pyramid is labeled *physiological needs*: the need for food, clothing, shelter, and protection from harm. If these basic needs are not met or are inadequate, the human may die. *Basic* needs are necessary for *survival.* Sadly, many persons in our world will not survive this day because of a lack of basic need fulfillment. But those who read this book will probably be able to check off this need with a flourish.

Stimulation. The stimulation of the five senses (hearing, sight, touch, taste, smell) is necessary for *growth,* mental as well as physical. New technology has allowed for the advanced study of brain development in newborns. We now know that the infant's brain is not fully formed at birth. It is in a state of plasticity. Neurons in the brain are waiting to be stimulated in order to form pathways of thought, memory, reasoning, and association.[2] That's why warm and gentle talking to an infant–even though he or she has no idea what you are saying–is so vital. It stimulates the brain to form connections and actually raises the IQ! Research has shown that premature babies who are touched, patted, rocked, and talked to actually gain weight and recover much faster than those who are left in incubators without stimulation. Human development specialists John Bowlby and Mary Ainsworth studied children raised in overcrowded orphanages where emotional and physical growth was stunted by neglect. [3] It was the beginning of their work on the importance of parent-child attachment. An actual diagnosis: *failure to thrive,* defines infants who do not gain weight after birth and are listless and quiet. Although other things than neglect can cause this condition, most of the sufferers have had little sensory stimulation in their environment. Parents of such infants can be given special lessons on how to provide sensory stimulation. They can be shown the importance of holding the baby while feeding, of talking to the baby and making eye contact, and of playing little games which stimulate growth and attachment.

Do teens still need stimulation? You bet! And they will find ways to get it that are either productive (hopefully) or risky. They can still be hugged, hair brushed out, backs rubbed, or feet massaged. Adults of all ages also crave stimulation. Often vigorous adults begin to decline when forced retirement or illness takes away their options for stimulation.

Guidance. Instruction in social skills, protection, and necessary limits and boundaries are essential for *socialization*. Without guidance, a person has little chance of becoming a socially accepted and approved human being. Consider all of the things that parents or other adults must teach a young child: how to eat, how to dress oneself, use the toilet, talk (with respect), act (with kindness), share resources, respect other persons' rights, and on and on. Human beings are social animals. They crave interaction and acceptance by other human beings. Maslow termed this the *need to belong*.[1] The parental task of *guidance*, successfully accomplished, teaches children the socialization that will allow them to live peacefully and productively with others: siblings, parents, friends, spouses and co-workers.

Parents often talk of "disciplining" their children. In most cases they are referring to various forms of punishment: spanking, scolding, shouting, reprimanding, taking away privileges, criticizing, threatening or just ignoring misbehavior. Why not look instead at the root word of discipline, which is "disciple"? A disciple is the student of a teacher. And what are the characteristics of a good teacher? Think for a moment of the best teacher you ever had. What made him or her so good? I have asked this question of many students and the answers always include: she had a good sense of humor; he wanted us to learn and was excited about the subject; he spent extra time with us; she made learning fun and interesting; she was tough and expected a lot, but I knew she cared. The good teacher offers *guidance*: patient, loving, interested and caring, but setting boundaries and expectations.

Recent research of adolescents who avoid high risk behaviors has identified two important characteristics of parents: they provide a warm and loving climate of acceptance in the home, and they do "parental monitoring."[4] This is not to be confused with parental policing. Parental monitoring describes the parent who is a loving and concerned guide who wants to know where the teen is going and with whom and establishes reasonable boundaries and guidelines for be-havior. Whether we are 8 or 80, there is still a need for guidance in different forms and different amounts, because following the rules of society opens the door to social acceptance and satisfaction.

   Love and Affirmation. Love is best described as uncondi-tional positive regard of other persons.[5] When one is valued and af-firmed, no matter how he or she looks or performs, it provides the basis for the development of positive *self-esteem* and *self-actualiza-tion*. Human beings are so hungry for love that they often will be se-duced by shallow substitutes (praise, manipulation, promises), particularly if they have had little experience with "the real thing." A strong dose of *love and affirmation* that results in positive self-esteem and self-actualization makes it possible for adults to successfully par-ent the next generation. It allows them to feel comfortable putting aside their own needs to care for the very dependent and needy in-fants and young children, thus providing the basic needs, stimulation, and guidance essentials for the next generation. What is considered a strong dose of love and affirmation? Marriage relationship re-searcher John Gottman has observed that committed partners must have a 5 to 1 ratio of positive to negative interactions if they are to remain happy in the relationship.[6] Children need an even higher ratio of hugs, positive attention, smiles, comments of affirmation for who they are and what they do right (vs. the tendency to target what they do wrong).

   If a person's need for love and affirmation is unmet in the early years of life, he or she tends to become a self-centered, grasping adult: never satisfied with the attention given or able to anticipate or empathize with another's needs and pain. Is an adult who missed out on unconditional love and a high ratio of affirmation as a child then doomed to be incapable of freely giving these essential qualities to another generation? The good news is that adults have the capacity to grow beyond an emotionally abusive childhood, but not without intentionally working on it, with desire.[7] The end result is definitely worth it.

   To recap, every growing person has four essential needs:
- Basic–for survival
- Stimulation–for growth
- Guidance–for socialization
- Love and Affirmation–for self-esteem and self-actualization.

   So keep on growing for as long as you live while helping to guide your child!

References

[1] Maslow, A. (1954). *Motivation and personality.* NY; Harper and Row.

[2] Huttenlocher, P. (2002). *Neural Plasticity.* Cambridge, MA: Harvard University.

[3] Bowlby, J. (1953). *Child care and the growth of love.* Baltimore: Penguin Books.

[4] Walsh, Nancy. (2003). Early puberty, ethnicity may contribute to teen smoking: parental monitoring matters. *Clinical Psychiatry News. Vol. 31,* 32.

[5] Rogers, Carl R. (1959). A theory of therapy, personality, and interpersonal relationships as developed in the client-centered framework. Reprinted in H. Kirschenbaum & V. Henderson (Eds.). *The Carl Rogers reader.* (1989). Boston: Houghton Mifflin.

[6] Gottman, J. (2000). *Clinical manual for marital therapy: A research based approach (rev. 2001).* Seattle: The Gottman Institute.

[7] Johnson, D.W. (2006). *Reaching out: Interpersonal effectiveness and self-actualization* (9th ed.). Boston: Pearson.

Empowering Children

Dorothea M. Rogers, D. Min., CFLE
Professor of Family Life Education,
Spring Arbor University, Flint, MI

"Don't spank your child." "Spare the rod, spoil the child!" Many people have their formula for raising the perfect child, but the fact is parenting is demanding, and the parenting process itself is complex, as well as downright scary. Parenting is not for the faint-of-heart, or the slow to find humor.[1] Children do not come with a set of instructions. Moreover, children are not the same; clearly, children are unique little beings with what we almost consider blank slates ready to be written on. Parents desire that their children mature into productive human beings. Parents also truly care for their children's social, physical, cognitive, psychological, and spiritual development. Therefore, the staggering responsibility to help children mature into valuable members of society rests upon the responsibility of the parents. As parents empower their children, that is, give children a sense of control over their own lives, both parents and children can feel a sense of personal power, confidence, self-worth, and wholeness.

A common definition of power is the ability to influence another person. "Most research of the use of power in the family has focused on a person's attempting to influence or control the behavior of another" (p. 28).[2] Empowering, on the other hand, attempts to establish power in someone else. "Empowering is an active, intentional process of enabling another person to acquire power. The person who is empowered has gained power because of the encouraging behavior of the other" (p. 28),[2] by giving such persons a growing sense of self-control and the ability to determine their own future.

Steffen Saifer defines empowerment in children as, "Giving someone the ability to have control over a situation, themselves, or their lives. Children are empowered when they are given choices and encouraged to make meaningful decisions" (p. 188).[3] The affirmation of children by empowering them gives them the ability to learn and grow and become all that they can be. Additionally, empowering children will help them be aware of their strengths and how to best use these strengths.

Several ways in which parents can help empower their children are:

- Showing children love, concern, and respect at all times.
- Giving children choices when possible, such as deciding between different outfits for school or selecting the menu items for a family meal.
- Having rules that are understood and allowing children to be part of the rule-making process, and if consequences are involved, helping to determine what might be the most effective deterrents for them.
- Helping children to express their feelings and really listening to them with undivided attention.
- Being a good role model in actions and speech. Realize, children may mimic their parents' negative qualities as well, regardless of all efforts to teach them good manners!

Parents have the awesome responsibility of raising their children to become all that they can be. Steps can be taken to aid parents as they endeavor to affirm their children's journey through childhood by empowering and encouraging them to make the best decisions. Henry Ward Beecher summed up admirable parenthood as: "Whoever makes a home seem to the young [to be] dearer and more happy, is a public benefactor" (p. 215).[4] The greatest reward to parents and children comes when those who have been empowered go on to help empower others.

References

[1] Walker, L.B. (2001). *Humor for a woman's heart*. West Monroe: Howard Publishing.

[2] Balswick, J.O., & Balswick, J.K. (1995). *The family, a Christian perspective on the contemporary home*. Grand Rapids: Baker Book House.

[3] Saifer, S. (1990). *Practical solutions to practically every problem*. St. Paul: Redleaf Press.

[4] Beecher, H.W. (1868). *Village life in New England*. NY: Charles Scribner.

Invest 5 to Save 10

Karen DeBord, Ph.D. CFLE
Professor Emeritus, North Carolina State
University, Raleigh

Parenting is hard work. And it seems as if life just keeps getting more and more rushed. Although we know that finding quality time with our children is critical, there are so many things usurping parents' time at work, at home and in the community. These challenges can add stress to our lives and make us feel overwhelmed!

Whether it is the first thing in the morning or as soon as you walk in the door in the afternoon, children, toddlers or middle-schoolers, want to share their stories and they want the time and attention of their parents or primary caregiver. By devoting a few minutes to focusing on the child as soon as you are together, it will help your relationship and keep the doors of communication open early in life. Later in life you will be glad you devoted this short amount of time to connecting.

Invest 5 minutes to save 10 minutes

Try to spend at least 5 minutes with your children right after you get home. Your kids have been looking forward to seeing you, and they need your full attention for a few minutes just to help them feel more secure and loved. This also may help keep them from getting upset later in the evening when you may need to pay attention to other things, like cooking dinner or doing housework.

For young children, spend those first 5 minutes with your children on an activity that they choose, like reading, coloring, playing a game, or telling you about their day. Get down on the floor with them or sit close to them and give them your full attention. Kids won't be as satisfied if you are distracted or focused on something else.

After you have spent a little time with them, help get them to start activities that they can do themselves or with siblings. Television should not be the preferred activity. They may be able to just continue what they were doing with you, or what they were doing when you came home. This will give you some time to yourself to rest or start household tasks.

For older children, ask them to respond to specific questions or inquiries. "Tell me about your day" is not as effective as "Tell me about what you did in your science class today," or "What was for lunch?" or "With whom did you sit?" Be sure to take the time to sit down with them to see what homework or school announcement may be in their backpack. Once you share their day, they may be ready to help you with some household chores you can work on together.

Create short morning and evening routines including a regular bedtime with some quiet time together before sleep. When possible, have your work time follow family time, or, better yet, after the children have gone to bed, separating work time from family time. Those "5 minutes" together can relieve family stress and save time you will need later for your own work.

Teaching Kids to Lie?
What Parents' Actions Really Say

Jody Johnston Pawel, LSW, CFLE
President, Parents Toolshop® Consulting, Ltd.,
Award-winning author, top-rated speaker and nationally-recognized parenting expert to the media,
Springboro, OH

Most parents want their children to be honest and moral, but many times their day-to-day actions show children it is okay to lie. So, despite their words, many parents *inadvertently* teach their children to lie. To gain insight into this intriguing idea, we will summarize research, theory and practical tips from three highly-respected and proven-effective resources.

Paul Ekman, Ph.D., has been studying lying for more than thirty years and published his research results in the thought-provoking book, *Why Kids Lie: How Parents Can Encourage Truthfulness.*[1]

The Parents Toolshop: The Universal Blueprint for Building a Healthy Family[2] is a one-stop comprehensive book that compiles proven parenting theories and research results, then translates them into practical language and action skills that parents can use to get proven-effective long-term results.

Rudolf Dreikurs presented a theory of the "Four Goals of Misbehavior," involving goals children use for the purposes of achieving attention, power, revenge, or feelings of inadequacy.[3] The Parents Toolshop blends Dreikurs' theories with Ekman's research on lying and the result is an essay on lying (2000, 337-340). This essay reveals some surprising discoveries that describe how easy it is for parents to accidentally model lying and respond to lies in ways that accidentally perpetuate the problem. It also offers practical tips for preventing and responding to lies in ways that teach truthfulness.

The following summary identifies key points often neglected but important for parents and parenting professionals to consider.

WHAT IS A LIE?
The dictionary[4] defines a lie as "a false statement made with deliberate intent to deceive; an intentional untruth; a falsehood."

Ekma[1] further says, "There isn't much difference between saying something false and concealing the truth. Both are lies. The purpose is the same–to deliberately mislead" (1998, 14).

Given these definitions, even "white lies," the excuses we give to spare others' feelings or to get out of a jam, and fictional stories, like the Tooth Fairy and Santa Claus, are all lies, technically speaking. So parents must ask themselves two hard questions: "Do I ever lie?" and if so, "What am I *really* teaching my children about truthfulness?"

WHEN DO CHILDREN UNDERSTAND LYING?

Most parents and parenting professionals know that children develop their understanding of lying and truthfulness slowly, as they move through developmental stages. In his book, Ekman[1] identifies five stages of understanding and practicing truth and lying, including the *reasons* children lie or tell the truth. The stages beginning with Stage I, for children to age 4, where they may be honest or lie to get their own way; ages 5-6 to please adults; ages 6-8 for what may benefit them; ages 8-12 for others to think well of them; and, Stage 5, 12 and older, for the desire to be good citizens or lying as a habit (1998, 93).

Ekman found that when people feel strong emotions, they may revert to an earlier stage. Most surprising, he found that not everyone reaches the final stage and many adults never go beyond the second stage, ages 6-8 years old (1998, 92)!

WHY DO PEOPLE LIE?

Lying is *intentional;* it has a motive or purpose. Rudolf Dreikurs[3] theorized that *all* misbehavior serves one of four purposes or "goals." If we sort the motives for lying that Ekman[1] identifies into Dreikurs'[3] four "Goals of Misbehavior" categories, we see that the first question we need to ask ourselves when children lie is, "What purpose does this lie serve?" The answer gives us clues that help us choose the best way to prevent or respond to *that type* of lie.

The following list includes the motives for lying identified by Ekma[1] and their related goals (Dreikurs[3]) as presented in *The Parents Toolshop.*[2] Note that these motives can apply to both children and adults when they are involved in telling a lie:

Lying for *Attention* to:
- Get a reaction to exaggerated or imaginative stories.
- Be accepted by or "cover for" one's peers.

Lying for *Power* to:
- Fool people into believing false stories.
- Avoid harsh punishment/lectures. In fact, Ekman's research

shows that this is the *main* reason children lie (p. 19).
- Protect one's privacy.
- Get something that's forbidden.

Lying for *Revenge* to get justice for a hurt.

Lying as a *Display of Inadequacy* because they feel discouraged when their truthful statements are not believed.

PREVENTING LIES

Parents can prevent lying by using these *verbal* approaches:

- ***Teach the value of truthfulness*** by pointing out the benefits, such as how it builds trust and promotes justice.
- ***Teach truthfulness repetitively,*** not only after children already have lied. Share events from the newspaper and read fairy tales such as Pinocchio and "he Boy Who Cried Wolf." Discuss the hardships people experience because of their lies.
- ***Acknowledge children when they tell the truth,*** especially when it was difficult.
- ***Avoid unintentionally rewarding lying.*** When there is too little parental supervision, children can get away with lying often, so they become more skilled at it.
- ***Handle mistakes calmly and non-punitively.*** When parents overreact to mistakes and accidents, children become fearful and are more likely to cover up or lie about future mistakes. Instead, focus on solutions, not blame. What can the child do to fix the mistake and prevent it from recurring?

WHAT ARE PARENTS *REALLY* MODELING?

Unfortunately, conversations about truthfulness aren't enough to set a child on the path of permanent honesty. We must tell the truth ourselves, even when it's not convenient or makes us "look bad." Not surprisingly, Ekman's research showed that children who lie most often have parents who also lie frequently (p. 52). Most parents think they don't fit this criterion, but if they look more closely, they may discover they lie more often than they think!

Here are the Top Ten Ways Parents Accidentally Teach Their Children to Lie:[2]

1. Having your child tell a caller you're not home when you're standing next to them.
2. Making up excuses to the traffic cop about why you were speeding.
3. Lying about your children's age to gain free entry into special events.
4. Protecting kids from upsetting news by telling them inaccurate details.
5. Lying about an ex-spouse to gain the child's loyalty.

6. Failing to tell a sales person she gave you too much change.
7. Covering up or blaming others for your mistakes or accidents.
8. Lying to avoid conflict.
9. Lying about why you were late or forgot something.
10. Telling children a lie to get them to behave, with no intention of following through. ("I'll leave you at the store!")

Such commonplace deceits often go unnoticed–by parents–but children are sponges who soak up these unspoken lessons.

IS LYING EVER OKAY?

If lying is wrong, is the brutal truth okay?

There are ways to be both truthful and tactful when the truth might hurt someone's feelings. For example, children can say, "Thank you for remembering my birthday," even if they don't like the gift.

You can also tell the truth without telling the whole truth. For example, when children answer the phone, it is fine to tell them to say, "My parents can't come to the phone right now." The child doesn't have to add that the parents are in the shower or not home.

Ekman's research shows most parents think two kinds of lies are acceptable (pp. 17-18):

1. If the child is home alone or needs to escape a potentially dangerous situation and telling a lie may keep the child safe, safety trumps truthfulness.
2. It's okay to lie so you can surprise someone later with something nice, like a surprise birthday party.

TRUTH OR CONSEQUENCES?

Even if we teach our children to be truthful and are good role models, it is likely that a child will lie at some point. *How* we respond to these lies can help determine whether the child continues lying or comes clean permanently.

There is not one perfect response to every lie. Instead, we can use Dreikurs[3] guidelines to identify the goal, avoid reactions that give the goal a payoff or escalate the situation, and show children how to meet their goal without lying.

Here are some helpful tips for responding to children's statements:

* ***Believe children,*** unless you have good reason to be suspicious. If their truths are not believed, they will be discouraged from telling the truth in the future. If their *perception* of the truth differs from yours, it doesn't necessarily mean they are "lying." For example, if children say they did a chore and did do it, but not as thoroughly as adults might have done it, the children aren't "lying." They believe they did it. Instead of

disciplining for lying, it would be more appropriate to provide additional instructions on how to do the chore.

- ***Question children in ways that encourage them to be truthful,*** rather than trying to trap them in a lie. For example, if a parent finds an empty bottle of alcohol in the trash, instead of asking, "What did you and John do while I was gone?" be up-front and respectful, "I just found . . . I need to know the truth about . . ."
- ***Reassure children that you won't be as angry if they tell the truth.***
- ***Don't punish truth telling.*** Consequences for coming clean should never be so severe that it's worth it to the child to take the risk and lie.
- ***Children need to understand that if they lie, they are in "double trouble."*** There will be two separate disciplines: one for the actual offense and one for lying. The discipline for lying should relate to the breakdown in trust. For example, when teens miss curfew and lie about why they were late there are two problems. An appropriate discipline for the missed curfew is to give up social privileges for one or a few nights. Teens can rebuild trust by agreeing to call home once or twice during the evening, when their privileges are restored.

When parents understand what lying *is* and *why* children might lie, they can prevent and respond to lies in ways that encourage truthfulness. By teaching truthfulness not only in words, but by their deeds, parents can raise children who are honest, moral, truthful, tactful and trustworthy.

NOTE: A special five-page report on Lying, with more details of Ekman's research (such as the five stages of developing truthfulness), explanations, and examples is available at: http://www.parentstoolshop.com/HTML/lying.htm.

References
[1] Ekman, Paul, (1992). *Why kids lie: How parents can encourage truthfulness.* NY: Scribner.
[2] Dreikurs, Rudolf, & Soltz, Vicki. (1987). *Children: The challenge.* NY: E.P. Dutton.
[3] Pawel, Jody Johnston. (2000). *The parents toolshop: The universal blueprint for building a healthy family.* Springboro, OH: Ambris Publishing.
[4] lie. (n.d.). *Dictionary.com Unabridged (v 1.1).* Retrieved October 27, 2010, from Dictionary.com website: http://dictionary.reference.com/browse/lie.

If you tell the truth,
you don't have to remember anything.
–Mark Twain

Tune in, Turn off

Karen DeBord, Ph.D. CFLE
Professor Emeritus, North Carolina State
University, Raleigh

Children spend more time watching television than in any other activity except sleep.[1] Research has shown that "mindless" television or video games may impoverish the development of that part of the brain that is responsible for planning, organizing, and sequencing behavior for self-control, moral judgment, and attention.[2] In one study,[3] twenty percent of 2- to 7-year-olds, 46% of 8- to 12-year-olds, and 56% of 13- to 17-year-olds have TVs in their bedrooms. Excessive television viewing is interfering with family time and children's healthy development.

According to the American Academy of Pediatrics,[4] children under six spend about two hours a day with screen media, about the same amount of time that they spend playing outside, and three times as much time as they spend reading or being read to. Never has the passive distraction of the computer, television or electronic entertainment been so readily available for our children.[5]

When children are young, placing them in front of the television seems harmless enough; however, as they age, the viewing patterns and their seeming addiction to television has detrimental effects on their behavior and learning.

- They grow accustomed to short entertaining sequences making attending to school work or tasks more difficult.
- They begin to fill their time with television and later in adolescent years learn to relate to others through messaging and social networking online.

Parents say TV is convenient, keeps children busy, reduces conflict and avoids boredom. Some parents say they children have anger fits when the TV is turned off or limited.[6] Parents who are tired or stressed with work tasks and home chores may turn to television to provide them a break. But later they may find that using television to buy time for them gets out of control.

Time spent in front of television could be time spent in building a foundation for relationships that will benefit the child and their well being throughout their lives. When large amounts of time are devoted to watching television, children have limited opportunity to experience a supportive family that values open communication and warm connections.

Setting limitations on television must start in the early years.

- Turn off the television and tune in.
- Disallow, or greatly limit, video games.
- Keep the computer and television out of the child's bedroom where they can isolate from the family and retreat without knowledge of their interactions.

What to do instead of TV!

Instead of learning to depend on the media raising children, consider the influence parents can have with children. First stop and ask–what do I hope for my child? What values do I want to convey? How can I convey those values without the influence of myself and our family?

Start by making family time a special and fun time which is part of who you are as a family. These times may include family mealtime, planned and impromptu family outings, and if you view television, view it together; then talk about the life lessons in the program. Select programs that are consistent with your values or the values you hope to build in your children.

Young children want time with their parents. Sit on the floor or stoop to their eye level and play with them. Activities such as stacking blocks, putting things together, scooping, pouring, scrubbing, rearranging, and putting in order are all skills they will need in order to understand science and math in school. Make it fun! Talk together. Ask how things work and use your imagination to create stories.

Other ideas:

Toddlers: Allow kitchen play in one designated drawer or cabinet that hold plastic ware, read together, take stroller walks, put music on to bop about the house as you do your chores at home, look through family photos, look at picture books, and stack blocks.

Preschoolers: Allow safe kitchen help, read together, take a walk with a collecting container, go to the library, tell stories where they name the characters and the setting to get started, use extra large drawing paper on the floor to draw together, play dress-up, and erect a puppet stage with a sheet and table.

School-agers: Play outside, bike, take walks, read together, read or tell stories into a tape player, make things in the kitchen or with miscellaneous things in the house (egg cartons, cardboard tubes, tape, glue, play doh), plant a garden together, and start an aquarium.

Teens: Play ball, bike, work on the car, work together to learn to pay bills and understand a check-book, learn to change a tire, learn how to check the oil, develop a family website, take photographs, plan a vacation or a weekend for the family, teens plan the meals, go to the grocery store, and plan a family website.

As children become more verbal, ask them open-ended questions, which require more than a yes or no answer. Challenge them to think. Look up answers together. Go to the library and check out books with pictures. Brush up on conversation starters. Keep the lines of communication open in the early years so they will be more likely to communicate with you in their teen years when social issues get much tougher to manage. Television will not hold the answers.

References

[1] Huston, A. C. and J. C. Wright. 1989. The forms of television and the child viewer. In *Public Communication and Behavior,* ed. G. Comstock. Vol. 2. Orlando, FL: Academic Press.

[2] Healy, J. (1998). Understanding TV's Effect on the Developing Brain. American Academy of Pediatrics, *AAP News.*

[3] Gentile, D.A., Walsh, D. A. (2002, January 28). A normative study of family media habits. *Applied Developmental Psychology, 23,* 157-178.

[4] American Academy of Pediatrics, *Television & the Family.* Retrieved Jan. 16, 2011, from http://www.aap.org/family/tv1.htm.

[5] DeBroff, S. (2002). *The Mom Book, 4,278 Tips for Moms.* NY: Simon & Schuster.

[6] Walsh, D. (2006, November). *Media use.* Plenary Session presented at the annual conference of the National Council on Family Relations, Minneapolis.

"Can You Afford It?

Elizabeth B. Carroll, J.D., CFLE
Associate Professor, Department of Child
Development and Family Relations,
East Carolina University, Greenville

You are out shopping with your child when they spot a new toy they want very badly. How many times have you asked him or her, "Can you afford it?" One of the most important skills for the transition to adulthood is the acquisition of money management skills. Learning to manage money is something that comes with practice. An essential part of guiding the child into adulthood is providing opportunities for the child to practice making decisions about spending. In order for the child to learn financial management skills, it is necessary for them to have money and the opportunity to make decisions about spending it. Consequently, asking a child "can you afford it?" is one of the wisest things a parent can do.

Children receive money in the form of allowances, spending money, gifts, incentives, and earnings. Many view allowances as an effective way of teaching money management skills. Both children and adolescents seem to have more money to spend than formerly, with teen spending averaging more than $100 dollars a week.[1] In view of this, it is apparent that one of the major responsibilities of being a parent is to impart consumer education to children. Unfortunately, only 25% of children report that their parents have actively taught them to manage money.[2] Parents are role models and should be aware that children will learn through imitating their attitudes and behaviors about spending and saving money. It is easier for the child to learn to be a good money manager if they watch parents who use good money management techniques. In addition, the lessons about financial management should be developmentally appropriate for the child's age. Preschoolers can sort coins; elementary grade students can practice math skills by counting the change after they buy something; and, teens can consider how peers and media influence their purchases. An understanding of what money is and how it is budgeted is an essential component of successful adulthood. The long-range negative impact of poor financial skills can be mounting debt and bankruptcy. The life-long advantage of teaching children to be wise financial managers is worth the effort.

Teaching about money management and spending choices begins from the time the child is old enough to go shopping and say, "I want that." Most parents cannot afford everything the child wants and even if they could, indulging every whim can set up unrealistic expectations for the future. Planned shopping trips with a child, where the parent sets limits on how much they are willing to spend, can provide the child with the chance to learn to stay within a preset limit.

Many parents will choose to give their child an allowance as they mature. Allowances offer opportunities for discussions about saving and making wise financial decisions. Children should be allowed to make some choices on their own and learn from the consequences if a choice they make turns out to be a mistake.

As children grow older, they may begin to earn money through special tasks that the parent or a neighbor may hire them to do and later through part-time and summer jobs. The older adolescent still needs parental guidance with regard to savings as well as spending choices. This is an excellent time to discuss future financial goals such as college, buying a house or car, and creating long-term savings. It is important for late adolescents, those 18 and older, to realize that they are considered legally an adult. They need to realize that poor financial decisions may have significant long-term effects such as creating high levels of debt or negatively influencing their credit rating.

For the parent, lessons in money management are a constant balance between giving the child the freedom to make decisions and the need to provide adequate instructions along the way. Just as children are not born knowing how to manage money, parents are not always automatically equipped with the knowledge to teach money management skills. This offers an opportunity for learning together.

"Can you afford it?" is one of the wisest things a parent can ask a child. It teaches them that there are limits on financial resources and that they need to stay within them. It provides the opportunity for the child to learn to budget and plan for purchases. It also allows children to learn to be responsible for their own behavior. It prepares them for the transition to adulthood when they will be responsible for "affording it."

References

[1] TRU. (2003). *Teens spent $170 billion in 2002.* Retrieved December 13, 2010, from: http://www.teenresearch.com/pressrelease.cfm?page_id=152.

[2] Diekmann, F.J. (2004). NCUA chairman: "Most Americans, especially the young, failing finance." *The Credit Union Journal, 8 (30),* 9.

Did You Have Fun?

Jean Illsley Clarke, Ph.D., CFLE
Author and parent educator, Minneapolis, MN

"Did you have fun?" the parent asks when the child comes home from the playground, or school, or a friend's house, or wherever. It is the question often put to children by adults who care about their children and want them to be happy. When young Charles came home from school, his mother may ask, "Did you have fun today?" If Charles said, "No!" his well-meaning mother may stop her activity and take him to the park so he can have fun. She wants him to be happy.

Happiness is a worthy wish, but the path from pleasurable activities to happiness is not direct. Exposing children to a constant stream of entertainment may provide some fun, but it may not lead to the happy state for the child that the parents intended.

Many adults who, as children, had been overindulged (described in the previous article) and who participated in the first three Overindulgence Research Studies,[1] indicated that when they were growing up their parents made sure that they were entertained. Some

who reported a high level of entertainment also reported:
- *On the whole, I am not satisfied with myself.*
- *At times I think I am no good at all.*
- *I certainly feel useless at times.*
- **I do not feel that I'm a person of worth.**
- *I wish I could have more respect for myself.*

Not what the parents intended! Why doesn't constant entertainment lead to happiness? Writing about the phenomena in *What Happy People Know,*[2] Baker and Stauth say:

Once we become accustomed to any pleasure, it no longer has the power to make us happy. ... Neurologically, it overloads the brain's pleasure centers, prohibiting further sensations, and depletes the feel-good neurotransmitters serotonin and dopamine. Psychologically, it creates inflated expectations and a sense of boredom (p. 62).

If fun and pleasure are not the basis of happiness, what is? Foster and Hicks in *How We Choose to Be Happy*[3] describes the nine components of happiness. One of those is accountability, holding ourselves accountable or responsible for how we respond to our world and nurture ourselves.

As a high school junior, Charles–yes, the same Charles whose mother made sure he had fun every day when he was little–was surprised that she was upset about his "D" in French. He explained that the class wasn't interesting and the teacher was boring and not any fun so he couldn't be expected to learn from her. Charles's mother had not only presented having fun as a value, but also that it was someone else's responsibility to provide it. Charles did not believe he was accountable for his learning.

Instead of asking "Did you have fun today?" Charles' mom might have encouraged accountability by asking:
- Tell me about something you did today.
- How did you do that?
- Tell me one thing that happened to you.
- What feelings did you have when . . .?
- Did you play games (or do things) that you already knew how to do?
- Did you play any new games (or do new things)?
- Tell me about one thing you did for someone else.
- Tell me about something someone else did for you.
- Tell me about one thing you did well today, and I'll tell you one thing I did well.
- Tell me one thing you could have done better today, and I'll tell you one thing I could have done better.

- How did you take care of yourself? (If something was distressing.)
- Was there a way that you could help others?

Consider Dan who tells his child how to be competent. As she leaves for school, instead of saying, "Have fun today," Dan encourages her to be accountable or responsible by saying:
- Be smart.
- Do something kind today.

The directive to *be smart* includes not only learning classroom lessons, but keeping yourself safe on the bus and handling yourself responsibly on the playground. *Do something kind today* encourages an empathic attitude and signals the parent's expectations about the child's developing social skills. These two directives offer the child her parent's assessment of how to be competent, or even how to survive in her time and place, thus telling her how to succeed in her childhood world. It does not tell her to have fun or how she is expected to feel. She may like it or not; she may feel competent or inadequate; she may feel happy or sad, and she might even have fun. But she is not obligated to have fun. She is not a failure if she does not have fun. She will not have to defend herself if she did not have fun. She will not need to find a way to blame someone else for not "making it fun."

If we haven't been encouraging accountability, we can start today. Of course we want our children to have fun. But pleasure is an outcome, not an activity. We need to remember that everything can't be fun. Sometimes: "Life hurts. If it doesn't hurt some of the time, it's not life" (p. 159).[2]

Our job is to teach children how to be accountable and to responsibly handle hurts. They can have fun without our making that a priority or a job or even a burden.

References

[1] Clarke, J. & Dawson, C., & Bredehoft, D. (2004). *How much is enough? Everything you need to know to steer clear of overindulgence and raise likeable, responsible, and respectful children.* NY: Marlowe& Co. NOTE: Also participating in the research studies were: Sheryll A. Mennicke & Alisa M. Potter.

[2] Baker, D. & Stauth, C. (2003). *What happy people know.* NY: St. Martin's Press.

[3] Foster, R., & Hicks, G. (1999). *How we choose to be happy.* NY: Putnam's Sons.

For more information about the Overindulgence Research Studies, see www.overindulgence.info.

Giving Allowances

David J. Bredehoft, Ph.D., CFLE
Professor of Psychology and Family Studies,
Concordia University, St. Paul, MN

Am I overindulging, that is, doing too much for my children if I give them an allowance? is a question I have been asked at each of my last three speaking engagements. In fact, one mother told me her little entrepreneur surveyed his neighborhood age-mates on how much money they were getting, then went online and googled it to see if in fact his neighborhood was above or below the national average. Next he asked for a meeting to bargain. At this meeting he no doubt shared with his mother that in a Junior Achievement/Allstate Foundation poll of nearly 1,000 13- to 18-year-olds in 2004, 35 percent are collecting an allowance.[1]

The answers to the questions on "the allowance issue" seem to be divided. Parents and so-called experts are all over the map. Should we give an allowance or not? If so, how much? Should it be tied to chores or not? Should parents have veto power over what the money buys? What do parent dollars buy? What do the allowance dollars buy? What are other parents doing? What type of values are we trying to instill in our children? What are our goals?

After discussing this issue with parents and children, as well as from what I have learned from a quick literature search, there seems to be a variety of plans today's parents are following, if choosing to give an allowance. Let me describe five of them for you. Oh, by the way, I was raised with the "You've got to be kidding me" Plan. Here are my thoughts on the topic of overindulgence and giving an allowance.

1. The Free Ride Plan

Your child's weekly allowance has no strings attached. He didn't have to do anything for it, and in some cases he can spend it on whatever he likes without your input. In such case, it might be well to tell him that each family member has an important contribution to make to the family well-being, involving chores and such, and we do so because we love each other, not because we will get paid for it.

2. The Budget Plan

Your child's weekly allowance requires no duties or chores. The money is expected to pay for her weekly expenses (for example, entertainment, school lunch, gas money, snacks etc.). With good planning, she can spend any money left over, however she wants.

3. The Allowance with Required Responsibilities Plan
Under this plan your child is required to fulfill a set of specified responsibilities each week in order to receive his allowance. For example, if his room is cleaned by Saturday noon he will get his allowance, if not, no.

4. The Free Ride with Incentives Plan
Your child's weekly allowance has no strings attached. However, you make it clear that if she wants more money, here's the chore list she has to do to earn it.

5. The "You've got to be kidding me" Plan
No allowance. This is on the other side of the continuum from the Free Ride Plan. Everyone in the family (parents and children alike) has chores, jobs, and duties that they do, and they are not paid. They do them because they are a member of the family and they are expected to contribute to the family.

Let's Apply the Test of Four[2]
The Test of Four, an assessment method, was developed in a study involving college freshman who were identified as being overindulged by their parents. When viewing allowances, this assessment suggests that parents may be overindulgent if the behavior:
1. Interferes with the child's development. (With plan 1, a child is not learning self-control, or to be responsible. To some degree this is true of plan 4.)
2. Gives a disproportionate amount of family resources to one or more of the children. (Plans 1-4 all might do this depending on how much money parents give for the allowance.)
3. Exists to benefit the adult more than the child. (Possibly plans 1, 4 & 5 might do this but in different ways; 1 and 4 to get the child to stop nagging, and in the extreme case, 5 could be used as a form of child slavery.)
4. Potentially harms others, society, or the planet in some way. (Any harm done? Plan 1 and possibly Plan 4 teach children just to be consumers without thinking about others or the environment.)

Plan 1 definitely is overindulgence; the others could be depending on the specifics.

Think about Goals and Values when Giving an Allowance?
I believe that it is important for parents to consider what their goals are in giving an allowance, as well as what values they hope to teach. Once they decide this they need to create a plan that achieves

them. For instance, if you want your child to become a saver and at the same time learn to be generous and give to others, consider using the Share, Save, Spend formula developed by Nathan Dungan, author of *How Not to Be Your Child's ATM*.[3] He suggests parents decide a set percentage of every dollar a child earns, receives in gifts, or is given in allowance to be given to charity, saved, and spent.

Are you trying to teach your child how to manage money? If so, make a list of what you expect the allowance is for. Attach estimated prices and then discuss it with your child. Monitor the process and readjust, discussing money management lessons as they are learned. Recent research found that fewer than 25 percent of parents think their children manage money well, while at the same time only half of the teens 14 to 16 surveyed said their parents have talked to them about money or how to manage it.[3] So, the lesson here is that it takes time and repetition for children to learn how to manage money.

Huge Stakes on the Line

Marketers are coming after your children's dollars whether you have prepared them or not! Children under the age of 18 wield combined spending power of about $250 billion in the U.S. alone (all disposable income). With all of these allowance dollars on the line for the taking, it's no wonder children are bombarded with 40,000 commercials each year.[4]

Tips for avoiding overindulgence with allowances

- Select an allowance plan that best fits you and your family's values.
- If you choose to tie chores to an allowance, tell your children why.
- If you choose **not** to tie chores to allowance, tell your children why.
- Clearly have in mind the goals and values you hope to teach with an allowance and frequently review them with your children.
- Talk about money management with your children.
- Educate your children about the manipulative effects of advertisements.
- Model good money management techniques.

References

[1] JA Economics for Success. (2005). *The 2005 JA interprise poll on teens and personal finance: Executive summary.* Retrieved October 27, 2010, from the Junior Achievement web site at http://www.ja.org/files/polls/personal_finance _2005.pdf.

[2] Clarke, J., Dawson, C., & Bredehoft, D. (2004). *How much is enough? Everything*

*you need to know to steer clear of overindulgence and raise likeable, respon-
sible, and respectful children–from toddlers to teens*. NY: Marlowe & Co.
NOTE: For more information about the Overindulgence Research Studies, see
www.overindulgence.info.
[3] Dungan, N. (2003). *Prodigal sons and material girls: How not to be your child's
ATM*. NY: John Willey & Sons, Inc.
[4] Gavin, M. L., & Dowshen, S. *How TV affects your child*. Retrieved October 27,
2010, from the Kids Health web site at http://www.kidshealth.org/parent/pos-
itive/family/tv_affects_child.html.

Raising Sexually Healthy Children

Sharon M. Ballard, Ph.D., CFCS, CFLE
Associate Professor, Child Development & Family
Relations, East Carolina University,
Greenville
&
Kevin H. Gross, Ph.D., CFLE
Program Evaluation and Research Consultant,
Eastern NC Evaluation & Research Services, Wilson

Many parents react with horror when the word "sexuality" is used in the same sentence with their child's name, particularly if their child is a preschooler. "We have a long time before we have to worry about that!" is the sentiment of many parents. The reality is that we are all sexual beings from the time we are born (actually, even before birth!) until the time that we die. Children are no exception. Children have difficulty achieving sexual health as an adult if sexuality is ignored throughout childhood. The Sexuality Information and Education Council of the United States (SIECUS), in a comprehensive writing on sexuality education, identified several life behaviors of a sexually healthy adult (pp. 16-17),[1] including: the ability to "develop and maintain meaningful relationships"; "appreciate one's own body"; "interact with all genders in respectful and appropriate ways"; "express love and intimacy in appropriate ways"; and, "express one's sexuality in ways that are congruent with one's values." Using these criteria, most parents would agree that they want their children to be sexually healthy.

Both parents and children report wanting to talk about sexuality together,[2] and the positive outcomes of effective parent-child sexual communication are well documented within the research literature.[3] Families are the primary socializers of their children. Not only are parents the preferred sources of sexuality information for many young people, but children do listen to their parents! It is important for you, as a parent, to remember how influential you are in your child's life. However, children and their parents have difficulty discussing sexuality.[4]

How do you overcome potential barriers and help your children achieve sexual health? First, ideas of sexuality need to be expanded. As the above description of sexual health states, sexuality includes more than just intercourse. It incorporates such things as body image, love, relationships, and gender issues. When you give your infant daughter a warning that you are going to wipe her nose rather than coming up behind her and taking her by surprise, you are conveying a respect for her body. When a preschooler sees his parents touch, hug, and kiss, this illustrates positive ways of showing affection. These examples illustrate the fact that sexuality education is already occurring in most families even when it is unintentional. It is helpful to think about additional actions that are intentional which can build on this foundation. What messages do you give regarding gender roles? Where appropriate, do you allow your child to make decisions, particularly decisions regarding his or her body? For example, if he doesn't want to kiss Aunt Edna, don't force it. Are your children learning correct names for body parts as a way to instill respect for the body and provide a common language?

Second, there is a common idea that sexuality education occurring in the home consists of "the talk" that often is an awkward and ineffective conversation. Sexuality education should be an ongoing and intentional process. Rather than having one talk, parents can take advantage of teachable moments (e.g., potty training is a great teachable moment!) to discuss sexuality-related topics with their children. For example, when a little boy is learning to use the bathroom, he might ask "why does Mommy sit down when she goes potty but Daddy stands up?" This provides a great opportunity to incorporate proper names for body parts into a discussion of the differences between girls and boys. Another example of a teachable moment might be when a three-year old asks about a pregnant woman. It is a good time to say that "she has a baby growing inside her–babies grow in a special place called the uterus." This is generally all the three-year olds want to know. But, by providing this information in an accurate manner, you have laid the foundation for future conversations about reproduction.

Answer questions as they arise and provide information that is developmentally appropriate. The result is a sense that sexuality is a natural part of one's life and not something about which to be embarrassed or ashamed. Additionally, if conversation is ongoing, parents can give children small bits of information that can continually build a foundation for sexual health. Preschoolers are curious about their bodies and their questions should be answered in a truthful and thoughtful manner. Young children generally need only small bits of information. As they process each piece of information, they may then come back to you for more information. Answers can be given in ways that children understand and that are consistent with your values. By treating their questions with respect and giving truthful answers (e.g., babies do not come from the stork!), children will learn that it is okay to ask Mom and Dad questions and that they can be trusted to give answers.

The parent who reacts with shock or embarrassment to the four-year old who asks where babies come from and avoids answering the question will less likely be asked questions in the future. That child has learned several sexuality education lessons from such an awkward or negative interaction–it is bad to ask questions, it is wrong to be curious, the human body is something about which to be embarrassed, and most importantly, don't ask Mom and Dad.

Finally, talking to your child about sexuality can be an important way to transmit your sexual values to your child. Clarify your own values and identify the goals and outcomes that you want for your children regarding sexuality. Convey these ideas in the messages that you send to your child. Are you setting the stage for continued honest communication about sexuality? Expanding your own definition of sexuality, engaging your child in ongoing, developmentally appropriate conversations about sexuality, and making communication an intentional process that reflects your own values can go a long way toward facilitating sexual health in your child.

The Cooperative Extension office of the U.S. Department of Agriculture (USDA) has developed a number of facts sheets on a national web site, all of which are useful to families. At the bottom of the site are three that might be especially helpful for parents to review: *"Talking with your teen about sexuality," "Teaching our daughters about sexuality,"* and *"Teaching our sons about sexuality."*[5]

As your child enters adolescence, she or he will encounter more and more sexuality information from a variety of sources, and will be making difficult choices about sexual behavior. Remember that a positive and open dialogue about sexuality in your home when your child is young will increase the likelihood that as a teenager he or she is going to come to you rather than friends with questions and concerns.

References

[1] Sexuality Information and Education Council of the United States, National Guidelines Task Force (2004). *Guidelines for Comprehensive Sexuality Education* (3rd edition). Retrieved October 27, 2010, from http://65.36.238.42/pubs/guidelines/guidelines.pdf.

[2] Somers, C. L., & Paulson, S. E. (2000). Students' perceptions of parent-adolescent

closeness and communication about sexuality: Relations with sexual knowledge, attitudes, and behaviors. *Journal of Adolescence, 23,* 629-644.

[3] Miller, B. C., Benson, B., & Galbraith, K. A. (2001). Family relationships and adolescent pregnancy risk: A research synthesis. *Developmental Review, 21,* 1-38.

[4] Hutchinson, M. K. & Cooney, T. (1998). Parent-teen sexual risk communication: Implications for intervention. *Family Relations, 47,* 185-194.

[5] National Extension Relationship & Marriage Education Network. (2007). *Extension Resources: Fact Sheets & Educational Materials.* Retrieved October 27, 2010, from http://www.nermen.org/factsheets.php.

Teaching Children to be Peacemakers

Beverly Johnson Biehr, M.S., M.A., M.Div.
CFLE Emeritus;
Retired Elder, North Indiana Conference of the
United Methodist Church, Valparaiso IN

We hear the song, "Let there be peace on earth and let it begin with me;" and, it keeps playing in my mind. Seeking to become a peacemaker in my daily life, I am led to question the inter-play between nations and individuals. In family life, how are we parenting our children–to become peacemakers or to become very competitive, if not aggression-admirers?

Families exist in a culture which has endured many wars and we may soak up many competitive values by default. We:

- have children play video games which may lead them to be more aggressive;[1]
- motivate children/youth to work hard for a fund-raiser by offering a prize to the one who sells the most, and with much less recognition to the ones who also cooperated but didn't come in first;
- admire the tallest, the strongest, the smartest, the prettiest;
- watch the post-athletic event ritual that gives accolades to the team that wins by a few points while the other team that played very hard, if not just as well, sits there looking and feeling dejected;
- give a best player award in a team sport;
- make decisions in a group by "majority rules" or by "leader authority" rather than by "consensus" (which does take longer but likely will include compromises); and,
- embrace popularity contests, beauty pageants, music awards, entertainment idol contests.

Yet children's intuitive common sense approach to peacemaking can be a lesson for parents. A retired grammar school teacher reminded me of an incident from my childhood. We "country kids" were being harassed by some bullies. I remember us meeting in a group and deciding to stand up for ourselves and put an end to the mistreatment. During recess we all linked arms and made a long chain of country kids. Then the inside person circled the school building while the rest of us fanned out. We walked slowly around the school. All the rest of the kids had to get out of our way. The teachers watched all of this from the windows and were in awe of our determination to get more respect. In that case, the children taught the adults and other children the power of a united peaceful protest.

The wisdom that I have arrived at is that if parents default and follow parenting fads which lead us back to spanking[2] or if we cave in to societal pressures of competition models in making day-to-day parenting decisions,[3] we may end up allowing our children to become competitive aggression-admirers or war-admirers, whether we want to or not.[4] If we want our children to learn to be peacemakers, we must go against the tide and pro-actively teach them both non-violence and peacemaking skills.[3,5,6] And we ourselves will learn peacemaking skills in the process,[6] by providing cooperative learning[3] and conflict management,[6] as well as using a counseling-based parenting approach.[5]

Here are two suggestions for parents to begin to take the lead and be pro-active facilitators of peacemaking skills:

1. Do an analysis of your children's extracurricular or spare time activities. Which ones teach cooperation skills and which ones teach competition skills? Competitive skills are emphasized in sports leagues, spelling bees, science fairs, writing and art contests, county fair projects, etc. Cooperation skills are emphasized in sports such as hiking, camping, bicycling, playground activities, and in children's clubs, religious organizations, and character-building organizations such as Boy/Girl Scouts, 4-H Clubs, and Boys/Girls Clubs. There needs to be a balance, because our society is organized on the competitive model, but the cooperative model encourages harmony and peacemaking. The competitive model assumes there has to be win/lose and even settles for lose/lose or a tie as a last resort, whereas the cooperative model works toward win/win as the ideal.

2. Conflict resolution among children (and adults) is a window of opportunity for values-based problem solving. The goal is to turn conflict situations into peace-filled situations and the means must be in harmony with the end goal. The method I like the very best was taught to me by a counseling service,

based on "I-messages"[5] and an adaptation of Speed Leas' work in conflict management.[6] It works well with serious disagreements and requires thinking it through ahead of time. It is always based on stating the problem as your own.

- You say, "I have a problem and I want your help."
- "The problem as I see it is that _____ seems to be happening and I feel _____ (mad, sad, glad, or scared)."
- "My part of the problem is that I do or don't _____ (react or respond appropriately or use avoidance, denial, or passivity)."
- "As we talk about it, I want to protect or create _____, _____, _____(values)."
- "How do you see the problem?" Listen.
- The other person says, or you say: "In order to solve/improve the situation, I am willing to _____."
- "What I want from you is _____."
- Then, together, negotiate any differences, seeking compromise if appropriate, and clarify your agreement.
- Set a time for evaluation.
- Get together. Evaluate. Celebrate achievements. Plan for any further follow-up.

Any parent who utilizes this method of values-based problem solving will most likely move beyond the comfort zone. We can think through the presentation of the problem ahead of time, but we don't know the outcome ahead of time.

Nothing takes the place of the example we set for our children as we resolve conflicts in front of them. Our children are close observers of how we react to problems and other provocative situations, and it is never too late to change, if needed. I wish I would have started values-based problem solving earlier in my parenting, but I feel it was better to have started it when they were teenagers than not at all. Especially during times of conflict and war, we need to spend additional time and effort helping our children learn how to "make peace."

References

[1] Anderson, Craig A. & Dill, Karen E. (2000). Video games and aggressive thoughts, feelings, and behavior in the laboratory and in life. *J. of Personality and Social Psychology, Vol. 78, No. 4,* 772-790.

[2] Jones, B.F. (2007). Christian child abuse: spanking away sin. *The Christian Century: Thinking critically, living faithfully. May 1, 2007,* 8-9.

[3] Pepitone, E.M. (1980). *Children in cooperation and competition: Toward a developmental social psychology.* Lexington MA: Lexington Books.

[4] Swartley, W.M. (2006). *Covenant of peace: the missing peace in New Testament theology and ethics.* Grand Rapids, MI: Eerdmans.

[5] Gordon, T. (1975). *PET: Parent effectiveness training: the tested new way to raise responsible children.* NY: Plume Book.

[6] Leas, Speed B. (1997). *Discover your conflict management style.* NY: The Alban Institute.

Caring Parents Actively Teach Their Children to Care

Brian Jory, Ph.D, CFLE
Professor and Director of Family Studies,
Berry College, Mount Berry, Georgia
&
Rachel Breece, B.A.
Program Coordinator & Certified Instructor,
KidzArt – Akron, Akron, OH

Imagine living in a family where everyone is self-absorbed and self-indulgent. Trust, respect, love, and commitment are meaningless. Relationships are dog-eat-dog, every man for himself, and tit-for-tat. In this family, parents vow only to stick together as long as they are happy–not "for better or worse, in sickness and in health." Nobody in this family is interested in caring for the children, frail elderly, sick or disabled.

Fortunately, most of us do not live in selfish families like this. We know the joy of loving and being loved, and we can trust *someone* to care for us in times of need. In fact, human babies cannot survive without compassionate caretakers, and this *caring* affects both the quality and length of our lives. So who teaches us to care? The vast majority of people can thank a parent who established a caring environment. Parents should not assume that their children will learn to care by accident, though. They should actively teach their children to care.

Caring involves complex attitudes and actions like setting aside self pre-occupation, feeling what others feel, anticipating their needs, and taking action on their behalf. Parents begin teaching their children to care by responsibly and trustfully caring for them in infancy. The motivation to care for infants is stimulated in mothers during childbirth through a hormone called oxytocin, sometimes referred to as "the cuddle chemical" (p. 46).[1] While oxytocin gets the process going, parents fall back on what they have learned about caring through their lives. Fathers may not get the benefits of oxytocin, but they still play an important role in showing their children masculine images of compassion.

As children grow into toddlers, parents model caring when they make the effort to understand their child by asking questions such as: What do you want? What do you need? Parents also model caring in the ways they treat one another. Do you take the time to ask each other how you feel? Do you listen to one another as you discuss the crunch of family needs? Or, do you spend too much time blaming one another and passing judgment? Do you anticipate the moods and feelings of one another? Do you respect each other despite your differences? Does your child see that you care about how your actions and attitudes impact others in your family, neighborhood and community?

Along with modeling, parents can actively teach their children to care by looking for opportunities in their everyday routines. For example, when reading a book or watching television or movies, do you discuss the inner thoughts and feelings of the characters with your child? When your child plays with others, do you teach the importance of sharing, give and take, respect, and tolerance? When your child has a conflict with others, do you teach your child how to approach that individual, listen to their side of things, and look for win-win solutions? Do you hold your child accountable when he or she is selfish, disrespectful, intolerant, or unfairly aggressive with others?

One time-honored technique is to teach children The Golden Rule–the mindset of treating others the way you would want to be treated. For example, on the drive home from her dance class, eleven year old Tatiana started complaining to her father, William, about a younger girl in the class, Ashlyn, who is only nine years old. According to Tatiana, Ashlyn is a pain and a loser. Ashlyn talks too much, doesn't pay attention to the dance teacher, and distracts Tatiana. Tatiana wishes Ashlyn would be kicked out of dance class. Tatiana's father sees this as a teachable moment, and invites Tatiana to think about what it would be like if she were suddenly and mysteriously transformed into Ashlyn.

"Wow, you sound unhappy with Ashlyn. What do you think it is like being Ashlyn?" asked William.

At first Ashlyn defensively told her Dad, "You'll have to ask Ashlyn about that. I'm not a mind reader!"

William repeated the question as a subtle way of holding Tatiana accountable for caring.

"Everyone calls Ashlyn names behind her back," replied Tatiana. "The favorite name for her is baby-cakes because she is such a baby!"

"Names?" reflected William.

"Nobody likes having a little kid in the class, Dad. I ignore her because I don't want anyone to think I hang out with babies."

"So, if you were Ashlyn, people would be calling you names. Ok, what else?" probed William.

"Ok, Dad. If I were Ashlyn, I would be starved for attention," blurted Tatiana. "It seems like she acts stupid just to get people to pay attention to her."

At this point, William held Tatiana directly accountable for caring: "Tatiana, knowing how you treat Ashlyn, would you like to be transformed into her?"

At this point, Tatiana confessed she did not like the way she treated Ashlyn. Having put herself in the place of Ashlyn, it suddenly seemed important to Tatiana to be a leader in looking out for Ashlyn. She agreed with her dad to start helping Ashlyn feel part of the group, and to encourage the other girls to include Ashlyn, despite the age differences.

Parental expectations for caring should fit the developmental capabilities of their child. Empathy, the ability to see things the way others do, is beyond the cognitive capability of toddlers, but it is important to teach preschoolers to give up selfishness in favor of sharing. Story books like *The Selfish Crocodile*[2] and *Selfish Sophie*[3] can be great for young children. For children over five, there is the classic short story *The Selfish Giant*,[4] first published in 1932 by Oscar Wilde, but still popular with children and literature lovers.

Parents also should consider how outdated and harmful gender roles can affect children. We live in a world that not only tolerates male insensitivity, but sometimes encourages it.[5] Young boys can easily get the idea that the needs and feelings of others are not important. They may even believe that their own feelings are not important. Male energy can lead to aggression, disruptive behavior at home and school, competitive relationships, and emotional inexpressiveness. These are signs that boys need extra attention in channeling male energy into masculine compassion, and parents may need to open up more opportunities for boys to express caring. A strong, compassionate male role model can help boys incorporate caring masculine identities into their own personalities.

In comparison, traditional gender socialization of girls tends to encourage them to forget their own dreams and desires, and care too much about the needs and feelings of others.[6] Caring does not mean that a girl should become a conformist, give in to bullying, or make herself a doormat. Girls can be taught that by caring for themselves first, they will be able to effectively care for others. All children, regardless of gender, need to be taught the importance of caring. After all, where would we be without it?

References

[1] Kuriansky, J. (2002). *The Complete Idiot's Guide to a Healthy Relationship.* Indianapolis, IN: Alpha Books.

[2] Charles, Faustin (2002). *The selfish crocodile.* London: Bloomsbury.

[3] Kelleher, Damian (2002). *Selfish Sophie.* Mankato, MN: Picture Window Books.

[4] Wilde, Oscar. (2001). *The selfish giant.* NY: Derrydale.

[5] Gurian, M. & Stevens, K. (2005). *The minds of boys: Saving our sons from falling behind in school and life.* Hoboken, NJ: Jossey-Bass.

[6] Cohen-Sandler, R. (2005). *Stressed-out girls: Helping them thrive in the age of pressure.* NY: Viking Adult Publishing.

A Small World Families Live In:
Six Degrees of Separation

Kristie Chandler, Ph.D., CFLE
Chair, Department of Family Studies
Samford University, Birmingham, AL

This notion of "six degrees of separation" evolved from social network theory research (meaning how people are connected to each other), such as Stanley Milgram's small world experiment.[1] Although there is some debate about the actual number of connections, the theory suggests that any two people are connected to each other using six or fewer relationship links, thus indicating that it is indeed a small world. This idea has been incorporated into various formats, including the "Six degrees of Kevin Bacon" game, a play, film and television productions, and now a new web site, www.sixdegrees.org, launched on January 18, 2007, and designed to create a social conscious charitable network.

My children used to play a game based on a version of this concept. While in the car, one of the children would need to go to the bathroom, of course! One child would say something like, "I have to go to the bathroom, so please don't say anything that will make me think about it. Let's talk about something else to keep my mind off of it." Then the other child would say something like, "O.K. Let's talk about our vacation to New Mexico." Then the child who needs to go to the bathroom would connect New Mexico to deserts, deserts to thirsty plants, and thirsty plants to the lack of water, which would then remind him/her of needing to go to the bathroom. The topic chosen to distract from nature's call did not matter; it was always connected back to water and the need to go to the bathroom.

Most things in this world seem to be interconnected, and parenting is no exception. In order to understand the functioning of family systems, it is necessary to examine the individuals in the family, as well as the society influencing those individuals and their relationships.[2] I use a version of the "Six Degrees" concept in my Marriage and Family class to help college students understand this interconnectedness. For example, a student will bring up a current news topic, an advertisement, a magazine article, a television show topic, a recently passed law, etc. Then, I will legitimately connect that topic to a concept in the marriage and family textbook, using six or fewer links. For instance, a student might comment that a local news show segment was on self-defense. I then connect the self-defense topic to dating violence or family violence, whether or not there is a biological or social reason that men usually abuse women, the fact that violence occurs frequently within the family, and so forth. Most topics are usually pretty easy.

On a slow news day, one of the students said that the new T.M. Elmo (Tickle Me X-treme Elmo) was just released. I sat there for a minute trying to think of a connection to the Marriage and Family class. Then, I remembered the topics in the class that related to the socialization of children. This led to a great discussion regarding the impact television and toys have on children. We had a talk about whether Elmo was male or female and how you make the determination through clues like name, voice and actions. We discussed what makes a toy appropriate for boys, what is appropriate for girls, and whether there should be any differentiation. The conversation evolved into a discussion about parenting authority, instilling values, and the process of raising children. All of this advanced from the announcement that T.M. Elmo was now available.

One of the primary functions of the family is to socialize their children. Although parents are still the primary socializing agent, some parenting experts believe that there are other socializing agents, including advertisers, toy and video game manufacturers, and other media, hoping to influence your child's desire for a certain toy, snack, or television program.[3] While this type of societal influence may seem more obvious to some, there are other ways which may be less obvious.

I was reminded through this discussion about Elmo how we sometimes defer the privilege of shaping our children to television, toys, peers, etc. Oftentimes, we are unaware of the influence some of these issues can have on our children. A societal issue can seem so far removed from our personal families that we don't make or want to make the connection that this may affect our family. So far, I have been able to relate every issue back to the family, usually using fewer than six connections. It is a reminder to me as a parent, that it is indeed a small world families live in and that I need to become more aware of the impact this has on my children.

Not all of these societal influences are necessarily bad; nonetheless, they are still influences. Our job, as parents, is to become aware of the ways our children can be socialized and to make conscious decisions which will sway their socialization process positively. Without this awareness, parents may be unable to fulfill one of their primary responsibilities.

When it comes to families and society's influence on families, I'm convinced there are fewer than six degrees of separation.

References

[1] Blass, T. (2004). *The man who shocked the world: The life and legacy of Stanley Milgram.* Cambridge, MA: Basic Books.

[2] Garbarino, J. & Bedard, C. (2001). *Parents under siege: Why you are the solution, not the problem, in your child's life.* NY: Free Press.

[3] Benokraitis, N.V. (2005). *Marriages and families: Changes, choices, and constraints* (5th ed.). Upper Saddle River, NJ: Pearson Prentice Hall.

Nurturing Traditions: Nurturing Family

Arminta Lee Jacobson, Ph. D., CFLE
Professor & Director of the Center for Parent Education and the annual International Conference on Parent Education and Parenting,
University of North Texas, Denton

Holidays remind me of the importance of nurturing and maintaining *traditions* and *rituals* in the lives of our children, our families, and our communities. Several years ago our oldest son, Trey, arrived home for Christmas after his first semester in college. My husband, his younger brother, and I were waiting for Trey to carry out our family "traditions" of decorating and cooking as a family. Trey let us know dramatically and in no uncertain terms how disappointed he was. He said "I have been cooped up in my dorm studying for finals and couldn't wait to come home and have Christmas. I thought you would have Christmas music playing when I drove up, the tree decorated, and cookies baking." For him, what was important for a slightly homesick college freshman was Christmas as he remembered it. After that year, we made sure the Christmas tree was decorated and music was ready to play when he arrived home from college for winter break. And to make sure, we carried out another family tradition, joking and having fun, Trey heard his favorite Christmas music record from early childhood when he walked in the door–"Christmas on the Farm."

Our family holiday traditions are examples of the kinds of rituals important to families, as studied extensively in the 1940s by James Bossard and Eleanor Boll in their book, *Ritual and family living.*[1] William Doherty, in his 1997 book, *The intentional family: How to build family ties in our modern world,*, says we have rituals for *connections or bonding, love rituals, & rituals that bind us to the larger community.*[2] According to Doherty, *connection rituals* help families feel closer together and build trust and loyalty. Connection rituals can be as simple as our routines at family meals to ways we celebrate holidays. *Love rituals* are how we express intimacy and make other members of the family feel special. How we celebrate birthdays and tell each other goodbye are examples of love rituals. *Community rituals* include family events such as weddings and funerals that involve the larger community. Early in the history of this country, most ritual celebrations were carried out in the larger community.

Holidays for most faiths include all three of these rituals. *Connection rituals* include the special traditions and routines we have at home, like drinking hot chocolate while we decorate the Christmas tree. *Love rituals*, making each family member feel special, include traditions such as hanging our children's tattered hand-made Christmas ornaments on the tree year after year, hand-making a gift, and calling distant family members on Christmas afternoon. Community rituals and traditions include worship services and also yearly observances such as Christmas Lighting and the Fourth of July parade. Families are part of the larger whole–the community, where we live our traditions and rituals.

Why do family rituals have so much importance for us? Why do we repeat them over and over again? Think of families as a whole– not just a group of individuals. Routines and rituals are how we stay organized as families and how we maintain equilibrium. We have *rules* about how we do things, the structure for our rituals and traditions. They make it clear how we are supposed to act and celebrate. Our rules may be related to culture, our religious beliefs, or may be passed down by families through generations.

Doherty says family rituals and routines are important to us in four ways: for *predictability*, for *connection*, for *identity*, and for *enacting values*. Rituals and routines are important for children of all ages, especially infants and young children. We know that young children like to read the same books over and over and the same way each time; that grandchildren like to play the same games every time they visit. Through *predictability*, infants and young children learn to trust their caregivers and their world. This is the basis of secure attachment and emotional and social development. Children also learn basic principles of life, particularly cause and effect. They learn concepts about people, objects, time, and social relationships and strengthen their memories through the repetition of ritual.

Traditions and rituals also build individual and family *connections* The shared experiences of traditions and rituals are a way of strengthening ties and bonds and building a sense of family and community. Through shared family and community experiences, children develop a sense of family, cultural, and community *identity*. The child knows "This is who I am. This is where I belong." Families *enact values* that are dearly held and reinforce them through family traditions. This is especially true when cultural and religious beliefs are expressed through ritual and celebration.

What is the message for parents? Be intentional and develop rituals and routines to which you can commit and maintain and reflect your most important values and beliefs. When parents include ritual and traditions in their family life, they model and teach children that the world and others can be trusted. Children learn that the most important people in their lives care about and take time for them. They also develop a sense of who they are as a member of their family and community, what is important, and what is valuable.

As rituals and traditions involve routines and organization, they also provide children important structure for their lives. They help regulate their behavior, provide clear expectations about what is expected, and facilitate building ties and bonds and a sense of community and loyalty.

As you celebrate holidays, family celebrations and religious traditions, look beyond the *work* of getting ready and reflect on how traditions and the rituals express who you are, what you believe, and how we care about others in our families and communities.

References

1 Bossard, James H., & Boll, Eleanor S. (1950). *Ritual and family living: A contemporary study.* Philadelphia: University of Pennsylvania.
[2] Doherty, W. J. (1997). *The intentional family: How to build family ties in our modern world.* Reading: MA: Addison-Wesley.

Where I'm From

I'm from applesauce, Tonka, and toy trucks.
The bunk-bed that was my tall fortress, and hideout
from my big brother Sami.

I am from the sycamore tree which I used to climb,
higher and higher as I grew older.
The maple syrup that my dad would get off a tree
and we would eat in front of a fire.

I am from the coconut that my family had to drill
open to get that sweet milk.
I am from funny uncles named Chuck, beach trips,
and waiting for that huge wave that could sweep me
off to shore.

I am from my cousins Gabe, Charlie, and my little
brother John.
From birthday songs and Easter eggs that we
colored every year.

I'm from washing before you eat, and look before
you cross the street.

I am from my favorite Lebanese foods that mom
made when I grew up, jaj ou riz and fasoulia.
I'm from the berserk firework that almost hit my
friend's dad.
I'm from Raffi tapes, Puff the magic dragon, and
being tucked in at night.
I'm from Christmas presents, family movie night,
and campouts in our backyard.

I'm from the Simpsons at 6:00 sharp every day,
dragon tales, and animal crackers.
I'm from starting small fires on my patio with
magnifying glasses, and reading Harry Potter.
I am from playing tag to running cross country.
I am from Preschool to Middle School.
Toddler to young adult.

–Mark Sfeir, Winchester, VA
Then, a 13 year old grandson of CFLE Emeritus,
Bob Keim

Imperfection Is Perfectly Fine

Margaret E. Machara, Ph.D., CFLE
Assistant Professor, Tennessee State University,
Nashville

When I played sports in high school my coach, probably like
many coaches or drill sergeants, used to say, "Practice doesn't make
perfect, perfect practice makes perfect." While I understood the point–
that you have to actually be able to do something, and keep doing it, in
order to do it when necessary–this idea isn't really very helpful in the
ever-changing, circus side-show in which most families are trying to
survive. Therefore instead of recommending becoming a Perfect Parent, I believe that imperfection is not only tolerable but perfectly fine.
In fact, I think that imperfection will nurture better kids.

First, take care of yourself; stop trying to be the Perfect Parent. While we read every day about neglectful or abusive parents,
some parents have the opposite problem. They are trying to be Perfect
Parents and feel guilty for taking care of themselves. It is important
to use some common sense, however. You obviously can't decide not

to get up and feed your infant during the night because you don't feel like it. Scheduling spa appointments Monday through Friday from 3:30 until 7:00 also is not a wise choice if those are the only hours that you see your kindergartener. Nevertheless, aside from the extremes, parents need to take time for themselves and not feel bad about it. When parents focus all their attention on their children, several negative things happen. (1) The children start to feel like the center of the universe–not a good trend to start–and the children don't learn how to be empathetic to other people's needs. (2) Children start internalizing the pressure to be perfect.[1] Instead of getting to be kids, they have the added weight on their shoulders of having to be good for the sake of the family. (3) Kids have stressed parents who aren't taking good care of themselves.[2] Therefore, consider hiring a babysitter occasionally and go shopping without a stroller or schedule a massage or a manicure. Take time to workout at the gym after work or plan a night with friends. But most of all, do these self care activities without feeling guilty. You can be a better parent if you take time for yourself and don't feel like you need to be a Perfect Parent.

Second, make mistakes. Since everyone does make mistakes, give yourself permission to make mistakes without guilt or remorse. Children do not need Perfect Parents. In order to develop and thrive, children need loving and consistent care but not perfection.[3] Parents tend to feel like they have ruined their children if they lose their temper or break a promise or make an occasional mistake. Rather than feeling like a failure when you make a mistake, use it as a teachable moment. No child is perfect, so use your mistakes to show them how to recover gracefully. It won't lower you in the eyes of your children to admit that you were wrong and apologize to them. You've just shown them how to take responsibility, apologize to others and try to make things better. By making mistakes gracefully, you show your child that it isn't the mistake but how you handle it that matters.

Therefore, imperfection is perfectly fine. Keep teaching kids that they don't have to be perfect and show them it is important to take care of themselves. When parents model how to take responsibility for their mistakes, imperfection can even be superior to perfection.

References

[1] Elkind, D. (2001). *The hurried child: Growing up too fast too soon* (3rd ed.). Cambridge, MA: Perseus Publishing.

[2] Edwards, C.D. (1999). *How to handle a hard-to-handle kid: A parent's guide to understanding and changing problem behaviors.* Minneapolis: Free Spirit Publishing, Inc.

[3] Fabes, R., & Martin, C. (2003). *Exploring child development: Transactions and transformations.* Boston: Allyn and Bacon.

Chapter II

Wisdom for Family Interaction

Many of the articles in this book relate to family interaction; however, the following ones focus upon it most directly.

Parental Investment

Jerry Cook, Ph.D., CFLE
Associate Professor, Family and Consumer Sciences, California State University, Sacramento

Many of us were taught that it was better to give than to receive. In reality, it was because of what we received *by giving* unconditionally that made the effort worth it. By giving and sharing qualities of happiness, friendship, and *a closeness to the community,* we can make the world a better place.

Parents give an enormous amount of time, energy, and resources to their children. Many children are blessed to have wonderful parents. But it is my impression that we as parents can do even better. And sociologists from many different ideological perspectives believe that children need more from us.[1,2]

In a world of "haves" and "have nots" to divide us, the one thing we have in common is the desire and ability to improve our children's lives. It may seem a bit ironic that the best way for us to obtain the rewards from our parenting journey is by giving away much of what we have. I call this principle "parental investment."

Most people understand investment to be an avenue for making money. What is sometimes forgotten, and perhaps the reason why so few Americans invest their money, is because something else needs to be sacrificed in order for that investment to occur. Instead of buying new furniture or eating out as frequently, that money goes into an account for the purpose of reaping a greater reward in the future.

This same attitude needs to be with us as parents; we are often sacrificing many things (e.g., money, time, sleep). Do we fully understand the purpose or power of that sacrifice as an investment in the future?

Below is a brief list of things parents can sacrifice for the purpose of benefiting their child's life.

- We can give up pride. Pride has many connotations, but often occurs when feeling superior to another. Age and experience give us wisdom, but it does not give us the right to belittle our children in private or public. Another (perhaps more common) expression of pride is worrying more about what others think of us as parents rather than on the energy we give to our children. We can worry less about our image as parents (which appears to benefit us) and focus more on what benefits our children.

- We can give up unnecessary duties and activities. Years ago I asked my son, if there was only one thing I could give him, what he would prefer to have. I have to admit, I was a little nervous, asking this question around Christmas! To my astonishment, he said, "I just want more time with you, Mom and Dad." Children crave attention and time from their parents.[3] Those who do not receive it will go to great lengths to receive it from somewhere or someone else. Things we think may be important now will not seem important later when our children are grown. Who will care what we watched on television, or went shopping for, or even provided service to a community, if it meant losing an opportunity to spend time with our children? Children notice the sacrifice their parents make, at least to some extent, by the parents' response to others' demands. Replacing "I have to" with "I choose to" in our conversations with others about our time with our children will say more than words.

- We can give up guilt. None of us are, nor will be, perfect. We will make mistakes as individuals, parents, employees, and marriage partners. We cannot change the past, but we can choose how to respond to it without having to live in it again. Guilt robs us of our ability to parent effectively, so it is a loss without any purpose. Making a decision that our relationship with our child is more important than our need to feel guilty for mistakes is a first step, but often we need additional validation through meditation, prayer, and a positive support group of friends or family. The removal of guilt may not happen instantaneously, but constantly reminding yourself that you and your child's welfare is of more value to you than any guilt you can feel will help.

While sacrificing for the purpose of improving your child's life is an important practice, it doesn't mean that we give up everything that is of value to us. We need to balance the principle of "parental investment" with our need to stay healthy and other responsibilities in life. But the core idea is one of power, and with practice, it will work.

References
[1] Pipher, M. (1996). *The shelter of each other: Rebuilding our families.* NY: Ballantine Books.

[2] Popenoe, D. (2005). *War over the family.* New Brunswick, NJ: Transaction Publishers.

[3] Chapman, G., & Campbell, R. (1997). *The five love languages of children.* Chicago: Moody Press.

Surprise: Our Children Still Need and Want Us

Sterling Kendall Wall, Ph.D., CFLE
Associate Professor, Family & Consumer Sciences,
University of Wisconsin–Stevens Point

About a dozen years ago my small young family took a Saturday off from the routine of graduate study and work and went down to the Garden of the Gods, in Colorado Springs, to eat lunch amidst the amazing natural architecture of the red rock outcroppings for which it is famous. We selected a camp site that was off the beaten path with a picnic table and shade. After we set up the food and had fixed lunch for our three and a half year old son, Sterling, he announced that he was going to go eat by himself, up in the rocks. We helped him pack up his plate and watched as he wandered off. I struggled slightly with feelings that it had already started, "he doesn't want to be with us," I thought.

The rest of us continued to eat our lunch, converse and, after a few minutes, noticed that atop of the rocky mound into which our son had headed we could just barely see his head and face as he ate his lunch. He had situated himself in a precise location where, in his own lunch spot and mostly hidden from our view, he still had a line of sight directly to our table.

I realized then that he needed us after all, just perhaps in a different way. It may be surprising for some parents to hear that even as teens our children still want and need us. This is contrary to how the media all too often portrays parenting during the teen years, as a constant battle between parents and independent young adults. Indeed, one survey of 200 teens found that 21% rated "not having enough time together with parents" as one of their two top concerns, ranking this concern equally with the teens' expressed educational worries.[1]

That children and teens still want and need direct connection with their parents seems to run counter to the current "hurry up" and "materialistic" consumer culture within which we live. Indeed, some have observed that the role of parents appears to be transforming from friend and mentor to provider of consumer goods and services.[2] The good parent is no longer seen as the close confidant or mentor, or even the parent who plays catch in the back yard. Rather, we sometimes feel that the good parent is the parent that can provide the goods and services to their child, such as driving them to baseball practice where they can play catch with someone else. Not that there is anything wrong with sports, but, sometimes the direct time with parents does seem to be squeezed out by a plethora of activities for our children. An old adage often has been repeated that "things are to have, and people are to love, as long as you don't get that mixed up, you'll do okay." Sometimes we do get it mixed up as we start to believe that possessions, success, and achievement are the main conduits to happiness. This even starts to play out in our activities with our children.

For example, several years after eating lunch in the Garden of the Gods, I found myself pursuing the final leg of my academic career in Auburn, Alabama. We lived in a nice apartment complex with a small fishing pond near the entrance gate. At this time, I was working 3 jobs, going to school, and our family had grown to four children. Sterling, now about six years old, had it in his head that he wanted to go fishing. Day after day it seemed that he would ask me to take him fishing. Day after day I would find some excuse about how I was too busy, or that it was raining and the fish don't bite in the rain. Finally he asked, "Can't we just try, Dad?" I had 30 minutes, so I packed him and his five year old brother Taylor, the fishing pole, tackle box, and their two year old sister, Mariah, into the pickup. It was sprinkling just a bit, but we were going to "try" anyway.

We got down to the fishing hole and I baited his hook with a hunk of bread (the bluegill seemed to love it) and he and Taylor went over to the bank to try their luck while I helped Mariah throw bread to the ducks from the pickup bed (it was safer, the ducks couldn't jump up on her from there). I watched as the boys would take turns casting and reeling, with the other holding the umbrella over the person fishing. It was so cute, but I didn't even see a glimpse of the usual school of bluegill, and they did not receive a single bite on their line, "due to the rain" I told them, just as I had warned.

Well, the time was up, and we piled into the cab of the pickup, slightly damp, but having tried. As I was trying to formulate some wise "I told you so" to my son, thinking that our trip was a failure since we had not caught a single fish, he piped up first saying, "This was the best day of my life!" I was surprised! I reminded him that we had not actually caught any fish, to which he replied, "Yes, but we went fishing!" It was an eye opener for me; I thought the goal was to catch a fish, to obtain a prize, to achieve. He had only said he wanted to "go fishing"; he'd never actually said he needed to "catch a fish."

I have been reminded of the priority of spending time with my children, even in seemingly simple and menial activities, on numerous occasions. Once while lying under our van making some repairs, I saw two little legs appear by the side of the car. Our 4 year old, Meaghan, wanted to know if she could help. "Not this time Meg, this is important and I have to get it done. Why don't you go ask mom if you can help her with dinner?" She went in and received the same response from mom, "Not tonight Meg, I'm in a hurry, why don't you go play?" Fortunately, children are persistent, and forgiving. Before long I saw the two little legs again and she picked up a wrench and started pounding on the car door (mimicking my sounds from under the car). I quickly slid out and showed her how she could help me by hitting on the tire and rim instead. Her smile was priceless that night as she told everyone around the dinner table how she had helped dad fix the car. She smiles just as big when she also gets to make special desserts or dinners together with mom.

Spending time with parents in seemingly simple activities is not only important just for little children. When asked to think back to when they were a kid, and picture the best time they had as a family, many adults mention such activities as singing songs together in the living room, camping out two hours from home, playing games on Friday nights, or even scrubbing the kitchen floor with mom.[3] Trips to Disney Land and other expensive vacations are not mentioned as often as these seemingly simple times together.

In summary, contrary to the popular notion among some parents that children and adolescents want nothing to do with them, children still need and want to be directly involved with their parents, perhaps in different ways than before, and perhaps in ways that are different from what we expect as parents.

Furthermore, most children and parents report having strong relationships and sharing similar values–and are not characterized by the high level of conflict that seems to be so popularized in the media of today.[4] Indeed, as long as parents can maintain connection, guidance, and love, even when the going may get a little tough in the teen years, things tend to turn out just fine more often than not.[5]

Yesterday I went to Sterling's track meet, he is now 15. I made my way into the stands, and he hung out on the field with his team mates. However, once the call was made for the "boys 200 meter dash," he went across the field and started warming up and getting ready to race. I was distracted by our three year old, Hannah, and when I looked up, I saw that Sterling had broken away from the group and was slowly walking towards us, from across the field, waving his arm until I saw and responded with an answering wave. He then went back, got set, and ran the race. It appears that whether they are sitting just barely out of sight on that rocky ledge, or out on the field getting ready to run the race of life, our children still want us to be there, and to be a part of their life.

References

[1] Global Strategy Group, Inc. (April, 2000). *Talking With Teens: The YMCA Parent and Teen Survey: Final Report.*

[2] Doherty, W. J., & Carlson, B. (2002). *Putting family first: Successful strategies for reclaiming family life in a hurry-up world.* NY: Henry Holt.

[3] Olson, D. H., & Defrain, J. (2000). *Marriage and the family: Diversity and strengths.* Mountain View, California: Mountain View Publishing.

[4] Demo, D. H., & Cox, M. J. (2001). Families with young children: A review of research in the 1990s. In R. M. Milardo (Ed.), *Understanding families into the new millennium: A decade in review* (pp. 95-114). Lawrence, KS: NCFR and Alliance Communications Group.

[5] Walsh, D. (2004). *Why do they act that way? A survival guide to the adolescent brain for you and your teen..* NY: Free Press.

Lessons Learned Around the Family Dinner Table

Peggy North-Jones, Ph.D., CFLE
Associate Director, Caregiver Connections,
Quincy, IL

At the family dinner table, I grew up knowing that my father, a son of Southern parents, did not like his food hot. In fact, he preferred turning everything into a "salad" by covering it with mayonnaise. My mother, a New Englander, liked her food pure and piping hot. The negotiations that went on between them on how to live with these differences characterized the time we spent at the dinner table as a family.

On my first visit to meet my future in-laws, I had just returned from the West Coast where I had fervently joined the ranks of bra-burning feminists. Seated at the dinner table in a mid-western town, I was handed 2 rolls on a plate. I watched as both of my soon-to-be sisters-in-law and mother-in-law carefully buttered one roll for themselves and then handed the other *split and buttered* roll to their spouse. I looked at my fiancé with incredulous disbelief, and said "You have got to be kidding." Only later did I realize that this dinner table experience was an introduction into the study of contrasts between my new family and my family of origin.

I knew that on every holiday, my grandmother would arrive in her pretty dress and high heels and place a cut-glass bowl of ambrosia on the dinner table. It was not important what else was for dinner. She brought this dessert that stemmed from her own family tradition.

From these experiences and others, I learned about marriage, conflict, communication, compromise and life's blessings at the dinner table. There is a wonderful Norman Rockwell painting, *Freedom from Want*. It depicts a smiling family at Thanksgiving dinner, and highlights parents who are proudly presenting the perfectly cooked turkey. For many today, this illustration would have little meaning other than nostalgia. The family dinner up until about the last 20 years punctuated family life with both a sense of time and of a shared meaning; it now seems to be disappearing for many. The image that might come to mind for a painting today would be cars in a fast food drive-through lane or parents serving "take-out" to their children.

With families today eating an average of only 4 meals a week together in the home, family dinners have declined by one third since the mid 1970s.[1] The percentage of food consumed by children in restaurants and fast-food outlets nearly tripled between 1977 and 1996.[2] According to Hoffert and Sandberg, mealtime, when children and parents come together to share the stories of their day, tends to correlate with overall child well-being.[3] It seems important to reflect on the apparent impact of these changes in family meal time.

The family dinner represents time shared and a place to pass on rituals, customs, and special-occasion traditions to the next generation. On a daily basis, manners can be taught, gossip shared, adult relationships modeled, and sibling rivalry expressed and resolved. Even when meal time takes on an unpleasant tone, the experience is still a sharing of who we are as a family. It provides a definition and experiences to remember, as well as predictability: dinner is at a specific time and everyone in the house is expected to be there. The routines and rituals around meals and the family table are components of the characteristics that underlie each family's uniqueness.

Nutrition can be taught at the family dinner table. Parents in many cases have stopped being the primary source of information for their children on what and when to eat. I grew up with no pantry, no snacks available, and I asked my parents if I could have something to eat before I could have it. The lack of fast food places meant that except for a special treat-trip to the corner market, my mother and father controlled food availability. And, although, I saw some food advertisements in magazines or the newspaper, I did not have a television or computer offering information to me about food. The dinner table then, provided a time to eat and to learn about what I liked, what was good for me, and what my mother was willing to supply. The kitchen and dining tables provide key learning opportunities that can represent family values.

Manners can be taught at the dinner table. Although the lessons often evoke eye-rolling on the part of children, they go with us as we venture out in the world. These include how to act: "If you don't have anything nice to say, then don't say anything"; how to look: "Sit up straight and put your napkin in your lap"; how to manage food: "Chew with your mouth closed"; and, how to be social and conversational: "You need to stay at the table until everyone is finished." Few of us are very tolerant of sharing meal time with those who did not have the experience of this training in table manners and etiquette, even if we found the learning tedious at the time.

Family time happens naturally at the dinner table. With today's multi-tasking, often over-extended dual-career or single parent families, time together is often lacking or at a premium. Now, even restaurant eating may find families together but with one parent on a cell phone and a child engaged in playing a hand-held videogame. The experience of dinner table conversation, of shared time where nothing can interrupt the family togetherness, is not a frequent occurrence today. Televisions are on, telephones ring, and family members come and go and often eat different foods at the same meal. The sharing, of so many types, that is fundamental to the experience of the family table seems to have been replaced–if family members even get to the table.

What lesson have I learned from listening to families with whom I have worked over the last 35 years? It is that there is *so much* to be gained by taking the time and putting forth the effort required to get family members to the dinner table. Family bonding, communication, good nutrition, and the sharing of family values all increase when this simple routine is created. According to Brendtro and others,[4] the sense of belonging that is fundamental to a child's healthy development is supported when she or he is made to feel an important part of a daily event in the life of the family. "Everyone please come to dinner"–what delightful words!

Change is part of life. So are lessons. I wonder… if the lessons outlined above are not being learned at the dinner table, where will there be learned?

References

[1] Doherty, W.J. (2000). *Take back your kids: Confident parenting in turbulent times.* Notre Dame, IN: Sorin.

[2] St.-Onge M., Keller, K., & Heymsfield, S. (2003). Changes in childhood food consumption patterns. *American Journal of Clinical Nutrition, 78,* 1068-73.

[3] Hofferth, S. & Sandberg, J. (2001). How American children spend their time.

Journal of Marriage and Family. May, 295-308.

[4] Brendtro, L.K., Brokenleg, M., & Van Bockern, S. (2001). *Reclaiming youth at risk: Our hope for the future*. Bloomington, IN: National Education Service.

Family Stress: Don't Dodge it

Mumbe S. Kithakye, M.P.H., Ph.D.
Adjunct Faculty, Department of Human
Development & Family Science,
Oklahoma State University, Stillwater

When I first played dodge ball as a child, I spent a lot of time ducking and hoping I would not get hit. Soon I realized that it was to my advantage to catch the ball and feign courage (even when I wasn't feeling it). I noticed that if I caught the ball there would be fewer members of the other team trying to hit me and I might even get somebody else out in the process. It took a bit of work but I eventually developed the skills necessary to catch, throw and dodge the ball and ultimately find more fun than fear in the game.

Life can sometimes feel like a game of dodge ball, with troubles and challenges coming at us from all over the place. As in dodge ball, sometimes a small side step is all that is needed while other times a dive to the floor is the only sure path for survival. Some challenges encountered by families are easy to deal with, requiring minor harmless adjustments; for example, eating dinner a little later so as to allow for all members of the family to return from their after school activities. Other challenges result in major and sometimes negative changes in the family; for example, a death in the family may lead to depression and conflict among family members. To further complicate things, families often experience several different challenges at the same time. And while some families may struggle to cope with challenges, others appear to take challenges in stride, adapting to trouble and overcoming difficulties.

Why is it that some families are able to adapt their lives and cope well with potentially devastating challenges and others are not? This question is at the core of family risk and resilience research. In an effort to help families cope during troubled times, scholars try to understand the things that assist a family in navigating challenges and adapting positively in times of trouble.[1] There is no exact recipe for overcoming trouble, but just like in the game of dodge ball, we can develop skills and characteristics in our families that will better prepare us for the challenges that lie ahead. A family environment that is *supportive, flexible, well-connected and* reliant on a *shared belief system* is better able to cope during troubled times than one that is lacking in support, overly rigid or unconnected.[2]

A *supportive* **environment** relies on healthy communication between family members as a means of providing emotional support and promoting collaborative problem-solving. For example, as some children pass through their teenage years, the whole family may experience a period of difficulty. Parents may feel that their child is intentionally choosing to challenge their authority and the rules of the home. In turn, the parents may become more demanding and restricting, causing more stress for the whole family.

In a supportive family environment, members of the family would be willing to address the changes in the family members' lives that may be contributing to more stress in the home. Children would feel safe enough to discuss problems they encounter at school or with friends and how those affect their lives at home. Parents would be willing to listen to their child without taking things personally and parents may even be able to help children navigate the murky waters of adolescence. This supportive environment would allow for information to be relayed clearly about challenges and for members of the family to be able to actively participate in addressing the challenges together.

In a *flexible* **environment,** families would be willing to adapt or change so as to better be able to address challenges without falling into unhealthy patterns. For example, if the sole breadwinner, maybe a father, was to lose his job suddenly the family members would need to be willing to be flexible so as to cope. A father who prefers to keep quiet about problems at work would need to openly discuss the job loss with his spouse. A wife who prefers to stay at home may need to temporarily join the workforce. And the children in the family may need to take on more household chores so as to keep the home functioning while the mother is working and the father is looking for a job. This flexibility would allow the family to positively adapt even during the crisis.

It also is to the family's advantage to be *well-connected* during times of trouble. A sense of unity enables the family to address challenges together, gaining strength from one another. One individual's area of weakness may be another's area of strength. And being well-connected in the community would allow for access to social and economic resources that may be necessary during times of trouble. For example, in an area prone to hurricanes, a well-connected family would have access to information about the best times to evacuate, the best routes, whom to contact in case one is stranded and which stores to go to for those last minute needs before evacuation.

Finally, a *shared belief system* allows the family to make meaning of the troubles they encounter, providing hope and a will or belief in the ability to overcome. For example, a family may experience the death of a family member and their shared beliefs could serve as the foundation for coping with the loss. The family may find hope and strength in their beliefs about the afterlife, believing that the deceased person is only temporarily separated from them and that a reunion will occur. With a shared belief system, troubles also can be seen as opportunities for learning new life lessons, such as the importance of patience, love, courage, etc. A shared belief system also could allow for challenges to be addressed as opportunities for growth or action, providing purpose and motivation to address and overcome challenges.[3]

Even though our families encounter challenges and cannot dodge all the difficulties that come our way, we can strengthen and prepare our families to adjust to challenges and overcome troubles. We can do this by cultivating supportive homes, flexibility in dealing with challenges, promoting a shared belief system and staying well-connected to one another and to our communities.

References

[1] Cowan, P.A., Cowan, C.P., & Schulz, M.S. (1996). Thinking about risk and resilience in families. In E.M. Hetherington & E.A. Blechman (Eds.), *Stress, Coping and Resiliency in Children and Families* (1-38). Mahwah, NJ: Lawrence Erlbaum Associates.

[2] Walsh, F. (2002). A family resilience framework: innovative practice applications. *Family Relations, 51*, 130-137.

[3] Walsh, F. (2003). Family resilience: a framework for clinical practice. *Family Process, 42*, 1-18.

Problems are opportunities in work clothes.
–*Henry Kaiser*

"I'm Sorry"

Robert E. Keim, Ph.D., CFLE Emeritus
Professor Emeritus, Northern Illinois University
Clinton, TN

While teaching Parent Education at the university, I frequently asked students how many of them recalled hearing their parents say to them, "I'm sorry." Quite honestly, at first I was astonished to find that only one or two (out of 30-40) would raise their hand. For a reality check for myself, I once asked my youngest daughter (then still living at home) how many times she recalled me saying it, and she responded by saying: "Gobs and gobs of times." It might sound like I must have been a terrible parent, having to say "I'm sorry" so many times. However, somewhere in the distant past, I seem to have been fortunate to have been impressed with the merits of saying "I'm sorry" when it seemed to fit–with my kids, and with others.

This notion of saying "I'm sorry" is well supported over time by various authors and scholars, by responding rationally to our self-talk (cognitive behavior theories[1,2,3]); by being open and honest (the "transparent self"[4]); and, by communicating our own feelings to another person with good "I" messages.[5]

"I'm sorry"–these two simple words, when said with sincere meaning and feeling, can make a world of difference in a relationship. Saying "I'm sorry" (with warmth in the voice) can help to make the hurt, offended, or injured person feel as if the person speaking these words really cares, that the person is being genuine, that he or she is reaching out to the other person, trying to make amends, trying to reestablish more honest and open communication. We occasionally experience this with others in our lives–we usually know how it feels, how it can bring back a warmer feeling between two people who were previously being pushed apart by some conflict or misunderstanding. Ample research indicates the power of forgiveness in relationships,[6] and this can best happen when someone says, "I'm sorry."

When should we say it? Probably when our self-talk tells us something like: "that wasn't nice," "you shouldn't have said that," or "done that"; or "would be good to tell them 'I'm sorry.'" We need to act on those messages to ourselves, whether they are to our children or another adult. Saying "I'm sorry" to our children can begin when they are young enough to understand (which is usually younger then we think), on up through their teen and adult years. And it will usually pattern the ability on their part to respond, as well, to the parent with "I'm sorry" when appropriate.

Occasionally, I've heard people express concern that they might lose respect from another, or their child, if they admitted that they had done something "wrong." On the contrary, people usually seem to respond positively when we express a sincere apology. As it applies between two adults, it also can apply to parents and children.

Yes, saying "I'm sorry," conveyed with sincere meaning and feeling, may be crucial in building a healthy relationship between parent and child.

References

[1] Ellis, A., & Harper, R.A. (1975). *A new guide to rational living*. Englewood Cliffs, NJ: Prentice Hall. Note: a classic on avoiding stupid thinking.

[2] Stoop, David. (1996). *Self-Talk: Key to personal growth* (2nd ed.). NY: Fleming H. Revell.

[3] Morin, A. (1993). Self-talk and self-awareness: on the nature of the relation. *The Journal of Mind and Behavior, 14*, 223-234.

[4] Jourard, S.M. (1964). *The transparent self.* NJ: Van Nostrand.

[5] "I messages," perhaps are to be first attributed to Martin Buber in his 1958 book, *I and Thou* (2nd ed.). They are most thoroughly described by Thomas T. Gordon in his 1970 classic book, *P.E.T. Parent effectiveness training*

[6] Fincham, Frank D., Hall, Julie, & Beach, Steven R. (2006). Forgiveness in marriage: Current status and future directions. *Family Relations, 35*, 415-427.

"I Forgive You"

Sharon McGroder, M.S., Ph.D.
Family Researcher, Sterling VA

I enjoy reading advice columns in my local newspaper, and a recent entry caught my eye. The reader wanted to know the appropriate response when someone says "I'm sorry." Intriguing as this question was, I found the response even more interesting—not because of what the advice columnist said, but because of what she *didn't* say. The advice columnist said that a sincere "thank you" is perfectly appropriate. While I don't disagree with this response, especially for a minor issue, it struck me as somewhat limited, and a missed opportunity to discuss the power of forgiveness and how to convey it.

Like most parents, I taught my young children the importance of saying "please" and "thank you." I viewed this not only as a common courtesy, but also as an opportunity to teach my children about the inherently reciprocal nature of human interaction. Sometimes we request assistance ("please"); sometimes we receive assistance ("thank you"). Likewise, I taught my children to say *"I'm sorry"* when they offended or hurt someone (which happened frequently enough between my energetic young sons!)...and to say *"I forgive you"* when the apology was accepted.

Forgiveness involves abandoning our angry feelings and thoughts toward a person, and replacing those feelings with understanding and compassion.[1] This may be easier said than done—especially when the hurt is deep, recurrent, or inflicted by someone we love. As Gandhi once said, "The weak can never forgive. Forgiveness is an attribute of the strong" (p. 301).[2] However, the benefits of forgiveness can be great; research has documented the importance of forgiveness for one's mental and physical health.[3] Forgiveness is a key ingredient in all close relationships—friendships and family relationships. We, as parents, must therefore teach our children the importance of forgiveness...and *how* to forgive.

A critical first step is showing our children that we ourselves know how to forgive. One of my more humbling moments as a parent came when I chastised my 7-year-old for spilling his orange juice on the carpet. I was angry–how many times had I told him not to take drinks into the living room? But while I was ranting about the rules and how he knows better, I almost didn't hear him apologizing; he felt really bad. I should have stopped, taken a deep breath, acknowledged his apology, told him I forgave him, and then cleaned up the mess together. But instead, I continued to rant, talking about the importance of following rules and being responsible. My son went from sad and apologetic, to mad and resentful–and his words went from "I'm sorry" to "I *SAID* I was *SORRY!*"

Just as a sincere "I'm sorry" builds and maintains a healthy relationship between parent and child (see Keim's "I'm Sorry," in the article above), so too does saying and teaching the power of a sincere and genuine "I forgive you."

Granted, we parents shouldn't force an "I'm sorry" or "I forgive you" out of a child. We want the child to understand their meaning and be earnest when finally saying them. And, if a deep hurt has occurred, it may take a little recuperative time before one is able to say "I forgive you."

Young children may not understand the full meaning of all of this. Indeed, most adults struggle with humbly requesting and graciously offering forgiveness. But as occasions arise through the years, no doubt there will be more opportunities for discussing and learning the meaning of an apology, of saying those words, "I forgive you." As parents, encouraging our children to request and grant forgiveness is one of the best things we can do. They will be healthier, and their lives richer, as a result.

References

[1] Fitzgibbons, R. (1998). Anger and the healing power of forgiveness: A psychiatrist's view. In R. Enright & J. North (Eds.), *Exploring forgiveness*. Madison: University of Wisconsin.

[2] Gandhi, M. (2000). *The collected works of Mahatma Gandhi* (2nd rev. ed.). New Delhi: Veena Jain.

[3] Harris, A.H.S. and Thorsen, C.E. (2005). Forgiveness, unforgiveness, health, and disease. In E.L. Worthington (Ed.), *Handbook of forgiveness* (pp. 321-334). NY: Routledge.

Change: One Step at a Time

Wendy Middlemiss, Ph.D., CFLE
Associate Professor, Department of Educational
Psychology, University of North Texas, Denton

Wisdom: As a parent, try to keep things simple and find small steps to take when you feel overwhelmed.

Theory: Families are systems of interaction,[1] or as one of our early scholars, Ernest Burgess, noted, a unit of interacting personalities.[2] These systems are very complex involving not only interactions and happenings within a family, but also interactions between members of a family and outside systems, such as other families, the parents' friends and jobs, the children's friends and schools, relatives, etc.[3] The complexities of these systems can impact our ability to parent in the manner we would like to parent.

One step we can take to create a well functioning family system and support our children's growth is to try to reduce the complexities that often stand in the way of positive parent-child interactions. How? As parents working within these complex systems, it may be helpful to realize one change in a system can lead to other, hopefully positive, changes elsewhere.

I recall a time working with one family when the importance of one small step in helping to change a family system became very clear. While I was teaching a parent education class, a couple came in late. It was apparent that they were very flustered and unhappy. As they sat down, they explained their week and why they were late. As I listened, I realized that, yes, there were a lot of difficulties being faced by this family, many parenting choices being made that were less than ideal, and many family interactions that were unhelpful or hurtful to positive development.

At the end of their discussion, my first thought was that this system was not working and perhaps was too chaotic to help with a basic parent education class. But, there sat the parents, waiting for some sort of wise guidance, and me feeling less than wise! However, they had made time to come to the class to see how to best parent their children. So I mentally reviewed the difficulties that they faced. I remembered my often-stated-advice to find something small to change, something that might be solvable with a few easy steps that the parents would be able to complete, even with the challenges they faced.

The small, definable problem and related possible change: knowing whether the dogs had been fed. For this family, feeding the dogs was one of the chores the children were to complete before the parents came home and it had become a chronic, annoying problem.

As the parents had explained, they never knew whether the dogs had been fed because if they asked, the children always said, "yes." But, it was apparent on some days, or after a few days, that the dogs had not been fed. So, how could the parents know? How could the parents make a small change in their system? One way would be to create a concrete marker of whether the dogs had been fed instead of relying on the reports of their children, who were punished if they had forgotten to do this chore. A concrete marker? ...make bags of food for each dog for each day of the week, with the day clearly labeled. Bag empty, dogs fed; bag full, dogs not fed.

Although feeding their dogs was by no means the most salient system change that could help this family, alleviating this concern had many potentially positive outcomes. First, the dogs would be fed. But more importantly, the parents would not have the issue of trying to determine whether their children were being honest in their responses. As parents, they could check the bags and then be free to address the question of responsibility and truthfulness with their children. Perhaps more importantly, however, making this change successfully and seeing the change in the system would give the parents, and family, hope that they could identify and change other small things and have an impact on their family's functioning. Overtime, this would allow them to put in place many of the parenting techniques they might learn in class, thus continuing to change the system.

The value of taking simple, small steps to help ease family difficulties also was noted by a colleague working with a family of four. This family, with children ranging in age from four to ten years, were having a chaotic time in the morning, trying to get everybody dressed, fed, and ready for the day. After reviewing their saga of morning events, it was apparent that getting up 15 minutes earlier might help. They tried this and all of a sudden, peace seemed to reign in the morning. Their moods were more pleasant and the annoyances the parents formerly felt disappeared.

Other ways to take seemingly overwhelming situations and make them more manageable and less stressful for a family are to introduce simple steps into how we teach our children to be independent as they grow. For instance, having a 3-year-old make their own choices about food or clothing, toys or activities, may be important to how they grow and develop. However, without some simple limitations, these activities can add stress and complexity. One simple step to reducing the stress and yet endorsing the activity is to provide a child with 2 or 3 choices acceptable to the parent. This helps the child grow autonomous, but avoids the difficulties that might ensue when shorts are chosen on a very chilly day, since shorts would not have been one of the choices!

Often, the complexity in families can be helped by looking at ways to change just one component of the scenario. These simple steps can include: making certain an overwhelmed parent has some time to relax or transition home after a long day; assigning chores and setting aside a specific time for chores to be done; using a "chore checklist chart"; or other simple step. Although all of these are just simple changes, each may have a lasting and positive impact on a complex family system.

Reference

[1] Whitchurch, G. G., Constantine, L. L., (1993). Systems theory. In. P. G. Boss, W. J. Doherty, R. LaRossa, W. R. Schumm, S. K. Steinmetz (Eds.), *Sourcebook of family theories and methods: A contextual approach* (pp. 325-355). NY: Plenum.

[2] Waller, Willard, & Hill, Reuben (1951). *The family: A dynamic interpretation* (Rev. ed.). NY: Holt, Rinehart & Winston.

[3] Bell, Norman W., & Vogel, Ezra F. (1960). Toward a framework for functional analysis of family behavior. In Normal W. Bell & Ezra F. Vogel (Eds.), *A modern introduction to the family* (pp. 1-34). NY: Free Press.

Parenting in the African American Middle/Upper Middle Class

Susan D. Toliver, Ph.D.
Professor and Chair, Department of Sociology, Iona College, New Rochelle, NY

Social scientists and other scholars of various disciplines have for many decades studied parenting. In their scholarship they have looked at cross cultural goals and practices and parenting in a variety of social contexts including racially and ethnically diverse communities, as well as values and behaviors across class lines. While research on African American parenting, especially with respect to class differences and parenting among Blacks, has been comparatively sparse, we can glean some facts about parenting in the African American middle and upper middle class, and can identify some important goals for parenting within this community. Various writings were used as resources for some of the following thoughts.[1,2,3]

What's different about African American parenting? While there are some goals that are important to achieve in parenting in any Western context (fostering self-esteem being high on the list), there are some goals or elements of goals that are unique to the African American parenting experience. As parenting is ecologically and socially situated, different groups in our society will need to formulate different goals, and will need to employ different strategies to reach some of the universal, overarching goals of good parenting.

One of the unique challenges faced by African American parents is how to develop in their children a strong positive sense of self as Black. This is absolutely essential to their developing high self esteem. The pervasive significance of race in contemporary society dictates that race be incorporated in the goals of Black childhood socialization. In some respects this is an even more difficult task to achieve for middle and upper middle class Blacks as isolation from the Black community is frequently an artifact of upward class mobility.

After the legal mandate for social desegregation was enacted, Black parents thought integration was the path to upward mobility for themselves and their children. Middle and upper middle class families moved to the suburbs to secure better housing, schools, and surroundings. While such residential shifts enabled them in many cases to escape the problems of segregated urban neighborhoods and reap the advantages of suburban living, the benefits did not come without costs. Chief among the costs was and is physical or geographic isolation from the Black community. In racially integrated neighborhoods and in predominantly Black neighborhoods it is not as hard to foster in children a sense of self as Black, but as social class and economics isolate middle and upper middle class Black families from other Blacks, developing this sense of self and being part of a Black community in the social sense of the word becomes even more difficult to achieve.

Black children need to know who they are, and how they are connected to the Black community, with others like themselves. They need to have knowledge of and appreciation for African American culture and grow to value it. In short, the racial socialization of Black children needs to incorporate elements that are directed toward the development of a positive sense of self as Black. African American parenting behaviors need to reflect this.

Strategies to foster the development of a positive sense of self as Black in African American children include the following.

- Teach children about and prepare them to encounter racism. Black children must learn to survive in a society that pervasively devalues them.
- Educate children in the home about race matters.
- Work with their schools to foster awareness and knowledge of race and racism, and to support and value diversity in the curriculum, school culture, and programs.
- Expose children to Black culture in and outside of the home. Instruct them in Black cultural behaviors, traditions, history, art, and artifacts.

- Engage in Black cultural activities as a family.
- Create Black social opportunities for children with others—i.e., Playdates, dinner parties, etc.
- Connect children with extended family.
- Form groups and join groups for Black children—civic, social, cultural, and educational.
- Assist children in the formation of friendships with other Black children. Foster opportunities for children to meet, get together with, and develop relationships, and support them in these endeavors.
- Connect children with the Black Church. The African American Church has been identified as a major source of strength for African Americans historically and contemporarily. If there is one in your area, that is consistent with your family's religious beliefs, join one. Otherwise, expose children to the Black Church when it is possible to do so. Foster a faith-based connection to other Blacks.
- Identify with and embrace the researcher recognized strengths of Black Families (e.g., Robert Hill, 1999[4]), especially the importance of religiosity, and extended family. Develop these strengths in one's individual family.

As the number of Black families entering the middle and upper middle class increases, parenting strategies that actively foster the forging of a real and perceived connection to the Black community will become necessary and important for a growing number of families. Such a connection is and will remain essential in effecting the wholesome psycho-social development of African American youngsters and ensure their high self esteem. Only until and if race becomes a less important factor in our society will African American parents be able to deemphasize the importance of this focus on the formation of racial identity and sense of self as Black in their parenting goals and strategies.

References

[1] Hill, S.A. (1999). *African American children: Socialization and development in families.* Thousand Oaks, CA: Sage Publications.

[2] Hopson, D.P. & Hopson, D.S. (1990). *Different and wonderful: Raising Black children in a race-conscious society.* NY: Prentice Hall.

[3] Toliver, S.D. (1998). Childrearing: Black Middle-Class issues and concerns. In S.D. Toliver (Ed.), *Black Families in corporate America* (pp. 121-43). Thousand Oaks, CA: Sage Publications.

[4] Hill, R.B. (1999). *The strengths of African American families* (2nd ed.). Blue Ridge Summit, PA: University Press of America.

Commuter Marriages with Children: Benefits and Cautions

Richard S. Glotzer, Ph.D., CFLE
Professor of Family Studies; Director, School of
Family & Consumer Sciences; Fellow, Center for
Life Span Studies and Gerontology, The University
of Akron, Akron OH

There are between 700,000 and a million *long distance married commuters* in the United States. Most commuters remain committed to their marriages, share child rearing and nurturance, including a common family residence. But by choice, they work a sufficient distance from the family residence that they must live away from home during the working week. Commuters travel to the family residence on weekends or at set intervals. Commuter families are challenged to develop unique ways of handling child rearing, family tasks, and other family routines. Commuting, most common among people in academic life, construction work, and corporate business, has become an option for many types of workers facing stable responsibilities in a fluid and unpredictable economy.

Research on commuter marriage is only now starting to grow. No one source tells the complete story. Two valuable accounts of commuter marriage are Gerstal and Gross's *Commuter Marriage: A study of work and family*,[1] and Winfield's *Commuter Marriage, living together apart.*[2] Both are readable accounts and available in many public libraries. The Employee Relocation Council (ERC), whose membership is primary drawn from large corporations, offers an annual *Family Issues Survey*, a synopsis of which is available on-line.[3] ERC *Surveys* track the issues families typically face in relocation, such as eldercare, locating schools, spousal employment, and home sales. These are issues related to making a commuting decision. Additional sources of information are the *Centers for Work and Family*, supported by the Sloan Foundation.[4] These centers, located at various universities, can be accessed on line and offer relevant papers that can be downloaded free or purchased at modest cost. Canadians may find Guelph University's *Centre for Families Work and Well-being* helpful.[5]

Families arrive at the decision to use a commuting strategy for a number of reasons. These include; a) the desire to maintain ties to their present community due to extended family, home ownership, a gainfully employed spouse in a secure and valued position, or/and not wanting to disrupt children school and social progress, b) local scarcity of professional employment for which one is trained and invested psychologically, c) financial need or crisis brought on by illness, debt, or family growth, and d) opportunities for occupational or income mobility.

Commuting is not as straightforward as it might seem. For example, physical and emotional wear and tear for all concerned are difficult to estimate. Working through the culturally laden assumptions of how married people with children should live can be surprisingly difficult. Dispelling notions of a family or marriage "in trouble" may be difficult to avoid, even with well-meaning friends and relatives.

In reaching a decision about commuting, family members should make a detailed inventory of the advantages and disadvantages involved, family strengths and weaknesses that may help or hinder handling it, and the pressures they believe they will face. Getting an informed and objective assessment of what the family likely is to encounter is an important second step. Working through various potential commuting scenarios with a family practice counselor or therapist offers an excellent way, which some may wish to consider, for identifying family strengths, potential stresses and conflicts, as well hidden or unarticulated problems.

The effect of long-distance commuting on children, the most vulnerable members of the family, is hard to assess until commuting actually starts. Commuting with pre-school age children and those in the early elementary grades is most difficult and should be avoided if possible. Younger children lack the capacity to fully understand the long absences of a parent. If a decision is made in favor of commuting there are helpful strategies for providing assurance to children and teens.

Predictability in scheduling trips home is important. Children should know parental arrival dates, have assurances of individual time with the parent, and have information about the departure and the next visit. Activities should center on the family, and it is a good idea, especially for shorter visits, to bring as little work home as possible. When possible, involvement in the children's school, i.e., attending performances, assemblies and parent-teacher conferences, is highly desirable. Avoiding the Santa Claus Syndrome, or bringing expensive gifts, is difficult to resist but important since the anticipation of gifts shifts the visit's focus from the parent and child bonding relationship to a material level. Commuting might however allow time for the commuter to search out creative and thoughtful gifts related to school projects and children's interests.

Having children visit the commuting parent is very helpful, replacing mystery with concrete experience and more readily understandable facts. Where commuting distances are substantial, the commuting parent can create a photo album of their *distant* residence, work place and people, and of the community. Photographs not only make the commuting parent's life away from home more understandable but may prompt interesting questions. Regular communication is equally important.

Telephone calls, e-mails and letter writing are all important for commuters. Communication should be routine and predictable. Supplying children with self-addressed stamped envelopes facilitates writing notes or sending pictures. Writing can become an enjoyable activity for children and should not be forced. School web sites provide a means for the commuting parent to stay informed about school activities, and staying in touch with teachers, homework, and class projects. It may be possible to collaborate on school projects by contributing learning materials and ideas. The home-based parent can provide guidance or hands-on assistance.

Ideally, commuter families should have a time limit for the commuting experience. Be reasonably clear about when the experience will end–and what will come next. The more flexible a commuter's schedule, translated into blocks of time for extended visits, the longer the family can accommodate the stress of commuting. Open-ended commuting with no clear plan articulated *or discussed* creates ambiguity and anxiety for children. Permanent commuting, with few opportunities for visits or participation in family life, is corrosive to marital relations and children's welfare. Additional income cannot make up for prolonged absence from the home and the lives of the people we love. Not surprisingly, commuting works best for adults with grown children. However, carefully considered, with limits, goals and strategies set, commuting can be a positive chapter in a family's development.

References

[1] Gerstal N. & Gross, H. (1984). *Commuter marriage: a study of work and family.* NY: Guilford Press.

[2] Winfield, F.E. (1985). *Commuter marriage: living together, apart.* NY: Columbia University Press.

[3] Employee Relocation Council, Washington, D.C. Retrieved Dec. 20, 2010, from: www.erc.org.

[4] Sloan Work and Family Research Network (links to other Centers), Boston College, Boston, MA. Retrieved October 27, 2010, from: wfnetwork.bc.edu/indephp.

[5] Centre for Families Work and Well-being, University of Guelph, Guelph, Ontario, Canada. Retrieved October 27, 2010, from: www.worklifecanada.ca.

2 Eyes, 2 Ears and 1 Mouth: Communication Tools

Deborah J. Thomason, Ed.D. CFLE
Professor and Extension Family & Youth Development Specialist, Clemson University, Clemson, SC

I've found that when individual family members are asked if they communicate with their family on a regular basis, most will say yes. When asked what they talked about, most can summarize what they contributed to the conversation. However, when questioned further and asked to recall or recount what the other family members said, few details are remembered.

I often begin a presentation on developing effective family communication skills with the statement, "We are born with 2 eyes, 2 ears and only 1 mouth. Why do you think that is important in family communication?"

Virginia Satir defined the communication process as a huge umbrella, covering and affecting all of the interaction between human beings.[1] Communication consists of much more than speaking. Effective communication will include an awareness of body language (non-verbal communication) and effective listening. It is reported that we are better thinkers (about 400 words per minute) than talkers (about 125 words per minute) which accounts for the practice of sometimes listening while "preparing" our refutation.[2] This results in not giving 100% of our attention to the speaker. Sometimes we only hear the beginning of what someone is saying and immediately we anticipate that we "know" what is going to be said and basically we have tuned out. This "jumping to a conclusion" can damage a relationship and prevent a real conversation from taking place.

Subtle body movements, position changes, physical stance or facial features can communicate volumes of information about an individual. One can determine reactions and feelings during a conversation simply by observing the "body language" of others. Becoming aware of your own body language will help improve your communication with your family. Take a moment and examine how you're sitting, what you are doing with your hands, your feet, and your overall posture. Maintaining eye contact with someone who is speaking conveys respect and reinforces that you are interested in what they are saying.

Hearing the words is not as important as actually listening and reflecting the intended message. Parenting experts define the humanistic or human potential model as valuing emotional maturity, empathy, and acceptance of self and others as well as promoting effective listening techniques.[3,4] In communication workshops to reinforce the importance of listening, I commonly use a STOP sign to convey the power of certain communication blockers. The following attitudes tend to "block" communication: insulting, judging, blaming, ignoring, accusing, stating opinion as fact, mind reading, interrupting, sarcasm and globalizing.

Youth as well as adults must be aware of their communication skills and deficits. Educational efforts to teach parents how to communicate with their children will be ineffective if children are not educated in communication skills as well. Communication is truly a "two way street."[5]

References

[1] Satir, V. (1982). *People Making.* Palo Alto, CA: Science and Behavior Books.

[2] Bolton, Elizabeth B. *About IFAS leadership development: Listening to learn.* Retrieved Dec. 3, 2010, from http://edis.ifas.ufl.edu/HE748.

[3] Ginott, H.G., Ginott, A., & Goddard, H. W. (2003). *Between Parent and Child.* New York: Three Rivers Press.

[4] Gordon, T. (2000). *Parent effectiveness Training: The Proven Process for Raising Responsible Children.* New York: Crown Publishing Group.

[5] Thomason, D.J.& Thames, B. J. (2001). Building Family Strengths Curriculum. Clemson South Carolina, Clemson University Cooperative Extension Service, Department of Family & Youth Development. NOTE: for sample lesson materials, see: http://www.clemson.edu/fyd/family_life.htm.

There are people who, instead of listening to what is
being said to them, are already listening to what
they are going to say themselves.
−Albert Guinon (1863-1923)

Communication: The Key to Student Success

Cynthia Jackson Small, M.Ed., CFLE
Family Dimensions, Inc., Carrollton, TX

Communication is one of the keys to building a lasting relationship between teachers and parents. It is the foundation of a solid partnership. When parents and educators communicate effectively, positive relationships develop, problems are more easily solved, and students make greater progress. While this may seem to be a simple process, it usually does not happen overnight and takes practice and time.

As a parent of three children, I understand that family schedules are often hectic and busy especially during the school year. We're living in such an instant, fast-paced world where everything must be done with such haste. Sometimes our daily schedules and journeys in life are so busy that it is often difficult to find time to sit down at the dinner table with the family. Despite our chaotic timelines and schedules, it's important to make priorities for our children from the early years to high school and keep the lines of communication open daily. One of the major items that must be at the top our busy schedules is to take time to build relationships with teachers and discover ways to communicate regularly, in a two-way process that will impact student learning and success.

Partnering with teachers is just one avenue for becoming involved in the education of youth today. One of the defining features of effective parent involvement is good communication between parents, school and community.[1] This can be a challenge for both parents and teachers, but can happen with the use of a variety of ongoing communication techniques including conferences, workshops, newsletters, telephone calls, e-mails, school websites, home visits, etc. Once parents begin to feel comfortable communicating with teachers, this invaluable relationship can grow into a meaningful partnership that can make a big difference in the teaching and learning process.

As a classroom teacher for more than 10 years, I know that parents' initial response to parent-teacher conferences is often somewhat cold, perhaps due to anxiety and fear. Even as a parent who also is an educator, I too have felt these uncomfortable feelings at conferences with my children's teachers, being hesitant in sharing information or asking questions. However, I found that regular communication builds trust, and we began to work more effectively as partners in the best interest of my children. I discovered that basically we, parents and teachers, are both on the same page with the primary goal of working together to help students learn. It was all about communicating care and concern for the success and well-being of the children.

Most importantly, I discovered the key to successful partnerships was effective communication. Consequently, I developed a list of sample questions to help parents begin the dialogue with their child's teacher and open the door to continuous two-way communication. The following questions were designed to stimulate discussions during parent-teacher conferences:

- What can I do to help improve my child's study habits and performance in school?
- Are there any areas of concern regarding my child's behavior or school work?
- What is the homework and grading policy?
- When is the next statewide achievement test given and what

is being offered at the school to prepare students for the test?
- What are some instructional strategies that I might use to reinforce skills at home?

Parent-teacher conferences provide an opportunity to strengthen relationships and improve communication between the home and school. Conferences need not and should not be an open forum for complaints and negative remarks about the school or the teachers. Conferences are avenues for teachers and parents to communicate and share information with student learning in mind. As parents, teachers, and community members work as a team, communication must be the center of the relationship that is formed. This is a two-way process that does not end with the parent-teacher conference but continues throughout the year, using a variety of communication methods.

As teachers and parents begin to communicate from the first day of school and throughout the school year, I think it's important to communicate and exchange good news between the home and school. Phone calls and notes sent to parents should not always focus on bad news but should reflect positive messages as well. I remember one occasion when my son's fourth grade teacher called me at home on a Sunday night. My first thought was "oh no, what has Jason done now?" But to my surprise, she was calling to let me know that she had just scored Jason's math test and that he had made an A. She wanted to let me know how proud she was of Jason. What a refreshing phone call! I must admit that I was initially shocked because I had been conditioned to expect bad news whenever someone called from the school. This one phone call changed my perception of schools and I began to view teachers from a totally different perspective.

Today as I conduct workshops in various school districts, I remind teachers and parents of this special story and the difference one can make when they communicate positive messages. Essentially, my message to educators is to catch students performing well and communicate good news.

In closing, I am confident that as teachers and parents make a commitment to communicate on a regular basis, we will see greater partnerships in education that will impact student success in school and in life. Together we make the difference!

When Parents Don't Agree

Donna Raycraft, M.A, CFLE
Executive Director, community agency,
Concord, NH

Parents frequently complain that they and their spouse don't parent the same way or about how their parenting differs, causing friction in their marriage. In fact, one of the most frequent causes of conflict in a marriage is about parenting.

It helps to understand where our ideas about parenting come from. Usually, we parent the way we were parented. At the very least, our childhood gives us a basis of what parenting should or shouldn't look like.

Some of the things about which parents disagree are: whether children should be paid for doing chores; what time children should go to bed; whether children should be able to sleep in their parents' bed; whether children should have to eat what foods are prepared for them; and, from my experience, most frequently, what consequences should follow negative behavior.

Many times, after taking a parenting course, one parent will ask how they can "get" the other parent to parent the way the course teaches. The answer is, "You can't." No one can control another's behavior. All we can do is control our own. And perhaps that will influence someone else's behavior.

The worst thing a parent can do if they want the other parent to use some of their new-found techniques is to lecture their partner. It usually makes that other parent defensive and even more entrenched in their old ways of doing things. Another ineffective strategy is to place parenting books or parenting articles in places the parent will likely see them. All that does is tip off the other parent that they are being manipulated.

The best thing a parent can do is to simply share with the other parent some of the things they've learned. Then they should stop talking and start acting in a way that the other parent can see what is happening. If the parent is successful, and if the wanted results are achieved, the other parent will see, and that will be what convinces them. Lectures only make the other parent even more resistant to change.

Sometimes parents become embroiled in a struggle over who is right and who is wrong. Then it's sometimes best to negotiate or compromise. If it's something that you can live with, just say something like, "I'll trade you allowances if you'll give me bedtimes." If it's very important to you and the other parent refuses to give in, you might say, "Look, this is very important to me, and I know you don't agree with me. So can I ask you to let me try this for two weeks without interfering, just to give it a test to see what happens? At the end of two weeks we'll evaluate the results and decide what to do next."

Once in awhile parents find that they come from such different parenting styles that it is sometimes helpful to get outside help. Couples counseling can be very helpful in unraveling where our ideas come from, why they are important to us and how parenting is affecting our marriage.

We all know that parenting is too important to be left to chance. And we all know that a child needs strong parenting from both parents. Negotiation and compromise around parenting issues are the biggest gift we can give our children. They learn from us the template for a healthy relationship that they will use in their own relationships and how they will parent when they parent. How we parent today will affect parents for generations to come–a pretty worthwhile project.

The Necessary Rules for Healthy Fighting

John H. Gagnon, Ph.D., CFLE, MFTL, ABMP
Private Practice, Stamford, CT

I have been a psychotherapist for 35 years. Throughout that time I have seen individuals, couples and families, including their children, in one configuration or another. Whenever I worked with issues of anger and fighting, I was taught to allow couples and families to express their anger without being "out of control." I had never seen a list by anyone that said, "Hey… wait a minute. There are ways that you can interact which will allow you to get through a fight without bashing each other to death or wounding one another beyond repair." And to the parents, we want to model better behavior than this for our children; they are apt to do as we do!

As the years went by, I began to insert rules in the way I conducted therapy. They first emerged in group therapy and before each session, I would lay out my rules of conduct for the group and if anyone violated one, I called them on it, they apologized and we moved on.

I can't remember what year I began to make a formal list of regulations for couples or families to follow but they were first called, "The Marquis de Gagnon Rules for Arguments," after the "Marquis of Queensbury" rules for boxing. I have worked on and refined the list a little bit but in the main, it has remained pretty much the same for some 20 years or so.

When couples or families get to the issue of having unsatisfying fights or hurtful fights, I introduce the rules on a sheet of paper.

I go through each one of the rules in the list while we are sitting in the therapy room. Next, I tell the clients to "... take your papers home and memorize them." I remind them that they are to use the rules at all times whenever they have a disagreement and to put the rules in a place where they can refer to them whenever necessary, as on the refrigerator door.

I require that each of the members of the family must keep track of the rules for themselves, catching themselves whenever they might call someone a name, for example, then stop the fight, apologize for the mistake, and continue. At first one person may yell, "... you aren't fighting by the rules," when they catch the "other" not using one of the dictums. I hear in the next session what happened and I encourage them to stop any fight by saying simply, "Rules!" Then, both parties are to go to their copy of the rules and continue the fight by them. No one may ever use the rules to show how "stupid" or "non-compliant" the other is.

Here they are:

1. **All fights exist in order to "reach good ground"** at the end of a disagreement. Therefore if one person "wins" a fight and the other "loses," the fight has not been conducted correctly ... and ...

2. Therefore, **trust, love, respect, caring and kindness are key** elements in every fight.

3. **Statements** of anger **may sound angry** but **must be simple**: "I resent that you left the dishes in the sink all day" is an example; and it is also **useful for one to express one's feelings**: "It makes me feel like I am expected to be the slave here." However, the simpler the statement, the better.

4. The **recipient** of resentment should **never defend him/herself**. Accept resentments and **understand them for what they mean**. Listen to what your behavior "means" to your significant other(s). **Imagine yourself** being the recipient of what you did or didn't do.

5. There **should be no name-calling**: "jerk," "numbskull," "asshole," etc. No one may be "wounded" in a fight.

6. There is **no swearing at the other person**, since swearing conveys a general lack of respect. Swearing as an adjective for an object may be okay as in, "... the damn dishes in the damn sink." Swearing at others, however, is forbidden.

7. **No insinuated insults**: the intelligence, body-image, opinions, ethics, spirituality, beliefs, or thinking of the other person are never "ridiculous" or "stupid," etc.

8. **No threats**: arrest (unless warranted), hospitalization (unless warranted), physical harm, punishment where not due, threat to leave, separate or divorce, or run away, etc. are not permitted.

9. **No intimidation**: no coming closer in a menacing manner, picking up a weapon-like object, raising your hand as if to strike, grabbing the other person in any manner, etc.

10. **No raising the voice** beyond a common angry tone, **no dominating** the conversation, **no attempts to control** by out-shouting or making louder noises to "drive home a point." Anger is louder than regular speech but it is not right to use loudness to shut the other person off. Therefore...

11. **Allow room for each person to speak.** It is not allowed to talk non-stop, breathlessly and not leave purposeful spaces for the other person to respond.

    In the simplest of fights, however, the entire thing might sound like this. First: "I resent your leaving the dishes in the sink all day." Second: "I don't blame you. I'd feel the same way." First: "Thank you for understanding. I don't want you to do that again." Second: "I will make every effort not to do that again."

    Here's another fight. First: "I resent that you told Billy he could stay up on a weekday night." Second: "I can understand how you'd feel like that. I figured that just this once wouldn't be a problem because this was a special TV show." First: "This was not a regular show that he could see again?" Second, "No." First: "This was not a series that he will want to stay up and see another time?" Second, "No." First: "Well, ... that makes lots of sense, then. Sorry." Second: "That's OK; I can see why you'd worry."

    Here's another fight. First: "I resent that you had Fluffy put down without discussing it with me! I loved Fluffy too." Second: "God... I'm so sorry... I can see how that would make you feel left out at the end. I'm sooo sorry." First and Second hugging and crying together.

12. **No leaving the present argument.** You may never bring up previous incidences of this event, nor talk about any previous fight, action, inaction, or behavior which has nothing to do with the topic of the current fight. You may not bring up any other topic to fight about. In fact, you may not project what will happen in the future if this ever happens again. Most wandering starts with, "OH YEAH, well how about the time when you..." That is forbidden. Each argument should be completely self-contained and limited to this instance of this problem right here and should not be allowed to go anywhere else.

13. **Also, no leaving the argument by walking out of the room.** Each fight must be concluded. The adage: "Never go to bed until you resolve a fight," is a great idea though it is sometimes impossible. When it is not possible to end a fight on a

particular day, time should be agreed on for the next day during which to end the fight. Good fighters will find, however, that it takes about 10 minutes to end most fights when conducted by this set of rules, as noted in 11 above.

14. **Agree always with the other's basic feelings**. "I understand how you could feel like that." "I don't blame you for feeling that way." "I would feel like that myself."

15. **Preserve** another's **sense of integrity and self-worth** throughout the fight. If you do not, you are "disqualified." Catch yourself, apologize and continue when the apology is accepted.

16. The **end** of a fight must **not be a "null sum (+1 and -1 = 0)."** **Both** parties should come away from the fight **feeling respected, understood and also wanting to change some behavior that may be irritating or difficult for another to accept.** Compromise is always an excellent resolution to a fight, but the first person to see that he/she is wrong and to admit that and to want to change is to be praised in the fighting process.

17. **Love is the outcome of a good fight** within the context of a family, friend or lover because with the reduction of anger, comes the return to positive feelings; and, one can't feel one's love for another when there is anger or resentment in front of it.

18. Finally, **if anyone leaves a fight feeling "hurt" or "injured," or "insulted," then** the rules of fighting were not used properly, or your fight was not conducted by these rules and **you need to seek help for improving your ability to deal with conflict and anger in a healthier manner.**

So it is also the job of the family to take a "time out" during which each member examines and discusses objectively what they did in the fight that caused it not to go well. No fighting may take place during this discussion. This is meant to be analytical and to permit people to "own" their respective problems. Anyone who starts a fight during this discussion is doing something wrong and must admit what he/she is doing wrong right at that moment. This discussion is designed to help "fine tune" the work of the couple or family to problem solve the manner in which they fight, that is not consistent with the rules given.

When couples or families use the "Necessary Rules for Healthy Fighting," they experience the value of this set of guidelines for all angry expressions or disagreements in their lives. Their ability to fight and share feelings improves, the acceptance of feelings increases and defensiveness decreases.

Now... go to your corners, come out for a healthy fight and then end up in a different corner than either of you came from. In fact, you will more easily learn to wind up in the same corner! ...
Dr. John

NOTE: One may find the following books to be helpful additional reading, but NO ONE has made a list like mine before: *The Angry Man*, by David Stoop, Ph.D.; *Anger, How to Live With and Without It*, by Albert Ellis, Ph.D.; *Letting Go of Anger*, by Ron Potter-Efron, MSW; and, *Angry All the Time*, by Ron Potter-Efron, MSW.

Covering For the Absent Parent

Kathy Lettieri, D.Phil., CFLE
National Certified Domestic and Registered Civil
Mediator; President and Consultant, Solution by
Resolution; President and Education Director, AIDS
Education Bureau, Huntsville, AL

How many times has one parent had to soothe the hurt feelings of a child when the other parent has not shown up for a planned, promised visit? Many! Both Moms and Dads have had to make the choice whether to cover–lie for the absent parent, telling the child Mom/Dad had to be away, or had to work, or any other excuse. Either decision–to cover for or to remain quiet, with the hope of the mere absence speaking for itself–offers a possibility of a child turning against the primary custodial parent. The resentment of being with one parent when the child wanted to have both or to be with the other parent can easily come out in blame and/or rebellion, such as, "Daddy says you won't let him come to see me."

Choosing to cover is love, parental love. Unfair? Yes! However, often the show of dignity and grace in the effort to save the feelings of children may be eventually recognized by someone, sometime and hopefully by the children.

What is not parental love is not keeping promises to a child. A promise is being on time for a visit, making an expected phone call, presenting the expected gift, or paying child support. Child support is a promise to the child? Yes. The money individually promised, or ordered by the court to be paid, is necessary. It is depended upon by some single head of household parents. The choice of a house or apartment rental may have depended upon the expected child support, as well as the budget for food, transportation, clothing and the fees for school activities and supplies.

Mothers and fathers (various parents, from anonymous personal communications) have stated that the hardest cover-up for the other parent was the reason for the divorce. One mother told of the phone calls from daddy to the children asking them to "talk to mommy; tell her that daddy wants to be family again. Daddy wants to be with you to take you to the movies and school activities. Mommy is keeping us apart."

"Of course," the mother says, "the children do not remember their father was never with them when we were married. But now they want to believe daddy. Where does that leave me? And how can I tell them daddy was abusive to me, controlling, demanding that the house be run as he wanted it–not that he would help keep the house or yard looking decent, or cook the meals, or...anything. My job brought in most of the money, giving him a chance to build and rebuild failing businesses, yet my husband did not like the job I had. He said it was too high profile, I should be more humble. I couldn't win, so I left him. I still can't win. He still causes chaos and hurt for the children and me."

Another mother said, "I finally got a good deal on a house in a good neighborhood and the kids and I moved in with little furniture. My ex-husband determined that if I could buy a house, I no longer needed the child support. It stopped."

A father said, "How can I tell a 7 and 4 year old that mommy is...just gone? I did not want to tell them she was in jail on a drug and prostitution charge. After we were married, she maintained relationships with her college friends, doing drugs, drinking and having affairs. I was afraid of AIDS. If anything happened to me, as a result of her activities, who would the kids have?"

In many books, mediators and counselors advise not to *bad mouth* the other parent.[1,2,3] Does letting the child know when the absent parent has fallen short of the agreement constitute bad mouthing? No. But parents need to do their best not to paint a negative picture of the other parent. Children are very tuned into their parents and know when something is not right. If you "bad mouth" the other parent, not only does it damage the child's relationship with the absent parent, but it also can damage the relationship with you. Your job as the parent is to preserve relationships for the child.

The seriousness of the possible lasting effects, to each parent as well as the children, will create the attitudes and actions for generations following.[4,5] At issue are: trust, the ability and/or willingness to love and trust; self respect; self confidence, the ability to concentrate on education and/or the job; and ultimately, ...what kind of parent the wounded child becomes.

Bottom line, a 43 year old daughter of divorced parents (the authors') said, "We know! We knew then, and we know now, so keep covering. It makes yourself look good. Some kids grow up and some will not be OK anyway, most of us will."

References

[1] Ahrons, Constance R. (1994). *The good divorce*. NY: Harper Collins.

[2] Benedek, Elissa P. (1995). *How to help your child overcome your divorce*, NY: New Market.

[3] Newman, Gray, M. (1998). *Helping your kids cope with divorce*, NY, Random House.

[4] Amato, P.R., (2000). The consequences of divorce for adults and children. *Journal of Marriage and the Family, 62 (4)*, 1269-1287.

[5] Zill, N. Morison, D.R. and Cioro, M.J. (1993). Long term effects of parental divorce on parent-child relationships, adjustment, and achievement in young Adulthood. *Journal of Family Psychology, 7*, 91-103.

Chapter III

Wisdom in Guiding Children: Suggestions for all Ages

Some of the more basic parenting discipline/ guidance approaches will be discussed in the chapter following this one. However, in this chapter you will find some more general suggestions that are not built on some big theory or system. You might also find them useful at various times in your child's life.

The very next article seeks to give an overall perspective to the various ideas or theories which you will be reading about in this and the next chapter. It is not essential that you read it first in order to understand other articles. After reading a number of other articles, you should come back and read it, if you haven't. It may answer some questions which you will have.

The Spectrum of Light: Element of Truth in Each Idea

Robert E. Keim, Ph.D., CFLE Emeritus
Professor Emeritus, Northern Illinois University;
Clinton, TN

As you read various articles in this book, at times you might get the impression that some of the authors' ideas or theories don't seem to agree with each other. They may seem to be suggesting different things or contradicting each other by emphasizing other ways to solve the same problem. This concern has been discussed previously in the Preface of this book as well as in the concluding chapter, "Wisdom of the Ages." Later in this article, I'd like to offer an analogy that will help explain this situation, giving some better understanding as to why this happens.

We also noted that these "experts," in truth, are not necessarily contradicting each other with their theories, as it may appear. In actuality, they most often complement each other; that is, they are sharing alternate approaches for dealing with the same issue or problem. We experience this all of the time in other walks of life: different styles of poetry conveying a similar feeling, varied arrangements for the same song, multiple ways to try to reach the goal line, a number of recipes for cooking supposedly the same dish, and so on. Parenting is no different. And as observed in the last chapter of the book, considering that so many of us have varying personalities, some approaches will appeal to one person and not to another. As in other aspects of life, we sometimes need to pick what makes the best sense to ourselves, what seems to fit and feel the most natural to us. And so, having this variety of approaches makes sense.

Now back to that issue of "contradicting each other:" Years ago I heard an interesting explanation of why theories of human behavior *tend not to contradict each other, but complement each other, with each theory containing some element of truth.* The concept was shared by Dr. A. Durwood Foster, Jr., a theology professor at the Pacific School of Religion, Berkeley (in a seminar, 1959). His contention was that when beliefs or theories originate, there is *an element of truth in each one.* This may sound like it is saying, "All ideas or theories are correct." However, the point is that within that element of truth, it may not have been interpreted correctly by the originator in the first place or distorted or misinterpreted by someone along the way, or by someone who is seeking to translate it into another language.

More precisely, Dr. Foster said that any theory evolves from the experience of some human being as a result of one of two things:

- The idea resulted from some personal experience of the person; or,
- The idea occurred to a person from having observed the behavior or interaction of others or some event.

With this perspective, there is some element of truth or reality within the experience of the person who originated the idea or theory. For a helpful further explanation of the development of theories, see David C. Bell's, *Constructing Social theory.*[1]

One can easily think of these complementing theories in an interesting analogy. Think of the different theories as being part of a spectrum of light. An excellent view of a colorful spectrum of light is located at the web sites noted in the second footnote below,[2] or just Google "spectrum of light" for results. Picture the authors or theorists on parenting as representing one thin line in that spectrum of colors, from violet through blending shades of blue, green, yellow and orange to red. Added together, the different theories make up the broad spectrum of light that fits together under the umbrella of all parenting approaches. We may pick and choose a variety of colors from time to time. In this manner, we can think of using various ideas of parenting, presented by an array of authors, adding up to one complete landscape of parenting and family life.

Now, given that notion of an element of truth within each idea or theory, imagine numerous persons "discovering" varied parts of that spectrum from their own experiences. These persons may be convinced, that, "Ah ha! This is reality; this is the answer, the way to do it!"–when, in fact, they have 'discovered' one aspect or way of doing something, a part of that spectrum of light. Think of parent educators as adding different layers or perspectives to the broad spectrum of parent education.

As for the articles in this book, or other books for that matter, you will notice in many of these articles some reference to *research*. Given the numerous ideas or theories that evolve pertaining to parenting, it makes sense to figure out which approaches are most effective. That is where research comes in, often referred to as "evidence-based parent education."[3] The results do not mean that the other theories have no merit, but that there might be better and different ways of packaging ideas to make them more effective for parents.

When reading this book try to stay aware that the ideas are merely reflecting a more complete picture of what is–the broad spectrum of the field of parenting. We may each walk through different doors to arrive at the end of the journey. As revealed from the results of research, in given situations, some approaches may work better than others; however, there are no totally proven right ways for all parents to use with all children for all of the problems that can be faced.

Many variables are involved, including mistakes or errors we sometimes will make ourselves. Thus, we will see different end results and may have to try some different approach–a good reason to know of several alternatives within that spectrum of parenting ideas. Nevertheless, our goal is to strive to achieve the best that we can as parents, given who we are. As Si Kahn, the talented song writer, wrote, "It is not what you have; it's what you do with what you've got."

References

[1] Bell, David C. (2009). *Constructing social theory.* NY: Rowman & Littlefield.

[2] To see a colorful spectrum of light, either Google "spectrum of light" or for a good example, go to:
http://www.learner.org/teacherslab/science/light/color/spectra/index.html or
http://hyperphysics.phy-astr.gsu.edu/hbase/vision/specol.html#c2.

[3] For more on evidence-based parent education programs, see: http://www.social
work.buffalo.edu/ebp/strategies/documents/ ParentingEducationLiterature-
Search.pdf.

Discipline–"To Teach"

Dawn Cassidy, M.Ed., CFLE
Director of Education, National Council on Family
Relations, Minneapolis MN.

When my daughter was still a toddler I came across an article in a parenting magazine about discipline. The article explained that the root of the word discipline is "to teach." That simple clarification had a profound impact on my parenting. Prior to that, I had always associated the word discipline with punishment. If a child needed to be disciplined, it meant they needed to be punished.

After reading this article I began to see discipline in a very different, and much more positive, way. When my daughter would do something that I wanted to change, such as a tantrum, not listening, etc., I found myself stepping back and asking "what is it that I want to teach her in this situation," rather than, "how should I punish her?" That simple approach made a huge difference in how I parented her and resulted in much more positive outcomes for most situations.

Instead of punishing her, I began talking to her, explaining to her what it was that I wanted or expected from her, and why. Times of *discipline* became moments of *teaching*. Instead of seeing hurt feelings and crying, I began to see the kinds of behavior for which I was hoping. Instead of moments of stress, there were moments of calmness and a feeling of cooperation between us.

Actions Speak Louder than Words: Being Role Models for Our Children

Kimberly Van Putten-Gardner, Ph.D., CFLE
Psychotherapist, Affinity: Counseling and Family
Life Services, Columbia, MD; and,
Family Science Instructor,
University of Maryland, College Park

"Do as I say and not as I do." This is a common inference that I've heard from bewildered parents during family therapy sessions as they plead with their adolescent children to be respectful by not cursing, to be less angry, not to use drugs, pursue a college education, not to engage in premarital sex....Unfortunately, this request is very hard for teenagers to follow.

As the social philosopher, George Herbert Mead, with his concept of *"taking the role of the other"* noted, children learn from observing their parents and others. All of the interactions within the family atmosphere communicate to children what is valuable and become blueprints for future relationships and individual choices.[1,2] During the adolescent years, teen children examine family interactions and values as they develop their peer relationships and begin to make their own life decisions.

Parents need to be vigilantly aware of the behaviors and attitudes that they model through parent-child and parent-parent interactions within the home.[3] Do you try to get your child's attention by cursing at him or her? Does your child see that the parent who acts out in anger by shouting and slamming doors is most effective in getting his or her own way in spousal arguments? If your son or daughter sees that such behaviors work for you, they will assume that those behaviors will work for them as well. Furthermore, teenagers are keenly attuned to the inconsistencies of their parents. For example, parents tell their children not to smoke marijuana, but parents will use and abuse other drugs, such as alcohol. Such behaviors send mix messages to teens.

I'm not suggesting that parents should be perfect examples.[4] That would be impossible. Often, parents have made choices that have created challenges in their own lives, and are attempting to instill values (e.g., values for education and marriage) in their children that would shield their children from the same difficult challenges that they have encountered.

Unfortunately, parents often attempt to instill values in their children by making demands. Rather than demanding that their adolescent child attend college or not engage in premarital sex, parents should clearly communicate their value beliefs to their adolescent children in a friendly, non-demanding way. By clearly communicating to your teenager what you believe, why, and the experiences in which your value beliefs are based, you are giving your child a message that may help him or her make future decisions.[2]

In summary, rather than saying "Do as I say and not as I do," parents should: (1) strive to be good role models for their teens through the things they do; (2) to say in a non-imposing manner what is expected of their teens; and (3) trust their teenagers to make responsible decisions.

References

[1] Mead, George Herbert. (1934). *Mind, soul, and society.* Chicago: University of Chicago Press.

[2] Shulman, B. H., & Mosak, H. H. (1988). *Manual for Lifestyle Assessment: Parental behavior and probable responses by child.* Bristol, PA: Accelerated Development.

[3] Dinkmeyer, Sr., D., McKay, G. D., & Dinkmeyer, Jr., D. (1997). *The parent's handbook: Systematic training for effective parenting.* Circle Pines, MN: American Guidance Service, Inc.

[4] Terner, J., & Pew, W. L. (1978). *The Courage to Be Imperfect.* NY: Hawthorn.

What was silent in the father speaks in the son, and
often I have found in the son the unveiled secret of
the father.
–Friedrich Wilhelm Nietzsche

Give Children Good Choices

Hilary A. Rose, Ph.D., CFLE
Associate Professor, Dept. of Applied Human Sci-
ences, Concordia University,
Montreal, QC, Canada

Sometimes we give young children confusing or too many choices, choices that can be overwhelming and inappropriate.[1] "Would you like to go inside and have lunch now?" I recently heard a well-meaning parent ask her five-year-old child this question, in effect, and no doubt unintentionally, offering the child the choice of going inside to eat or not. Lunch (or any meal, for that matter) should not be a choice, since eating (or having a bath, or brushing teeth) is not optional for growing children. The point here is the often misuse of terms such as "Do you want to..." or "Will you...," when the parent's intention is for the child to do what is being asked. Offering a child a choice in such cases is illogical.

If there is a choice at all, it should be a minor one that doesn't change the outcome. "Do you want your sandwich cut in halves or in quarters?" is a reasonable choice for a preschooler. For older children, of course, the choice should be more age-appropriate,[2] such as the choice between a tuna or egg filling. It is important that parents retain the ultimate control and responsibility for the outcome of the decision, all the while structuring the child's choices so that the child ultimately learns to make good choices on her or his own.[3]

Remember the five-year-old who was asked about going inside to eat lunch; on this occasion, the five-year-old didn't respond to his parents–and maybe not because he was being difficult. I think he didn't respond because the question itself is a difficult one. Here's what that five-year-old may have been thinking: "I'm having lots of fun now, so why would I want to stop? But I'm hungry, too, and I want to eat. How can I stay outside and play, and go inside to eat at the same time? This is confusing. I can't answer this question." And so the five-year-old says nothing, or whines, or says "No." Sometimes children don't comply with parents' expectations because they are confused or feel unable to meet those expectations.[2]

We sometimes think that we are doing our children a favor by giving them choices. But children, especially if they are young, tired, or hungry, can find choices overwhelming.[1] Young children are not cognitively or emotionally mature enough to make complex choices. We are not doing children a favor by giving them such choices; instead we are doing them a disservice. Think about a choice as a decision that has to be made. Good decisions require the ability to think logically, in particular, to consider alternatives and to anticipate outcomes. These cognitions, or thinking abilities, develop with age,[4] and it is inappropriate to expect that a young child is capable of complex thought processes.

Finally, we should think about the messages we are sending children when we give them choices: "You have the power to choose; I am deferring my authority to you."[1] While these messages may be appropriate for older adolescents and young adults, they are usually inappropriate for young children–unless the outcome of the choice is inconsequential, or it simply doesn't matter. We also need to remember that once the child is in a school classroom with 30 other children, there will be fewer individual choices to be made. Children who grow up with the expectation that they have choices about everything that affects them may be in for a rude awakening when they hit the "real world" of public school.

In conclusion, choices for young children should be:

a. Simple, not complex. Especially with young children, we need to structure choices so that the actual choosing is made easy for the child. Otherwise, the child can become overwhelmed and frustrated. The choice should be between two more-or-less comparable alternatives. Three or four carrots? Green or blue pants? Jam or jelly?

b. Minor and inconsequential. Choices by definition are optional. Children need to learn that some things in life are not optional–like going to bed on time. If we ask "Do you want to go to bed now?" we are implying that the child has a choice. Make sure that choices are truly optional, and that outcomes of those choices are minor.

c. Age-appropriate. Regardless of how intelligent young children are, they are still immature–cognitively and emotionally. Choices that are too complex are a burden, not a favor. Help your child learn how to make good choices by structuring them with the child's age in mind. As children get older, choices will get more complex or demanding.

d. Rare, not frequent. Having too many choices can be overwhelming and can lead to poor decision-making. Having choices all the time also sends the message that choices are an everyday right, not a once-in-a-while treat. Expecting to have choices about everything all the time is unrealistic, especially as children head off to school.

e. Thoughtful. We get tired and hungry, too. When we do, we often react automatically by giving children an order (telling them what to do) or a choice (asking them what they want to do). Try to take the time to think about the implications of giving choices (or orders) to children. Act thoughtfully instead of reacting automatically.

As parents, we should think about the choices we give our young children. As our children grow older, they will have to make many choices in life, often when we are not around to assist them. We can help them learn to make good choices when they are young by structuring the choices that we give them.

References

[1] Rimm, S. B. (1997). *How to parent so children will learn: Clear strategies for raising happy, achieving children.* NY: Three Rivers Press.

[2] Brazelton, T. B., & Greenspan, S. I. (2000). *The irreducible needs of children: What every child must have to grow, learn, and flourish.* Cambridge, MA: Perseus.

[3] Vygotsky, L. S. (1934). *Thought and language.* Cambridge, MA: MIT Press.

[4] Inhelder, B., & Piaget, J. (1958). *The growth of logical thinking from childhood to adolescence.* NY: Basic Books.

Which Way? Giving Toddlers Control

Dawn Cassidy, M.Ed., CFLE
Director of Education, National Council on Family
Relations, Minneapolis MN

We want our children to grow up with the ability to have control of their lives, while feeling comfortable with making choices. When my daughter was very little, I made a discovery of how to help her do this. As a young parent I read everything I could get my hands on about parenting. I remember reading an article that encouraged parents to allow their toddlers to have control and be able to make appropriate choices.

On our way home from pre-school I would put that advice into action and allow my daughter to decide which way the car would turn. I also used this technique when we would be out for a walk with her in her stroller. "Which way?" I would ask. "That way!" she'd shout and point right, or left, or forward. We even turned around on occasion! It sometimes took us a bit longer to find our way to our house, but it made her so happy to get to be the one in charge. My daughter is now 15, but even now I'll sometimes ask, "Which way?" A big smile will come across her face as she decides and points!

Parenting Using "While Activities"

Jerica Berge, PhD, LMFT, CFLE
Assistant Professor, Department of Family and
Community Medicine, University of Minnesota
Medical School, Minneapolis

Parents frequently report in parenting workshops that they have difficulty teaching their children values, morals and interpersonal relationship skills. Parents usually easily identify with parenting techniques that use external motivators to alter children's behaviors such as disciplining through rewards/punishment, natural/logical consequences, and time outs. However, they have a harder time relating to skills used to impart intrinsic, or internal, motivators to guide their children's behaviors, so that the they wish to "do the right thing" for reasons or values which they have taken on as their own. Parents say that they typically approach the task of teaching values, morals and interpersonal skills through lectures or discussions with their children. For some, after this approach fails, they hope that their example alone will be enough to influence their children's behaviors. It is known that observational learning through modeling does have an impact on children's behaviors; however, we also know that enacting the behaviors themselves have an even more powerful effect on future repetition of the behaviors and eventual internalization of the behaviors.[1,2] This is somewhat similar to the adage: it is easier to act yourself into right thinking than to think yourself into right acting.

"While activities" provide the opportunity to model and enact behaviors that facilitate interpersonal relationship skills and also have a values/moral position either inherently attached to them, or easily created in the process of engaging in them.[3] "While activities" include any activity that most people would consider mundane, such as chores (dishes, laundry, gardening), driving in the car, shopping, or making dinner. These seemingly mundane activities can ultimately provide the context for improving family interactions, as well as nurturing and teaching children values and morals.[4] "While activities," such as household chores, while typically thought of as necessary, often go unnoticed or uncounted as relational activities.

For instance, many parents want their children to have a good work ethic–believing that it will enhance the future job opportunities available to their children and secure their career longevity. Household chores provide an optimal setting for such training. The key is that parents must engage in the chores with their child. This doesn't mean that the parent hovers over the child to make sure he or she does the job right; rather, the parent joins in the job itself or does a complimentary job alongside his or her child. In the "doing" the parent will be modeling and teaching how to have a good work ethic. This activity then becomes a relational activity in which the parent and child have social interaction, develop a value, and complete a necessary task. Chores also provide, at times, opportunities to gain conflict resolution skills and communication skills. Children may have differing opinions about who should do what, or how to do it. This is a crucial moment in which parents can model and teach conflict-resolution skills. Values such as love, unselfishness, and cooperation also are acquired during such encounters.

There also is a considerable amount of down-time during "while activities," because they may not require a lot of intellectual capacity to perform. This provides yet another optimal moment for interpersonal relationship skills, such as problem-solving, to be taught and modeled. For example, while gardening together a daughter may have a conversation with her father about whether she should continue to be friends with girls who have started to engage in risky behaviors. Or, a mother and son could have a conversation about drinking and smoking as they listen to a radio program discussing these issues on their way to dropping the son off at soccer practice. In both of these situations, the father and mother have the opportunity to use problem-solving skills with their child, while at the same time, imparting his or her values during the conversation.

Parents who use "while activities" as part of their parenting repertoire will be able to influence their children's values, morals and interpersonal relationship skills through everyday and mundane activities. Children may even wonder how they acquired their intrinsic/internal motivators without any noticeable effort.

References

[1] Berger, K. S., & Thompson, R. A. (1995). *The developing person through the lifespan.* NY: Worth Publishers.

[2] Brooks, J. B. (2004). *The Process of Parenting.* Madison, WI: McGraw Hill.

[3] Bahr, K.S. (1996). More than clean windows: The unrecognized value of housework. In K.S. Bahr, A. Hawkins, & S. Klein (Eds.), *Readings in family science* (pp. 211-216). Dubuque, IA: Kendall/Hunt Publishing.

[4] Webster-Stratton, C. (1992). The incredible years: A trouble-shooting guide for parents of children aged 3-8. Toronto: Umbrella Press.

"In a Minute"

Rebecca A. Adams, Ph.D.
Associate Professor, Department of Family and
Consumer Sciences,
Ball State University, Muncie, IN

My husband and I used the following bit of wisdom with our daughter. Now that she is a parent, we have observed her and her husband using the technique with their four-year-old son. Their results continue to be positive and once it becomes part of the parenting routine, daily or weekly, transitions can be less stressful than they might otherwise be. The technique involves giving children a "one minute heads up" to adjust to a change parents have planned for the immediate future. For example, when it is time for children to stop an activity because it is bedtime or because it is time to come inside, give children a "one minute heads up." Instead of saying, "Bryce, it's time for you to pick up your toys, because it's your bedtime," say "Bryce, in a minute, it will be time for you to pick up your toys, because it will soon be your bedtime." In the second scenario, the additional time gives children the opportunity to make the cognitive transition from playing to getting ready to end their play. Because they initiated the change, parents already have had the opportunity to process the upcoming transition.

This approach is very similar to that used by the Guerney's in their Filial Play Therapy.[1] During play, when needed, the child is cautioned as to what is, or is not, expected to be done. It has been found that when children are aware ahead of time as to of what is expected they are far more cooperative. They usually seek to follow what they know is expected of them.

By allowing time for the children to modify their thought processes, parents demonstrate respect for their children. They acknowledge that their children are separate persons and may need their own time to adjust to change. It may be unfair to expect them not to be frustrated when they are asked to make an immediate behavioral change. In many respects, their experience can be compared to an adult situation where two people are watching television and one is in charge of the remote control. The person without the remote can develop cognitive whiplash, if she is concentrating on a television show when her partner changes the channel. Children, too, may experience whiplash and demonstrate it through whining, crying, or angry outbursts when they are confronted with immediate change without prior notification.

As with other behavioral techniques used with children, consistency and follow-through are important. Parents need to be consistent with the timing (although, the minute does not need to be precisely one minute). When the time is up, parents should expect their children to begin picking up their toys, come inside, or whatever their expectation might be. If this does not happen, a time-out, or, better yet, a logical consequence of their behavior may be appropriate.

Logical consequences are the costs to children as a result of their actions. The consequences need to relate to the current problem, be respectful of the child, and be reasonable, as stressed by Dreikurs in his classic book, *Children: The Challenge.*[1] They should not humiliate or induce suffering, but teach the child proper behavior. For example, Bryce may decide that he does not want to come inside after his parent have given him an "in a minute" getting-ready-for-bedtime message. A logical consequence might be to say to Bryce that if he does not come in now, he will not be able to play outside tomorrow morning; or that you will only read one bedtime story to him tonight instead of the usual two.

I introduced the "in a minute" technique to our daughter when she was a toddler. I continued to use it throughout our daughter's childhood. Most daily transitions were less stressful when the technique was used. The "in a minute" notification is metaphorically, like a fastened seatbelt that prevents whiplash from occurring when an unexpected change occurs.

Reference

[1] Rye, Nina. (2008). *Filial Therapy.* Retrieved December 12, 2010, from: http://www.filialtherapy.co.uk/.

[2] Dreikurs, R., & Soltz, V. (1964). *Children: The challenge.* NY: Hawthorne.

Teaching the Right Lesson: They Will Do as You Do

Cameron Lee, Ph.D., CFLE
Professor of Family Studies, Fuller Theological
Seminary, Pasadena, CA

Seven-year-old Adam is lying on his stomach on the living room carpet. His crayons are scattered about him as he happily makes bold red swirls on a piece of paper. As he reaches for the purple crayon, five-year-old Eve comes running through the room. She accidentally steps on some of her brother's crayons, breaking them in two. Suddenly, Adam is furious. He flies into a rage at his sister.

You come running at the commotion, just in time to see Adam push Eve to the floor. Horrified, you immediately cross over to Adam and give him a firm and angry smack on his behind. And with the smack comes the rebuke: "That'll teach you not to hit your sister!"

As parents, we're confronted with questions of discipline when our children misbehave. But it helps to remember that discipline is more than just stopping unwanted behavior. It's about teaching our children values and molding their character. The word *discipline* comes from the same root as the word *disciple*.[1] What would change if we thought of our children as our disciples? Just by being around us, they are learning from us all the time. This is true whether we are consciously trying to teach them something or not!

If we were the parent in the story above, we'd want Adam to stop hurting his sister. That's the immediate change in behavior we'd be looking for. But beyond this, what else do we want him to learn? We want him to learn other ways to deal with his anger, so he can stop himself from hurting her in the future. And we want him to do this for the right reasons. We want him to do what's right *because* it's right, not merely because he's afraid of being punished.

In other words, we don't just want our kids to endure discipline. We want them to develop *self*-discipline. That's part of growing up. We can't chase them around for the rest of their lives, telling them what to do. Instead, we hope that they will take our values for their own, not just put up with our rules until they can get out of the house.

Researchers suggest that harsh, punitive methods of discipline don't help us accomplish these positive goals.[2] Merely punishing Adam may make him stop whatever he's doing. But it won't necessarily help him learn self-control.

In fact, he may be learning an entirely different lesson, one we didn't intend to teach. He may learn that the "normal" way adults handle anger (at least with their kids!) is by hitting. This is suggested in part by recent discoveries of *mirror neurons* in brain research.[3] In a sense, we are wired to perceive the intentions and emotions behind what other people do. That state can be recreated inside us. Thus, our intended goal may be to teach our child not to hit. But if we do that by hitting, ironically, we might actually accomplish the opposite!

This doesn't mean we can never show anger as parents. Anger is a natural part of any close relationship. Kids will inevitably do things that make us angry, and we will do things that anger them. The question is what we teach them about how to handle anger from the example we set.[4]

Parents who are consistently warm and nurturing are more likely to have kids who accept their values. They submit more readily to their parents' authority.[5] Mirror neurons are the basis of empathy, the ability to walk in someone else's emotional shoes.[3] If we take the time to try to understand what Adam is feeling, we will be better able to help him find other ways to deal with his emotions.

So we can be firm with Adam, and set limits on his behavior. He needs to know that pushing and hitting are not OK. More than this, if we want him to learn self-control, he will first need to see that in us. We must be good examples of the kind of behavior we expect to see in our children.[6]

The moral of the story is that "Don't do as I do, do as I say" simply won't get the job done. And discipline is more than punishing bad behavior. We can force children to comply with our demands. But good behavior isn't the same thing as good character. What do we really want our children to learn? Discipline is about teaching, in the context of a close relationship with our children. Sometimes, they learn much more than we intended! We must pay close attention to *how* we discipline if we want to teach the right lesson.

References

[1] Bettelheim, B. (1987). *A good enough parent.* NY: Knopf.

[2] Gordon, T. (1989). *Discipline that works.* NY: Plume.

[3] Siegel, D. J., & Hartzell, M. (2003). *Parenting from the inside out.* NY: Tarcher / Putnam.

[4] Doherty, W. J. (2000). *Take back your kids.* Notre Dame, IN: Sorin.

[5] Fisher, S., & Fisher, R. L. (1986). *What we really know about child rearing.* Northvale, NJ: Aronson.

[6] Faber, A., & Mazlish, E. (1980). *How to talk so kids will listen and listen so kids will talk.* NY: Avon.

Intentional Parenting: What's Your Goal?

Cameron Lee, Ph.D., CFLE
Professor of Family Studies, Fuller Theological
Seminary, Pasadena, California

You're at the grocery store with your child, ready to check out at the register. Wide-eyed, she spies her favorite candy, and asks for some. You refuse, but she insists. It's clear you won't be able to keep saying no without a struggle.

What do you do? And why?

Competing goals may pass through our minds. *I don't want to be the bad guy. But I also don't want her to spoil her dinner. I want her to learn to eat things that are good for her. I want her to learn self-control; after all, money doesn't grow on trees. And I wish she could just enjoy being with me, even if she doesn't get candy.* If the situation dissolves into a tantrum, many parents would have another major and immediate goal–*I want this to stop right now, because it's embarrassing me!*

Notice how the goals differ. Some are more immediate and short-term, while others are long-term goals. Some are about what we want for ourselves (called *parent*-centered goals) and others about what we want for our children (*child*-centered).[1] In the example above, stopping the tantrum because we don't want to be embarrassed is a short-term, parent-centered goal. Helping our children learn self-control and good eating habits are long-term, child-centered goals.

And there are also *relationship*-centered goals.[1] Negatively, I don't want to be the bad guy all the time. But what *do* I want, positively? What do I want our relationship to look like, not just this moment, but long-term?

It is common wisdom in the business world that successful organizations have clear and achievable goals, with short-range goals serving long-range ones. Goals are often embodied in mission and vision statements that guide strategic decisions. Without this kind of intentionality, precious energy and resources are squandered needlessly.

Something similar can be said of families. As therapist Bill Doherty has recognized, modern life poses many challenges to keeping a family together.[2] We are busy and fragmented, and can't take family life for granted. If we want our families to be a certain way, we will need to be intentional,[2] putting thought and effort into our pursuit of family goals.

To do this, we must know what our goals *are*. Long-term goals are particularly important, since they embody the larger vision that gives shape and context to shorter-term goals. Some parent educators even advocate a 10-year plan.[3]

Here's an example of a relationship goal as part of a 10-year plan. In teaching communication skills to parents of younger children, I often ask: "What kind of a relationship do you want to have with your child when s/he is 15 or 16 years old?" Imagine your teenager-to-be is in trouble. We would want our children to think, "I know I can depend on Mom and Dad to help. They might get mad, but they'll listen." If we want that kind of relationship in 10 years, then what are we doing now to build the proper foundations? What are we doing to show them that we can be trusted to love and help them in even the most difficult situations?

Long-term child-centered and relationship-centered goals can be particularly helpful in those situations where we are most tempted to overreact emotionally. When our goals are more parent-centered, we are more likely to use power to get our own way. But when we stop to think about what's best for the child or for the relationship, we tend to be more understanding, and rely more on gentler methods of persuasion.[1]

This is one facet of what is known as emotional intelligence, which includes the ability to manage our own emotions.[4] When we are upset with our children, stopping to consider our goals helps slow us down. We can be more intentional about what to do next, rather than simply reacting without thinking. And this in turn will help our children learn to do the same–itself a valuable long-term and child-centered goal!

Goals also can be shared as a family. Maurice Elias and his colleagues, for example, suggest that families can have *mottos, mission statements*, and *constitutions*.[5] A family motto is a short and memorable phrase that defines a core value of the family: "We are a family who…cares about others." A mission statement is a somewhat more detailed sentence that helps parents keep their most valued long-term goals in mind. A constitution is a simple set of principles and rules, embodying the motto and mission, usually posted somewhere for all to see and follow. Making goals explicit and shared in this way helps everyone to commit to a mutual vision of who we are and want to be.[6]

Thus, it's important to take some time by ourselves, when we're calm, to consider what goals we have as parents. Don't wait until there's a problem with your child to try to figure it out. Think about your goals, write them down, and keep them in mind. What kind of a parent do you want to be? What qualities do you want to help foster in your child? What do you hope for your relationship? Then, when thrust into a situation with your child that provokes an emotional response in you, don't just react. Be an intentional parent. Stop and ask yourself: "What's my goal?"

References

[1] Hastings, P. D., & Grusec, J. E. (1998). Parenting goals as organizers of responses to parent-child disagreement. *Developmental Psychology, 34*, 465-479.

[2] Doherty, W. J. (1997). *The intentional family: How to build family ties in our modern world.* Reading, MA: Addison-Wesley.

[3] Christopherson, E. R., & Mortweet, S. L. (2003). *Parenting that works.* Washington, DC: American Psychological Association.

[4] Goleman, D. (1995). *Emotional intelligence.* NY: Bantam.

[5] Elias, M. J., Tobias, S. E., & Friedlander, B. S. (1999). *Emotionally intelligent parenting.* NY: Three Rivers.

[6] Lew, A., & Bettner, B. L. (1999). Establishing a family goal. *The Journal of Individual Psychology, 55*, 105-108.

Is "Good Job!" Enough?

Jean Illsley Clarke, Ph.D., CFLE
Author and parent educator, Minneapolis, MN

"Good job!" has a nice ring to it. It is frequently used as a compliment in the Zeb family. However, Mother and Father Zeb have noticed that it doesn't necessarily encourage children to "do better." When teenage Zeb passes his driver's test and the family shouts "Goood jahab!" he starts telling how often he will *need* the car. When 4th grade Zeb passes her spelling test and the reward is "Good job!" she thinks, okay, that was good enough. I don't need to study more and bring my score higher. When two-year-old Zeb puts three crayon scribbles on his paper, big sister Zeb says, "Good job!" But little Zeb throws the paper aside, puts two marks on the next paper, looks up for his reward, and reaches for another clean sheet.

So why doesn't "Good job!" motivate children to achieve? Probably because it tells them that *we like* what they did instead of telling them what *they did well*, or finding out what *they* think.

But, but, you tell me, "I say 'good job' all the time because I want to encourage my child." Certainly you do, because you care, you love your children, and you want them to be successful. Your intentions are good, but try reading each of the following pairs of responses aloud. Say each of them with pride and pleasure in your voice, and think about how they might strike a child.

Teenager:
"Good job!" Or,
"You must be learning how to set priorities in order to get that long term paper done so well"

School age:
"Good job!" Or,
"Hey, you got an A on that paper. Tell me how you did that."

Four-year-old:
"Good job!" Or,
"I like the way you colored the flowers in your picture. What do you like?"

Two-year-old:
"Good job!" Or,
"You brought three books to me. Which one shall we read first?"

One-year-old:
"Good job!" Or,
"You got out from under the table all by yourself."

How was that? Did it help you understand that a constant barrage of "good jobs" can create praise-junkies where children perform to get praise rather than to enhance their own skills and learn to develop their own internal reward system?[1]

Other thoughts about "Good job!"
- "Good job!" is appropriate if we are teaching specific standards for a specific skill. Even then we need to point out specifically how the task was well done.
- "Good job!" is a way of telling a child to feel good about what he did. What if he doesn't feel good? Need he act like he does to please us?
- Too much praise can program children to expect to be praised for everything they do. That is debilitating for them and boring for the rest of us.
- "Good job!" is well meaning, but it is lazy parenting.
- We can say we like something without telling the child she must like it. "I love the valentine you made for me. How did you guess I would like a lace border?"

Over-nurture
Adults who have been overindulged as children (participants in the first three overindulgence studies reported in the *How Much Is Enough?* book[2]) told us their parents had given them "too much love." That is called over-nurture. What parents meant to have been helpful has turned out to be a liability, not an asset. So, let's remember that saying "Good job!" is for our need, not the child's.

Whenever we want to say "Good job!" let's hold fast to our good intentions, describing exactly what was well done, or asking what the child liked about it, and remember that our job is always to encourage growth and, only when appropriate, to evaluate.

References
[1] Kohn, A. (1993). *Punished by rewards: The trouble with gold stars, incentive plans, A's, praise, and other bribes.* NY: Houghton Mifflin Co.
[2] Clarke, J. & Dawson, C., & Bredehoft, D. (2004). *How much is enough? Everything you need to know to steer clear of overindulgence and raise likeable, responsible, and respectful children.* NY: Marlowe & Co. For more information about the Overindulgence Research Studies, see www.overindulgence .info.

Compassionate Parenting: A Case Study

H. Wallace Goddard, Ph.D., CFLE
Editor of the classic, *Between Parent and Child,*
Professor of Family Life, University of Arkansas
Cooperative Extension Service, Little Rock, AR

There is a nationally-syndicated columnist who regularly gives advice to parents on raising their children. His advice, it appears to me, usually encourages parents to be tough with their children. Many parents appreciate his no-nonsense approach; some may not–such as those who fail to set limits on their children's behavior because they fear losing their children's goodwill.

This failure to put limits on bad behavior has serious consequences for our society. The columnist and I agree on that point. Parents must let their children know that they are serious about the rules they make. The way children know we are serious is that we set reasonable rules and enforce them when they are broken.

Yet, I believe that there is a danger in focusing primarily on doling out consequences for misbehavior. If we are not careful, we will throw out the baby with the bath water. It takes more than consistent consequences to teach goodness, character, and compassion. Consequences are especially unhelpful when delivered with irritation and rejection. We should strive to replace our frustrations and annoyance when children break a rule with a feeling of compassion. Also, we need to realize that for any given situation, there usually are several alternative ways of dealing with it, which may get lost or not considered if we too quickly seek to exact a consequence for a broken rule.

A Case Study

To move this from an abstract discussion to a practical one, let us look at an example from the columnist's published column and contrast his approach to some alternatives which I believe would probably be more acceptable to scholars who study child rearing.

A mother wrote to the columnist that her 4-year-old daughter at some point during a meal would sometimes decide that she wouldn't swallow her food.[1] When told that she cannot spit it out, she would hold the bite for hours. The mother reported that they had tried many things to get the daughter to swallow: having her remain at the table for hours, skipping the next meal, returning the unswallowed food to her at the next meal, removing toys and privileges for weeks, banishment to her room without toys, spanking, praising (on those rare occasions when she swallowed), and withholding dessert.

Almost parenthetically, the mother noted that the girl was adopted internationally a year previous to her writing to the columnist. The problem began about four months after the adoption. The mother also mentioned that there were other children in the family.

Based on this information, what do you think should be done to solve the problem?

One Recommendation

Let's begin with the columnist's recommendations. He first suggested that it was not useful to look for a psychological cause for the behavior. "This is one of those weird, strange, inexplicable things that some children sometimes do, for no obvious reason at all." Further, "some of the things children do defy explanation. Some of the odd stuff in question is harmless to the point of being funny. What your daughter is doing is funny (to me, at least), but it's also a very clever, subtle form of defiance" (p. E3).[1]

One might wonder if all of this is funny to the child who doesn't swallow, or to the parents perplexed by the behavior–doubtful.

The columnist confidently gives a solution–offering to chew his hat if it doesn't work: "You simply tell your slyly defiant and highly intelligent little princess that you called her doctor and he/she said that not swallowing happens because a child is tired and doesn't even know it...Your doctor said that from now on, if you take a bite and you are so tired that you can't swallow, you have to go to the bathroom, spit it out and go to bed. If she balks at swallowing, and you begin the procedure, and she suddenly decides to swallow, you must still put her to bed. Just tell her the doctor said that even having problems swallowing means she's tired and doesn't know it. I predict that in a week or two, it will be a thing of the past, and I will still have my hat."

Testing the Counsel

Does this counsel sound good to you? If you were the child, would it seem helpful to you? Is it likely that a parent seeking to enforce reasonable rules would act this way?

Certainly there are many responses to these questions, remembering the idea of alternative solutions. I don't believe there is only one "right" answer. But if I were responding to the parent's question, my recommendations would be quite different from those of the columnist.

A Different Starting Place

First, I would recommend the kind of compassion and humility that comes from seeking to understand the child's experience. What were the first three years of the child's life like? How was she nurtured and nourished in those years? Did she have consistent and caring attention during those three years before she was adopted, or did she experience chaotic or stressful conditions? Was availability of food a grave concern for the girl during this time? Under what circumstances was she adopted? How has this little girl integrated with the other children in the adoptive family? Does she have friends? What is the child's personality or temperament like? Is there a certain food that she refuses to chew? Are there foods she enjoys? What kind of food did she have before the international adoption? Was there unusual stress in her life at the time the problem behavior began? How have siblings reacted to the non-swallowing? Has this girl been teased previously about her eating? How affectionate and appreciative do the parents feel about this child when not at the dinner table? Does the little girl have friends and activities she enjoys? All of these issues suggest the merits of considering the exploration of various alternative solutions.

To confidently recommend a certain remedy without knowing the child's history is not a good remedy. In addition, if the other children in the family are old enough, the above solution introduces the acceptance of lying into the family, as they may see through the approach their mother is using. While some sensible actions can be suggested in the above case, based on the scant information provided by the parent, it strikes me that humility seems to be a wiser stance than a dogmatic solution.

The Limits of Power

Apart from the limited information issue, there is another issue. Any parent who has ever been a child knows that the "put-the-child-to-bed" prescription is a power technique that can lead to long term conflict. The power technique may have a smile on its face but it is unmistakably a power play. No child will be fooled no matter how big the smile. Research on guiding children recommends against the strategy suggested above.[2]

The behavior recommended by the columnist may work in some narrow sense. It is likely that the child will start swallowing the food rather than be put to bed. Yet, in my opinion, the real problem will go untreated. Does this child feel desperately confused in her new country? Does she feel stupid and helpless (maybe even picked on) in a family that already knows the rules of American life? Does she feel lonely and unloved?

The Magic Cure

The most important factor in determining how well a child develops is love. Children who have people who understand, support, love, and teach them, are likely to become strong and able adults. By turning up the use of power on the annoying but harmless behavior, in my view, the columnist could be guaranteeing continuing trouble.

Worse yet, might the prescriptions almost guarantee that the root problems may get worse? Today's dinner battles may become tomorrow's eating disorder, anxiety problem, learned helplessness, or depression.

Based on the scant information provided by the parent, I would recommend minimizing the swallowing issue by unceremoniously providing a "discharge" bowl for the little girl while encouraging family members not to worry about the swallowing issue. She is welcome to eat as much as she is inclined to eat and may stop at any time. At the same time, I would look for ways to strengthen the parent-child relationship away from the dinner table. The Number 1 question for her parents is "What is life like for this 4-year-old?" I would recommend that the parents monitor the child's food preferences while noticing the child's areas of connection, expression, and joy as well as any particular difficulties.

The child is trying to tell us something. From the compassionate viewpoint, we will get the message best if we have the patience and wisdom to hear and interpret her message. As a side note, the best writing on the subject of families and eating is probably Ellyn Satter,[3] who underscores that we should not turn eating into a battleground. Many of us are still struggling with irrational eating because of ill-advised eating rules in our childhood homes.

Two Ways or More to Consider

The columnist's recommendations have a certain natural appeal. I wonder if that is because the natural instinct in each of us wants to be in control and obeyed. We do not even want to be inconvenienced. "Things should be done my way–and done promptly."

Yet we probably realize that there are ways that are more sensitive to the child. A loving parent might take the little girl on his or her lap and hum to her. He might ask her what foods from her native country were her favorites. I can imagine him making a bear out of peanut butter balls for her–if he knew that she liked peanut butter. Or raisin ants on a cheese and celery log. A compassionate parent will take time to discover what the girl likes–and will do it in the context of a loving relationship.

How do we know what will help the child feel loved? When we see an earnest, struggling child behind the imperfect behavior, when we feel compassion for the child, we are likely to act in ways that are loving.

Clearly, there are children's misdeeds that need "consequences" and teaching. But if we lead with correction rather than compassion in our responses to children, we may not be friends to many children. An over-riding feeling of love, even when correcting a child, is what distinguishes effective parents from all others.

We have far more power than children do. We rule over them. The question for all of us who are parents is whether we will choose to act in ways that are sensitive to the child or whether we will be brutish and demand compliance at all costs.

Of course there is more than love and compassion to effective parenting. My article in the next chapter, "First Compassion, Then Teaching," will expand on this theme.

References

[1] Rosemond, J. (2002, October 23). Obstinate daughter won't swallow food. *Arkansas Democrat Gazette*, 3E.

[2] Maccoby, E. E., & Martin, J. A. (1983). Socialization in the context of the family: Parent-child interaction. In P. H. Mussen (Ed.), *Handbook of child psychology, Volume IV (pp. 1-101)*. New York: John Wiley.

[3] Satter, E. (2000). *Child of mine: Feeding with love and good sense*. Boulder, CO: Bull Publishing.

Grounding–by the Rules

Joyce M. Buck, MS, CFLE
Instructor Specialist
Child and Family Studies Department
Weber State University, Ogden, UT

It was the typical parent-of-a-teen dilemma. Should I call for emergency help, get in the car and go searching, or just keep pacing the floor while the wee hours of the morning ticked away. My young son, just thirteen, was out with older friends, and it was way past curfew.

Family rules were swimming in my head. As Virginia Satir indicated,[1] established relationship rules, spoken and unspoken, guide individual responses in every situation. Did my rules allow me to "blast" this child right off the face of the earth as soon as he appeared? In all my efforts to be Baumrind's authoritative parent[2]– the one whose rules are clear and associated with consequences well understood–where had I gone wrong?

Baumrind has it down, I thought. "Influential and internationally recognized research psychologist Diana Baumrind ...asserted that normal parenting centers on the issue of control and that parent's primary roles are to influence, teach, and control their children" (p. 399)[2]: keyword: control. However, authoritative parenting (just one of four parenting styles) is tempered with warmth and flexibility and two-way communication.

As I paced the floor I rehearsed my speech. I would be angry. I took justification from Satir, who says emotional honesty is critical.

But I also felt that it was important to find out what was going on. "Seek first to understand" is one of Covey's habits for effective relationships,[3] and it was one of my primary rules for successful family relationships. I kept rewriting and rehearsing.

The young man finally came quietly slipping in the back door. I met him, hands on hips. Yes, I was angry, just as he had suspected I would be. But my "where have you been?" voice was not too loud (actually, not real soft, either), as I expressed frustration, fear, and sleeplessness. Then, I flopped down on the couch and motioned for him to sit by me and asked, "So how was it?" What followed was nearly an hour an animated retelling of the evening's adventures spiced with delightful detail and accented with sparkling eyes. It has been really fun! And the retelling was really fun for me, too. We felt happy and close.

The night was well spent when he finally asked, "Well, Mom, how long am I grounded for?" (grounding being the already established consequence for coming home late) and we negotiated the activities he would forfeit. There were teeth in this grounding (the rules said, you make Mom suffer, you must suffer, too), but it was delivered with a friendly swat on the back of the head, and a goodnight (or rather a good-morning) kiss.

There were some additional rules in operation here: It was clear that there would be no sleeping-in, and there were responsibilities to take care of when the sun came up, and repeat offenses would double the consequences, but as he went off to bed, my teen-age son turned around and said, "Hey, Mom, I love how you do grounding."

References

[1] Satir, V. (1988). *The new peoplemaking.* Mountain View, CA: Science and Behavior Books.

[2] Welch, K. J. (2007). *Family life now: A conversation about marriages, families, and relationships.* Boston: Pearson.

[3] Covey, S. R. (1985). *7 Habits of highly effective people.* NY: Simon & Schuster

Like Persian Carpets: Perfection Not Required

Clara Gerhardt, Ph.D., CFLE
Professor and Director of International Education,
School of Education and Professional Studies,
Samford University, Birmingham, AL

In my parents' house a Persian carpet covered the dining table. Antique Persian carpets were so precious that they were put on tables rather than floors to protect their beauty. As a child I had ample time to look closely at the intricate patterns. Every carpet, however beautiful it was, had a purposeful mistake knotted into the design. This would show that the artwork in the carpet had indeed been knotted by human hands, as only the Divine could achieve perfection. In fact, an old Persian proverb states that "A Persian Rug is Perfectly Imperfect, and Precisely Imprecise." Later in life it became a game to find these signs of humanness–where did the carpet makers place their mark into the landscape, where was that sign of authenticity, that imperfection that characterizes us humans?

As a parent, I frequently recall my own memories of being parented. I look back at my childhood with the eyes of a grown up. When my parents made mistakes, they were the errors of real, fallible people. I know that in my small world I was the apple of my parents' eyes. That is the part I felt and remembered; that made me resilient, able to overcome problems or bounce back from hardships. I believe that the woven core or backing of the proverbial carpet, of which I am made, is the fiber of parental love, upon which the intricate patterns of well intended but sometimes imperfect parenting are knotted.

As grownups and as parents, we may understandably feel that it is the love which our children bestow upon us that motivates us to be the best parents we can be. For me, of the many challenges in life, parenthood has been the most demanding, yet also the most rewarding. Even though we fail in many small ways, our children tend to trust and love us unconditionally–an immense gift we may hardly deserve, but which we try to honor.

In my heart I know that my best parenting contains that error in the carpet, the expression of humanness. I am imperfect, but I will give it my best effort, dedicated with every fiber of my being. If I had to apply for the job as a parent, I could only have the courage to take on the challenge if the job ad read: "Perfection not a prerequisite, nor a requirement."

Chapter IV

Wisdom in Guiding Children: Some Classic Approaches

As discussed above in the article, "The Spectrum of Light," there are a number of ways to resolve specific child behavior issues. This chapter presents a number of the more classic approaches. As suggested earlier, they don't necessarily conflict with each other. They merely indicate different ways to handle similar situations. Parents need to pick and choose the ones that appeal to them the most.

In fact, often parents may try to resolve an issue first by merely talking about it with their child, using good communication skills, listening carefully and sharing their desires. If that doesn't succeed, then a parent might try using some natural or logical consequence, as discussed below in this chapter. Sometimes that approach may seem not to work; then, a parent might try some more specific management plan, such as contracts or a reward/reinforcement system.

As parents, you likely realize that even now you probably use several different methods or approaches, from time to time, without realizing that they have a name. The following articles can help in adding to your alternatives.

Parenting with Style

Kevin H. Gross, Ph.D., CFLE
Program Evaluation and Research Consultant,
Eastern NC Evaluation & Research Services, Wilson

Parents have a style, which is to say that we all have a particular style of parenting. How we choose to raise our children often is related to whom we want them to be when they grow up. And while some parents spend a considerable amount of time thinking and learning about and shaping their own parenting style, others simply do mostly what their parents did. There are four basic parenting styles,[1,2] discussed below, which scholars have studied, based upon two primary dimensions: **responsiveness**, and **demandingness**.[3]

Responsiveness refers to the amount of warmth or acceptance that is characteristic of the parent-child relationship. It also is about respect for a child and his or her rights as an individual. **Demandingness** refers to the rules or expectation we parents have for our children's behaviors and the amount of structure we have provided for them.

Authoritative parenting, the first parenting style, is characterized by both a high level of responsiveness and a high level of demandingness. Authoritative parents have a clear set of reasonable expectations for a child's behaviors and they take the time to explain to the child why it is important to behave in such a way. For example, when faced with a preschool aged child who will not eat their green beans at dinner, an authoritative parent may say to the child: "It is important to eat your vegetables so that you can stay healthy and play with your friends." Or they might say: "You may either eat your green beans or your salad but you need to eat one to be healthy," however the child is not allowed to leave the table until they eat some sort of vegetable. While it sounds easy enough, in practice authoritative parenting tends to take more time and energy especially with young children. The payoff is that as they become older they become more autonomous or independent in their decision making and they tend to make better choices for themselves.

The **authoritarian parenting** style is characterized by parents who have a high level of demandingness, but a lower level of responsiveness. With an extremely authoritarian parent a child is not allowed to question why they are to behave in a particular way nor is any explanation usually given. Often an authoritarian parent will rely on physical punishment as a way to teach a child about what is expected of them. They tend to place a higher value on following the direction of an authority figure than they do on independent thought. An authoritarian parent may say to a preschool aged child "You eat your green beans because I said so" or "because that is what we have to eat tonight." Often authoritarian parents are overly critical of their children, focusing only on what they have done wrong or upon their failures. To the child it may seem like that no matter how well they do something, it is never good enough and so they may give up even trying. Children of authoritarian parents often will have a difficult time forming their own identity and are more susceptible to negative peer influences. They tend have trouble deciding for themselves between right and wrong and thus rely on others to tell them.

A **permissive parenting** style, in contrast to the authoritarian parenting style, is characterized by a high level of responsiveness but a low level of demandingness. Thus, there is a strong, warm emotional connection between the parent and child but there is little in the way of rules and expectations. Sometimes the parent seems more like a friend than a parent, especially as the child grows older. Using the green bean eating example again, a permissive parent is likely to say "You don't have to eat your green beans if you don't like them" and let the child leave the table without eating any vegetables. While these children tend to have good social skills and sometimes may seem more mature than their peers, they often struggle with forming a clear identity or purpose in life and so they spend a lot of time exploring different identities. They may drop in and out of college, change majors frequently, and/or try several different careers before they finally settle on something. At times they may seemed lost and unsure about what do to next and they may not be sure where to look for guidance or even recognize that they might need some. Generally, children who experience one of these three styles do well in life; however, there are some differences as discussed below.

Lastly, it should not be surprising that we refer to parents who are low in responsiveness and demandingness as having an **uninvolved parenting** style. Children who grow up with this fourth parenting style tend to have a much more difficult time. Not that these children are doomed to a life of misery, but the challenges they face seem to be more difficult to overcome when there is no one there to help. When they do succeed, it is often due to another adult in their lives stepping in the take on a parenting role.

There has been a considerable amount of research on parenting styles and the general consensus is that authoritative parenting works as a protective factor in reducing the likelihood of a young person participating in any of a number of "undesirable" behaviors.[4] Regardless of sex, ethnicity, social economic status, or family structure, children who are raised in homes characterized by warmth, structure, and high, reasonable expectations are more likely to be characterized as competent individuals. Specifically, children raised by authoritative parents are more likely to do well in school,[5] they are less like to engage in health risk behaviors (e.g., smoking, drinking, and drug use)[6] and they are less likely to have sex at an early age.[6] This all stems from the fact that these children are more likely to actually listen to their parents and truly internalize their parent's values and beliefs.

The distinction between an authoritative parent and other three types of parents is not just about what they do, it also is about how they interpret their child's behaviors. Authoritative parents often have a basic understanding of child development. They know that the way a child sees and interacts with the world around them is very different from the way they as adults see things. They do not expect their child to behave like an adult nor do they expect them to understand their environment from an adult perspective. This is what is meant by reasonable expectations.

It is important to understand that we are talking about increasing the chances that children will experience the sort of positive outcomes that we often want for our children and for all children in general. It is not a guarantee that everything will turn out okay. Even under the best of circumstances, children make mistakes–some big ones and some not so big ones. How we respond to these mistakes influences what our children learn from them. Do they learn to hide them from their parents so that they do not get into trouble, or do they learn to talk with their parents about them so that they can avoid making the same sort of mistake in the future? It also is important to note that often when we compare different parenting styles the differences that we see in child outcomes is not simply a matter of good outcomes versus bad outcomes, but more likely good and not quite as good. Nevertheless, sometimes, not quite as good can make a big difference in the opportunities that our children will have to be happy, healthy, productive adults.

To lump all parents into these seemingly simple four styles may seem like an oversimplification of the many ways in which parents at times parent. Depending on the circumstances some parents may actually switch from one style to another. For example, when it comes to keeping the child's bedroom clean the parent may be permissive, but they may be authoritative when it comes to how that child behaves when there is company over for dinner; however, most parents tend to emphasis one style over the others. It also may be that in two parent households one parent has one style and the other parent has a different style. In such a situation it is possible that the two different styles would complement each other. For example, one parent may be authoritarian and one may be permissive and together they create an authoritative home environment. The key is that for a situation like this to work, it is important that the parents be aware of their different styles and that they support each other in their different roles as parents.

Finally, it is important to keep in mind that we as parent tend to respond to the world in which our children are growing up. Thus, it may be that what worked for children a generation or two ago is not necessarily what is best for them today and what works for a child growing up in one setting may not be best for a child growing up someplace very different. Ultimately, what is most important is that parents be thoughtful about what style they mostly use and why, and that they make thoughtful decisions about the way in which they parent.

References

[1] Baumrind, Diana. (1971). Current patterns of parental authority. *Developmental Psychology Monograph, 4*, 4-103.

[2] Baumrind, Diana. (1991). Parenting styles and adolescent development. In J. Brooks-Gunn, R. Lerner & A.C. Petersen (Eds.), *The encyclopedia on adolescence* (pp. 746-758). NY: Garland.

[3] Maccoby, E., & Martin, J. (1983). Socialization in the context of the family: Parent-child interaction. In E. M. Hetherington (Ed.), P.H. Myssen (Series Ed.), *Handbook of child psychology: Vol. 4. Socialization, personality, and social development* (pp. 1-101). NY: Wiley.

[4] Blum, R. W., McNeely, C., & Nonnemaker, J. (2002). Vulnerability, risk, and protection. *Journal of Adolescent Health, 31,* 28-39.

[5] Dornbusch, S. M., Ritter, P. L., Leiderman, P. H., Roberts, D. F., & Fraleigh, M. J. (1987). The relation of parenting style to adolescent school performance. *Child Development, 58,* 1244-1257.

[6] Borawski, E. A., Ievers-Lands, C. E., Lovegreen, L. D., & Trapl, E. S. (2003). Parental monitoring, negotiated unsupervised time, and parental trust: The role of perceived parenting practices in adolescent health risk behaviors. *Journal of Adolescent Health, 33,* 60-70.

You must be the change you want to see in the world.
−Mahatma Gandhi

First Compassion, Then Teaching

H. Wallace Goddard, Ph.D., CFLE
Editor of the classic, *Between Parent and Child,*
Professor of Family Life, University of Arkansas Cooperative
Extension Service, Little Rock, AR

In the previous article, "Compassionate Parenting: A Case Study," the central importance of compassion in raising healthy children was described. Compassion is the first law of parenting. Nothing matters as much as compassion as a form of love in helping children develop into healthy adults. What's more, the quality of love has an impact on the effectiveness of all other parenting efforts.

In dealing with parenting dilemmas, it is hard to tease apart loving compassion and disciplining (or guiding, as we say in the field of child development). Many issues we think of as control issues are really, at root, relationship issues.

There is far more that can and should be said about effectively loving children. It is worthy of our most devoted and patient attention. But I promised to write in this article about the other key dimension in parenting. It goes by several names: control, guidance, or structure. I like to think of it as *teaching*.

The Control Dilemma

This discussion can begin with another bit of counsel from the same parent columnist described in my previous article. In a another column he responded to yet another inquiry about feeding children.[1] There are two parts of his counsel on which I would like to focus. First, he said that children should not be allowed to complain about the food they are served for meals at home. It is rude, he said. Second, he took to task a parent who would create an alternative meal for a child who was not happy with the offered one.

Before discussing his counsel, let's set the stage for thinking about control. What is its purpose? To prevent problems? To keep children out of trouble? To make life run smoothly?

The Purpose of Control

I believe that there is one primary purpose for parents to exercise control in their children's lives: to teach them to make good decisions. Certainly control also should be used to keep children safe from threats for which they are not prepared. But this fits within the larger purpose of parental control–helping children learn to make good decisions. We want them to make good choices long after they have left our homes.

There are many ways to abuse parental control, but the many ways can be classed into two broad categories for the sake of this discussion: too much and too little.

Too Much Control

Those who exercise too much control may be trying to prevent their children from making mistakes but, in the process, they hamper the development of their children.

Progressive Choosing

The solution to the control problem is not to provide unlimited choices to their children. The solution is progressive opportunities to make choices. We honor the baby's preference for goo-ing with the parent or resting time–but remaining available when the child is interested. We allow a preschooler to pick the book to be read at bedtime, but usually not the time for it. We allow a school age child to pick the clothes to wear to school–providing subtle coaching along the way and holding our complaints when they are not welcome. Most adolescents are allowed to make many decisions, under wise and gentle parental guidance.

Progressive choosing is much like helping a child learn to ride a bike. As children get ready to learn to ride, we provide a bike with training wheels. As they get more experienced, we might adjust the training wheels up or even remove them. For a short time we run alongside children as they learn–coaching on steering, braking and balancing. Eventually they learn to ride on their own. Along the way most children get some bumps and bruises. But wise parents provide just enough guidance to prevent damaging or discouraging accidents. We give children all the freedom for which they are prepared. We even coach them to help them be ready for more freedom.

Examples of Control with Progressive Choosing

Children should be given choices within the bounds set by loving and wise parents. And we do not have to become unpleasant as we set limits. One of our parenting mottoes has two vital parts: It is our job to (1) help our children get what they want (2) in a way we feel good about. We care deeply about our children's preferences. But we set some boundaries based on their readiness. We did not let our young children decide whether they wanted Hershey bars or green beans for dinner. But we might offer a choice between green beans and peas.

Another example: When 17-year-old Andy asked us if he could go to the lake with his friends on an upcoming Friday night, we took seriously our responsibility to help him make a good decision. But we also honored–based on good experiences with him–his good sense and maturity.

So I asked, "How do you feel about going?"

"I think it will be fine. We'll play ball and have snacks."

"So you don't see any problems with the gathering?"

Andy paused. "Well, I do have a question. I know some of the guys will be bringing marijuana but I won't be using any so it shouldn't be a problem, right?"

I managed my shock. We had a calm discussion about potential problems. I encouraged him to think about it for another day or two. He ultimately decided that he didn't need to be at a party with drugs. In fact, he offered an alternative gathering at our house.

The Gentle Art of Progressive Choosing

Progressive choosing is an art. It requires wisdom and faith to provide children abundant opportunities to make decisions while not setting them up for disaster.

When does setting bounds become too controlling? Perhaps the answer is when we fail to be sensitive to both their abilities and their limitations. But this is not a tidy answer. It is only when we have love, concern, and compassion in our hearts that we can set bounds wisely. Compassion must guide the purpose and enlighten the practice of progressive choice with *wisdom* as her fair companion.

Back to the Food Issue

So when we look at the question about food preferences, I disagree with the parenting columnist about children expressing their dislike for foods. Why? I do not consider it rude within a family for a person to express that he does not have a taste for a certain food. The expression can be phrased with consideration for the people who provide and prepare the food. But a child should be able to express feelings.

And we can model civility ourselves. We do not need to rant or shame them. We can set a standard that seems reasonable: "I ask that you try one bean. Then, if you do not want more, you may fix yourself a peanut butter sandwich" (or some other reasonable choice they prefer).

Even in making such simple requests, we can avoid stark confrontation. Psychology teaches us to minimize power as a relationship issue. It tends to get in the way of helpful guidance. As Wendy Grolnick, an insightful psychologist has observed: "[Humans] simply do not do well (or feel well) when we are made to feel like pawns to others, whether at work, at school, or in our personal relationships" (pp. 32-3).[2]

The best tools for effective parenting include persuasion and patience. Please note: A capable parent is not afraid to set and enforce reasonable limits. Yet this is done with the abilities and needs of the child in mind.

In the eating arena, we provide lots of nutritious foods and let children make choices. Yet, I agree with the columnist that a parent probably should not jump to prepare an alternate meal for the child. And I would not allow the child to eat just anything. I would probably have an alternate choice in mind that was acceptable to the child, which he or she might help prepare. That would set appropriate bounds.

So, having discussed the exercise of excessive control, with the introduction of progressive choosing, let's turn our attention to insufficient control.

Too Little Control

Many parents cannot tolerate children's displeasure. They are not willing to set firm boundaries. They may lecture and threaten but they do not deliver on their threats. What do children learn from such parenting? They learn that the key to getting what you want is to keep your parents constantly on the horns of your displeasure. They learn to be family tormentors.

Most of us have seen parents caving in. In fact, most of us have done such caving ourselves. For example, we likely have all seen a parent insist to a child in the supermarket that he cannot have a candy bar under any circumstances. But, after some whining, nagging, and maybe even a tantrum, the child gets the candy bar. What did the child learn? A little persistence pays handsome dividends. So children learn to become efficient tormentors of their parents.

Children learn just what combination of whining and demanding will get them what they want. And many parents learn to be endless lecturers. So both sides lose. Both parent and child lose dignity in the battle over a candy bar. We teach children to surrender character and become mercenaries. And we become chronic grouches.

There are other ways of exerting too little control. One of them is to use threats as a control technique. Frustrated parents may threaten to withhold Christmas presents or to keep a child home from a party. Both parent and child know that the threat is unlikely to be enacted. It is merely a stick swung threateningly in the air. Feeling insulted by the unjust attack on his or her dignity, the child resists. The parental anger and threats escalate. Childish indignity grows.

This can't possibly be the best way to teach children how to use their ability to make choices. The drama would be comical if it were not so tragic.

Guidelines for Guidance

Sensible rules for guidance include at least the following:

1. **Be careful about the rules you make.** Avoid idle threats. Do not make big issues out of little behaviors that should be ignored.
2. **Consistently enforce the rules you make.** The action behind the promise is the only way children learn that we—and nature—are serious about the rules we make.
3. **Use consequences.** Let nature—rather than angry diatribes—teach the law of the harvest. When we do not sow, we do not reap. If we do not finish our chores, we do not go out and play.
4. **Keep the relationship positive.** We should probably deliver at least five positive experiences for each negative one. And even the negative encounters should be done with persuasion, gentleness, meekness, patience, and genuine love.
5. **Give children lots of real choices.** It takes regular practice for them to learn to use their decision-making capacity well. (See Goddard, "Something Better than Punishment," in *Principles of Parenting* [3] for more details on these five principles.)

A Concluding Example

My wife and I once attended a birthday party for a graduate student. The hostess was greeting all of her guests even as she tried to finish preparations for the party and manage her two children. We tried to help as we noticed trouble brewing. Four-year-old Ellen (not her real name) was standing at the kitchen table, nose-to-nose with the cake. She clearly had designs on the frosting.

This is a crossroads in parenting. The mother may choose to do nothing. She may harpoon her with threats. Or she may set Ellen up for success.

In this case, Mom followed her poorer instincts of control without looking at other alternatives. She threatened. "If you touch that cake you're in trouble!" and shot the threatening glare. Ellen returned the glare with the hidden message: "I can make you suffer for treating me this way."

Having offered her threat, Mom returned to preparations for the party. Ellen returned to frosting-lust. Obviously the maternal injunction had not created a mighty change of direction for Ellen.

Ellen lingered near the cake and Mom continued to leer at Ellen. When Mom got busy taking snack items to the party area, Ellen snatched a frosting-rich corner of the cake. When Mom returned and spotted the telltale signs of the crime, she screamed, "I told you not to touch that cake!" Ellen felt mistreated and Mom judged her to be a bad child. This approach did not lead to a win-win situation.

Some would say that Ellen should be obedient. Some would say that she should be punished. An alternative: parents can set children up for success. When the Mom spotted the high-risk situation, she might have done any of several things:

1. She might have gotten Ellen a snack. This would be especially appropriate if Mom knew that Ellen was hungry; yet, maybe just giving her some of the leftover frosting might suffice.
2. Mom might have explained to Ellen that for a party like this, it is important to keep the cake looking nice and "whole" for the guests to see.
3. Mom might have gotten Ellen busy helping, inviting her to take supplies and snacks to the table.
4. Mom might have cut a slice of cake for Ellen to eat right away.
5. Mom might have moved the cake to the top of the fridge.

Which is the best response? It depends. It depends on Ellen's disposition and current state of hunger. It depends on Mom's need to deliver an uncut cake to the party. It depends on how long it will be before the cake is cut and served. That is the unique challenge of parenting. There are no simple, pat answers. There are just sensible, considerate processes.

Ideally Mom wants to help Ellen get the experiences she wants. In addition, Mom wants to help Ellen learn to make good decisions. We don't want to set her up for failure. We don't want to punish her into resentful submission for being a normal child. We want to help Ellen learn to make good decisions.

No Simple Answers

Hundreds of thousands of words have been written about parenting. This short article may raise more questions or objections than solutions. Parenting does not have a simple formula. Ultimately, good parenting requires us to be compassionate, to have kind hearts and wise minds. It also helps if we are feeling peaceful and purposeful.

There are clear principles. Grolnick's summary is compelling: "Providing rationales and clear consequences for behavior in the context of choice, acknowledgement of feelings, and minimization of pressure should facilitate the active process of [helping children do right things for right reasons]" (p. 64). [2]

Each parent can benefit from slightly different kind of suggestions. Parents who have a hard time showing compassion and understanding and are vary controlling might benefit from reading Haim Ginott's classic *Between Parent and Child.*[4] Parents who have a hard time setting limits might benefit from reading *How to Talk so Kids Will Listen and Listen so Kids Will Talk.*[5]

In the process of becoming better parents, we should remember, we are forming a relationship that can bless us for a lifetime—and can bless generations to come.

References

[1] Rosemond, J. (2005, March 2). Catering to children creates spoiled brats. *Arkansas Democrat Gazette*, 3E.

[2] Grolnick, W. (2003). *The psychology of parental control.* Mahwah, NJ: Lawrence Erlbaum.

[3] Goddard, H. W. (1994). Something better than punishment (HE-687). In *Principles of parenting.* Auburn, AL: Alabama Cooperative Extension System.

[4] Ginott, H. (2003). *Between parent and child.* NY: Three Rivers.

[5] Faber, A., & Mazlish, E. (2001). *How to talk so kids will listen & listen so kids will talk.* NY: Piccadilly Press.

Avoid Nagging by Using Natural and Logical Consequences

Hilary A. Rose, Ph.D., CFLE
Associate Professor, Dept. of Applied Human
Sciences, Concordia University,
Montreal, QC, Canada

An important life lesson for children is the cause-and-effect relationship between actions and consequences: when children behave in certain ways, certain things follow.[1] A new stepmother was telling me how frustrating it was trying to get her young stepdaughters (five- and seven-years-old) ready to go to their summer swimming lessons. She hated nagging them, and she hated yelling at them, but that's what she ended up doing on a daily basis. I suggested that she stop nagging and stop yelling; I told her to state warmly, but firmly, that she was going to leave the house to drive to swimming lessons at 8:30 a.m., and that they were coming with her, "ready or not." She asked me, "But what if they haven't gotten dressed yet?"

"Then they go to swimming lessons in their pyjamas. They have to change into their bathing suits at the pool anyway." Then I added, "I bet they'll show up at the pool in their pyjamas only once." A week later, my acquaintance happily reported that her stepdaughters had indeed arrived at the swimming pool in their pyjamas just once. After that one occasion, they always were ready on time–and there was no need for any nagging or yelling on the part of their stepmother. The girls learned that when they weren't ready on time (action), they would go to their swimming lessons in their pyjamas (consequence). They also learned that by changing their actions (getting ready on time), they could avoid the consequence of arriving at the pool in their pyjamas. Best of all, they learned this lesson on their own.

In a recent national survey, 92% of parents agreed that it is important to teach children to take responsibility for their actions.[2] What is the best way to accomplish this goal? Many child psychologists and parent educators agree that the best way to teach children to take responsibility for their actions is by letting them experience the consequences of their actions.[1,2,3] Learning the association between actions and consequences is the primary way in which we learn to take responsibility for our actions. As a benefit to parents, allowing the consequences to be the "bad guy" means that parents can, and should, avoid the nagging, pleading, yelling, cajoling, or preaching that often comes with being the disciplinarian.

Some parents, however, seem to want to "protect" their child from life's lessons.[1,4] Recently I heard about a teenage boy who was late to catch the bus for a school field-trip. His father, who had driven the boy to school, followed the school bus for one and a half hours on the freeway to get to the site of the field-trip. Was the father angry at his son for the inconvenience of spending three hours driving on the freeway? No–the father took his anger out on the teacher and the poor bus driver! According to the father, they should have waited for his son. By blaming others, and by not letting his son experience the consequences of being late, the father robbed his son of an opportunity to learn to take responsibility for his actions.

Consequences should not be a form of punishment.[1] Arbitrary punishment is something that parents do to try to deter children's negative behaviors. Natural consequences are simply the obvious outcomes or results of the child's behavior. If a child is late for dinner, the food may be cold–or all gone. These results would be the consequences of coming home late for dinner. In some cases (e.g., where safety or health is a concern), it may not be practical to allow the child to experience natural consequences. In such cases, the parent can use a logical consequence–an outcome logically determined by the parent (or even suggested by the child). If dinner is over when a child comes home, the natural consequence would be that the child gets no dinner; the logical consequence might be that the child makes his own dinner (and does the clean-up, too).

In conclusion, effective consequences are:

a. **Thoughtfully chosen.** Parents shouldn't use natural consequences if they are unsafe or unhealthy. In cases where safety or health is a concern, parents should use logical instead of natural consequences. What if a child misses the school bus? If it is unsafe to walk to school (the natural consequence), maybe the child could use allowance money for a taxi cab (a logical consequence).

b. **Experienced by the child.** In order for learning to take place, children have to experience personally the consequences of their actions. Sometimes parents want to protect their children from life's lessons, but parents can't protect children forever, and sooner or later children will be on their own in the world, expected to be responsible citizens.

c. **Not about parental control over children.** The goal of natural and logical consequences is to teach children about the cause-and-effect relationship between their actions and the subsequent consequences, not about punishment. Parents' concerns about being in control and having authority can undermine the effectiveness of natural and logical consequences.

d. **Originating in, and flowing from, the actions which lead directly to them.** Parents should avoid arbitrary punishments which have little to do with the child's behavior. In order for children to learn about actions and consequences, there must be an obvious link between them. If a child misses lunch, she can fix her own lunch instead of having unrelated television privileges revoked.

e. Rationally and clearly presented. In presenting consequences to children, parents should be warm and friendly, but firm. In particular, parents should avoid presenting consequences in anger or as threats, as this will be experienced as punishment by the child. Even saying something like "You see? This is what happens when you..." will sound preachy to children.

f. Forewarned, if feasible. Children are more cooperative and compliant with parents' requests when they know in advance what is going to happen. Just like the stepmother who announced that she was leaving at 8:30 with the girls, "ready or not," let children know what your plans are.

If you have not yet tried this approach, please do. You will likely find that you can avoid a lot of nagging, pleading, yelling, cajoling, or preaching, and have a more pleasant home life as a result. In addition, you will give your children an opportunity to learn one of life's most important lessons: taking responsibility for one's actions.

References

[1] Dreikurs, R., & Soltz, V. (1964). *Children: The challenge.* NY: Hawthorn.

[2] Bibby, R. W. (2006). *The boomer factor: What Canada's most famous generation is leaving behind.* Toronto, ON: Bastian.

[3] McKay, G. D., & Dinkmeyer, D. (1996). *Raising a responsible child: How to prepare your child for today's complex world.* NY: Fireside.

[4] Runkel, H. E. (2005). *ScreamFree™ parenting: Raising your kids by keeping your cool.* Duluth, GA: Oakmont.

Using Parent/Child Contracts

Alice B. Davenport, M.S., CFLE
Private practice in Las Cruces, New Mexico

Simple contracts can help parent/child relationships. Through the use of contracts, parents can learn how to listen and communicate with children at the child's level. Children can learn to listen, negotiate, make choices, take responsibility, and gain some control over their lives. Both parties learn respect for each other.

The idea of using contracts is supported by early behavioral scholars[1,2] and contemporary parenting authors.[3,4,5] Negotiating a contract sends the message that parents expect children to comply with family rules by having open dialogue about rules and behaviors. This child-centered approach is characterized by warm, positive feelings and the use of an authoritative parenting style.[2]

The use of a contract includes stating the behavior desired and the consequences of breaking that contract, not doing the desired behavior. The use of contracts calls for the parent to be consistent and remain calm when discipline is needed, that is, when the consequences are being carried out. According to behaviorists, changing the environment will change the behavior.[4,5]

Part of the contract process involves scheduling a meeting. The parent/s schedules the meeting with the child in a relaxed place without the distractions of television or mealtime. One problem should be selected to work upon. A timer can be used so each person gets equal, uninterrupted time while the terms of the contract are worked out, giving each one to three minutes. Ground rules for the discussion are important. "Because I say so" is not a valid reason and neither is "Because I don't want to," while discussing the reasons for the contract. Each person must listen while the other is speaking. Parents must use words the child understands. This gives children the opportunity to learn to form and articulate their thoughts, reasons and questions. Real communication is a vital part of working out these terms. Parents may realize the idea is flawed or the child may gain new understanding of the problem before the contract is even written.

Throughout the process, children need to have some feeling of control to maintain their sense of independence and personal dignity. Terms **must** be clear to each party. Issues such as "clean your room" can mean something different to each parent and each child. Define specifically what clean means (bed made, items picked up from the floor, etc.). Some portions of the contact may be more important than other portions, or they may take more time than other parts. Compromise is often needed to accomplish the needed results. Not following the rules may result in time-outs or age appropriate consequences and they should be written into the contract.

Children 3 and 4 years old love to negotiate and sign contracts with their names on them. They tend to follow the few simple rules to the letter, but at this age they may need many friendly reminders. They may tell anyone who listens about how well they are doing. Older children tend to feel honor-bound to follow the terms of the contract, especially when they have negotiated the terms. And they often tend to use their contract as the reason for refusing to be pushed or pressured by peers.

The parent may want to have two copies of a one-page form with blanks to be filled in when the terms of the contract are established. All parties sign and date both copies. Each person gets a copy.

One may be posted in a common area of the home (refrigerator magnets work well for this). The form of the contract can be very simple, such as:

Contract

Date: March 21, 2011
I, Alice, will take out the trash from the bathrooms and kitchen on Tues., Thur., and Sat.
If I do not, I will not be able to go to the Mall on Saturdays.
Signed and dated: Alice, March 21, 2011 (child)
Betty, March 21, 2011 (mother)

Children tend to establish new habits within a couple of weeks, but it may take older children several months, so contracts may go for 3 to 4 months. Parents **should not** nag and yell. Parents also **must** admit when they have violated the contract.

Often, it is the parent who learns the most from the experience. The contract allows the parent to stop yelling and nagging and gives the child the opportunity to take responsibility for keeping his or her contract. Sometimes more than one contract is in effect. A contract does what nagging does not do: It makes the home less stressful.

As mentioned, the use of contracts is a way for parents to learn to **stop** yelling at their children. Every "nag" or "yell" may be marked on the bottom of the contract by the parent. As the parents marks their behaviors, the child also marks on the contract each time they violate or break it, which we call "oops." Thus, "oops" is marked each time the child doesn't follow the contract. Also, it is important for children to be praised for good actions. Smiles, hugs, and acknowledging the commitment that the children have in keeping the rules of the contract are important.

Older children have different issues, but contracts work the same way for both parents and children. That is, conversation flows both ways with each having equal time to explain the why and why-not's on the issue. All discussions must be in terms the child can understand. **Parents:** Be sure terms of the contracts are appropriate for the child's age and development.

Teenagers often have the hardest time explaining their reasons and feelings. There may be accusations of various kinds. Parents need to **really** listen to see if they are true or make sense. Tears often fall. Parents **must not** resort to yelling and bullying. **No** bad language or other inappropriate remarks should be used. If there are, apologies must be made right then. Some complex issues need to broken into smaller bits, sometimes making more than one contract.

Through the use of contracts, when all parties show respect for each other, each does a better job of negotiating, and committing to and accomplishing desired results. Each party needs a copy of the contract in a prominent place as a reminder and handy to mark the "yells," "nags," and "oops" when they occur. Marks will lessen with time. After signing a contract, schedule another meeting in a week or two, using the timer again so each gets equal time, and discuss the progress from each viewpoint.

All parties should be present for the **signing off** at the completion of the contract. Take pictures of the event, show the smiles of a more connected family holding the contracts (complete with the negative marks on the bottom as reminders). Children can learn self-discipline, emotional self-control and have more friends and better school performance. Put simply, contracts are tools for better parenting.

References

[1] Patterson, Gerald R. (1975). *Families: Applications of social learning to family life.* Champaign: Research Press.

[2] Baumrind, Diana (1978). Parental disciplinary patterns and social competence in children. *Youth and Society, 9,* 238-276.

[3] Ballantine, Jeanne (2001). Raising competent kids: The authoritative parenting style. *Childhood Education, 78(1),* 46-47.

[4] Carlson, Richard (2001). *The don't sweat guide for parents: Reduce stress and enjoy your kids more.* NY: Hyperion.

[5] Peters, Ruth (1997). *Don't be afraid to discipline: The commonsense program for low-stress parenting.* NY: Golden Books.

Chapter V

Wisdom for Relationships in the Family

Many relationships exist within the family: between siblings, between a parent and a child, between the parents themselves. The following articles touch on a variety of these relationships at different times in a family's life. Find out if one speaks to you now.

First Time Parents:
Four Principles for Strengthening the Marriage

Jerry Cook, Ph.D., CFLE
Associate Professor, Family and Consumer Sciences,
California State University, Sacramento

Becoming parents for the first time can be an exciting, and perhaps frightening, time for many couples. New parents have many opportunities to grow closer as a family, but there also are challenges that exist, particularly for the couple's relationship. Because a substantial amount of energy and time is needed to care for an infant, couples may find it difficult to nurture their own relationship.

There are four principles that, if followed, will greatly benefit a marriage as couples become new parents. The first is *commitment.* Commitment to each other serves as the foundation of a strong and meaningful couple relationship. The second principle is *consensus.* Consensus is not an "either-or" principle; rather the idea is to find out how close you are to agreeing on major issues (e.g., finances, parenting roles), and then create a strategy for how to work through differences you have or will have. In other words, you and your spouse are in consensus for what to do when you disagree on things.[1] My wife and I learned long ago that this type of consensus is crucial for when children are trying to "work the system" with both parents. For example, our children will ask if they can watch television. If the first parent says "no," they will often go to the other parent to try to get a different response. Regardless of our parenting differences, we both agree that the first response always is the one that will be enforced. This not only strengthens us as parents, but our marriage as well.

The third principle is the *Golden Rule*. Most of us understand this to be "Do unto others as you would have them do unto you." Phillip and Carolyn Cowan,[2] pioneers of new parenthood research and intervention, explain that it is important to see from the other person's perspective in carrying out the Golden Rule. For example, just because my idea of relaxation from parenting stressors is watching a basketball game on television, I can't assume my wife would feel relaxed by watching it! It's a simple concept, but it's amazing how many times new parents forget to apply it.[3]

The fourth and final principle is *forgiveness*. Parenthood can be challenging, and new parenthood can be demanding. Many of us fall into the trap that we have to be perfect parents, and that if we fall short, we are in some way letting our children down, letting ourselves down, or letting God down. Nothing could be farther from the truth. New parenthood does not transform a person or their partner into perfection, but rather it does the best with the qualities we already have before we become parents. Accepting who we are–and accepting our spouse–our strengths as well as our limitations, and forgiving ourselves and, when appropriate, verbally apologizing to, or forgiving, our spouse, all of these helps build the foundation for how couples will love each other through the difficult times. It also sets the foundation for how one will love the new child when (and not if!) they make their own mistakes.

The journey into new parenthood can feel terrifying at times, and it often is easy to focus too much of our time and attention on the things that we don't like: the lack of sleep, financial challenges, and having less time together as a couple. However, when following these four principles (commitment, consensus, the Golden Rule, and forgiveness), couples will be able to draw upon their strengths in a way that builds unity, happiness, and appreciation for each other regardless of the challenges with which they will be facing.

Last but not least, I wish you and your new family the best in life!

References

[1] Jordan, P. J., Stanley, S. M., Markman, H. J. (1999). *Becoming parents: How to strengthen your marriage as your family grows.* SF: Jossey-Bass.

[2] Cowan, C. P., & Cowan, P. A. (1992). *When partners become parents: The big life change for couples.* Mahwah, NJ: Erlbaum.

[3] Chapman, G. (1995). *The five love languages: How to express heartfelt commitment to your mate.* Chicago: Northfield Publishing.

Best-Friend Parents

David J. Bredehoft, Ph.D., CFLE
Professor of Psychology and Family Studies,
Concordia University, St. Paul, MN

Ian Pierpoint of Synovate,[1,2] a market research company, surveyed 1,000 parents who lived with children ages 12 to 30, and an additional 500 children in the same age range in the US, UK and Canada. Pierpoint found that:

- 43% of parents say they want to be their child's best friend.
- 40% would buy their children everything they wanted if they could.
- 37% would prefer their kids at home at ALL times because they want to protect them.
- 71% of parental child purchases are made without any child request. Parents guessed what their teen or young adult wanted, rather than purchasing something for which he or she asked.
- 47% of the teens say they intend to stay home as long as they can.
- 41% of 20-24 year olds are living at home!
- 56% of parents are in no hurry for their children to leave home.
- 72% of parents would welcome their children back at any time.
- 65% of teens believe their parents "try hard to be a friend."
- 40% of teens indicated they would raise their own kids differently.

Pierpoint says that a best-friend parent "doesn't give you rules and tell you what to do." Best-friend parents interviewed for this study felt their own parents didn't understand them and that is why they want to be seen by their children as someone who is fun to be around, listens and is non-judgmental.

Best-Friend Parents

Best-friend parenting raises a number of questions. *What does it mean to be a friend? What does it mean to parent? Can parents be friends with their children, and in doing so, do they abdicate parental responsibilities in exchange for friendship? How is a friend-to-friend relationship different from a parent-to-child relationship? Is there a difference between being a friend and being friendly? Is being a best-friend parent good for children, or is it a form of overindulgence? If so, what type?*

I would argue that the role of parent and friend are very different—perhaps even conflicting. The Oxford English Dictionary defines a parent as "A person who holds the position or exercises the functions of a parent; a protector, guardian." Friends are on the same level with you, equal in power while parents should hold more power than their children. Parents should be friendly, but should resist the urge to become a best friend. This "best friend" can happen when the child becomes an adult.

When children are young, parents have very clear jobs. They make decisions in the best interests of children's development.[3] They say yes and no at appropriate times. They role model. They teach. They mentor. From time to time, they insist. They stand fast as consultants to their children as their children become ever more skillful and responsible. They act to keep children safe. They discipline. These are not the hallmarks of an equalized friend relationship. Friendly, yes. Best friend, no!

Let's Apply the Test of Four to Best-Friend Parenting

Is being a best-friend parent good for children, or is it a form of overindulgence? In a study conducted with colleagues, we developed "The Test of Four" to assess the extent of overindulgence. The Test of Four says parents may be overindulgent if the answer is "Yes" to one or more of the following questions:[4]

1. Will being a best-friend parent interfere with or slow down what my child needs to learn at this age? (*Yes.* Children in this study and our studies[5,6] reported growing up without many of the life skills needed to function as adults, because their best-friend parent did things for them).

2. Will being a best-friend parent spend a disproportionate amount of family resources on one or more of my children? (*Yes.* When asked, 40% said they would buy their children everything they wanted, and 73% guess and then buy things for their children without asking.[2])

3. Is best-friend parenting done to benefit the parent more than the child? (*Yes.* They said they were parenting this way because they felt their own parents didn't understand them. They want their children to accept them.)

4. Does best-friend parenting potentially harm others, society, or the planet in some way. (*Possibly.* Children raised by best-friend parents won't follow rules because their parents didn't set guidelines or rules.)

Best-Friend Parenting = All Three Types of Overindulgence

I believe best-friend parenting is a form of overindulge. It overindulges children in all three ways: Too Much, Over-Nurture, and Soft Structure.[4,6,7] Best-friend parents buy everything for their children: Too Much. They want to protect their children by keeping them home as long as they can and cater to their every desire: Over-nurture. They don't set limits or enforce rules: Soft Structure. Further, research shows that overindulgence harms children and they too are more likely to become less effective parents when they grow up.

References

1. I. Pierpoint (personal communication, November 1, 2004).
2. Hellmich, N. (2004, October 12). Parents want to be teens' pals: But loose style can backfire. *USA Today*, p. 8D.
3. Clarke, J. I., & Dawson, C. (1998). *Growing up again: Parenting ourselves, parenting our children* (2nd ed.). Center City, MN: Hazelden.
4. Clarke, J. I., Dawson, C., & Bredehoft, D. J. (2004). *How much is enough? Everything you need to know to steer clear of overindulgence and raise likeable, responsible and respectful children – from toddlers to teens.* NY: Marlowe & Co.
5. Bredehoft, D. J., Mennicke, S. A., Potter, A. M., & Clarke, J. I. (1998). Perceptions attributed by adults to parental overindulgence during childhood. *Journal of Marriage and Family Consumer Sciences Education, 16*, 3-17.
6. Bredehoft, D. J., & Leach, M. K. (2006). *Influence of childhood overindulgence on young adult dispositions – Executive summary: Study 2.* From the *How Much is Enough?* Web site retrieved January 24, 2007, from http://www.overindulgence.info/Research_Folder/Research.htm.
7. Bredehoft, D. J. (2006). *Becoming a parent after growing up overindulged – Executive summary: Study 3.* From the *How Much is Enough?* Web site retrieved January 24, 2007, from http://www.overindulgence.info/Research_Folder/Research.htm.

Helping Siblings Resolve Conflicts

Rachel Ozretich, M.S., CFLE
Independent Consultant and author of
Give Them Wings, a newspaper column on
parenting, Corvallis, OR

When I was about to give birth to my second child, an experienced friend told me to expect three times the amount of work that was required for just one child. After the birth I learned just how right she was! I discovered that I had to consider not only the needs of each child separately, but also the interactions between my two boys. In addition, I had to consider the interactions between all members of my family, including my husband and me. According to Bossard,[1] for our family, that would be 6 dyads, or relationship pairs to monitor

(10 if we had a third child). If one considers that each person has a unique perception of his or her relationship with each of the others, that would be 12 relationships (20 if we had a third child), according to Beaglehole's calculations.[2]

As each additional child is added to a family, all of the relationships between members of the family must adjust, and the interactions between parents and the children become more complex, as predicted by family systems theory. The importance of positive relationships between children, including brothers and sisters, to children's development, social skills, and family well-being is well supported by research[3,4] and a number of effective strategies for enhancing these relationships can be found in the parenting literature.[5,6]

While raising two children together, I began to realize the importance of their relationships with each other. Children in our modern culture usually spend more time each day with their brothers and sisters than with their parents. Sibling relationships are the longest-lasting close family relationship experienced by most people, so it is important that they be positive. In addition, there is a link between poor relationships among the children in a family and a decreased sense of marital happiness on the part of the parents.[4] My husband and I made it our goal to help our children build and maintain close relationships with each other, as well as with each of us. Our children are adults now and we are all very good friends, so our efforts paid off.

For firstborn children or older siblings, the birth of a brother or sister can bring about conflicting emotions. The excitement and joy of having a new member of the family is often tempered by a decreased amount of parental attention, as well as other difficult or confusing changes. Sometimes the older child is required to give up the crib in which he or she has always slept or to endure other stressful transitions when the new baby is born. Since the birth of a sibling can bring about so much stress for older siblings, children are likely to adjust better when family members try to reduce the level of these stresses by making only the most necessary changes as gradually as possible.

Firstborn children or older siblings may react to the stress of these changes by becoming withdrawn or unhappy, by seeking attention, or becoming more demanding. They may also regress both emotionally and physically for awhile, asking to be cuddled like a baby or have a bottle, for example, or having toileting or sleep problems. It is important that parents accept these temporary reactions and avoid responding to them in ways that might negatively impact their relationships with their older children. A child does best in many ways when he or she has a close relationship with at least one parent, and is likely to view his or her new sibling more positively as well.

It is never too soon to start talking to each child about the needs, feelings, and desires of their brothers and sisters, helping each take the point of view of the others. Children tend to be friendlier to each other when parents do this. Children who learn these social abilities early develop more positive peer relationships and friendships over the long run.[3]

Parents typically interact differently with each of their children, responding to their children's different personalities and ages. However, a child's perception that a parent treats him or her with less affection or more frequent control than a brother or sister is strongly associated with a decreased quality in the child's sibling relationships. This perception also is related to poorer child adjustment and well-being.[3] Note that what matters is the child's perception of the parent's behavior, rather than the actual behavior itself. This means that it is helpful to listen to and accept a child's feelings about their siblings, even though you may disagree with the accuracy of their perceptions. By accepting his or her feelings, the two of you can work together to find ways to address the situation that the child will perceive as effective.

There are many reasons for the daily quarrels between brothers and sisters. Children have reported being bored, being in a bad mood, or getting a sibling's attention as reasons for quarrels between themselves and their siblings. Other reported reasons for quarrels have included competition over toys and privileges, feelings of rivalry, showing power over a sibling, getting a sibling into trouble, getting a parent's attention, and having excess hostility or resentment toward a sibling.[7]

In many families, quarrels between brothers and sisters are the focus of a large portion of their interactions with parents every day. While the frequency of these quarrels varies from family to family, it seems that the ways in which parents respond to sibling quarrels influence the quality of family relationships. Therefore, it is important for parents to consider what the best ways of responding to these quarrels might be.

When I conducted a survey of 8- to 11-year-old children, they reported that their sibling relationships were higher in conflict and lower in warmth when their parents' typical response to sibling quarrels was merely to tell the children to stop arguing or to do something else, or their parents ignored or punished them. Alternatively, when children reported that their parent's typical response was a problem solving approach, that is, to help the children find a way to resolve the conflict in a mutually satisfactory manner, their sibling relationships were warmer and had lower levels of conflict.[7]

A problem solving response to sibling quarrels usually includes:

1. Each child learning about and taking into account the other's feelings, needs and desires–an approach related to greater sibling friendliness and individual social competence as stated previously;
2. The parent serving in the role of mediator, rather than referee or judge, and not telling children what to do;
3. The parent helping the children to understand each other, to identify the problem between them, and then helping the children to come up with various possible ways to resolve the quarrel;
4. The children then deciding on a solution;
5. The parent facilitating the implementation of that solution if needed; and,
6. If the solution doesn't work, then the parent helping the children decide on a different solution to try.

The problem solving process can be used many times a day in response to everyday quarrels. It can also be used more formally during a family meeting for conflicts that are more serious or long-lasting, or that involve more family members. The problem solving approach has worked very well in my family and I highly recommend it. I have used it not only for daily quarrels between my sons, but also to resolve conflicts between myself and my sons. Acting as a mediator with siblings does take a little more time than acting as a referee and telling the children what to do, but the payoffs in terms of close and more peaceful long-term family and sibling relationships are well worth the effort. Also, you will find that in time, children will learn to cooperate with each other more and more on their own and therefore, the need for your involvement in their conflicts will gradually decline as well.

References

[1] Bossard James H.S. (1945). The law of family interactions. *American J. of Sociology, January,* 292-294. **NOTE**: Bossard offered a mathematical formula, with "y" being the number of people in the family and "x," the number of relationships (dyads) within the family, so that $x = (y^2 - y)/2$. For a couple and three children, then $(5^2 - 5)$ divided by 2 equals 10.

[2] Beaglehole, Earnest. (1945). A critique of "the measurement of family interaction." *American J. of Sociology, 51(2),* 145-147. **NOTE**: Beaglehole gave his own equation, with "y" being the number of people in the family and "x" being the number of nonsymmetrical relationships: $x = y(y - 1)$. It yields double the number derived by Brossard's equation.

[3] Dunn, J. (2001). Lessons from the study of mothers and siblings in early childhood. In J. Gerris (Ed.), *Dynamics of parenting* (pp. 103-113). Leuven-Apeldoorn: Garant.

[4] Brody, G., Stoneman, Z., McCoy, J., & Forehand, R. (1992). Contemporaneous and longitudinal associations of sibling conflict with family relationship assessments and family discussions about sibling problems. *Child Development, 63*, 391-400.

[5] Faber, A., & Mazlish, E. (1987). *Siblings without rivalry.* NY: Avon Books.

[6] Crary, E. (1979). *Kids can cooperate.* Seattle, WA: Parenting Press, Inc.

[7] Ozretich, R., & Sugawara, A. (1999). Children's perceptions of parental responses to sibling quarrels and characteristics of sibling relationships. In F. Berardo (Series Ed.) & C. Shehan (Vol. Ed.), *Contemporary perspectives on family research: Vol. 1. Through the eyes of the child: Revisioning children as active agents of family life* (pp. 353-372). Stanford, CT: JAI Press.

Tact between Mother and Daughter

Mary Bold, Ph.D., CFLE
Department Chair and Professor, Digital Learning & Teaching
American College of Education, Chicago, IL

Mothers and other female relatives are often the supervisors for clothing shopping for early adolescent girls. The responsibility to supervise wise clothing choices sometimes leads to unwise comments about how the girl looks as she tries on items. With awareness and a little practice, the adult can adopt wise language that will spare feelings and avoid arguments.

Adolescent girls' self-esteem is related to many factors, and research findings tell us about some of them. For example, parent-child communication has been tied to self-esteem stability for 11- and 12-year-olds, suggesting that lower self-esteem is associated with critical messages from parents.[1] Likewise, body image has multiple influences. While findings suggest that family influences (such as pressure to diet, negative remarks about a child's body, or supportive communication about body shape) contribute to self-image and perception of body image,[2,3,4] it is important to realize that society's influence is also great. Mass media, especially information directed to younger audiences, carry messages about body shape, dieting, and fashion. Keeping in mind the broad context for self-esteem and body image, family members nevertheless can try to have as positive an influence as possible on their children's awareness of body shape.

Clothing manufacturers and designers do not provide all clothes for all body types. Still, teenaged girls may want to try on all the fashions. For the adult accompanying the girl into fitting rooms, an impulsive comment might be, "That looks awful," or "You can't fit into that." A more tactful response is in order: "I don't think it flatters you," or "I think this outfit looks better on you than that one."

As a mom who hates to shop, I had to pace myself in order to satisfy my daughter's interest in clothes shopping. I knew my own irritation with shopping likely was to influence my attitude and my language. When I happened upon the phrase, "it doesn't flatter you," my daughter reacted positively and I made the phrase my only comment when the fit was poor or the outfit was inappropriate. My daughter picked up on the phrase and soon was asking, "Does this flatter me?"

This simple phrase not only steered me away from hurt feelings and arguing, it also properly shifted the negative comment to the article of clothing, away from my daughter. She was not un-flattering; it was the clothing that was the problem. You may find another phrase that works better with your own daughter, such as "Does this compliment me?" or "What outfit looks best on me." Most importantly, try to come up with something that focuses on the outfit and not the person. This can help provide honest feedback but in a supportive way. It can avoid conflict and help your daughter more easily make decisions that are important to her.

Interestingly, this same approach can work in other areas of interaction with your daughter or son, by focusing on actions rather than the child. For example, instead of focusing on the child with put-down statements such as "Your are doing that stupidly," or "You did that all wrong," or "How dumb can you be," we can focus in the action and not the child by saying such things as "Is there a better way to do that?" or "How might you do that more effectively?"

The more tactful and thoughtful ways we speak with our children, the more we can help them keep a positive self-esteem and develop in a more mature way.

References

[1] Kernis, M. H., Brown, A. C., Brody, G. H., (2000). Fragile self-esteem in children and its associations with perceived patterns of parent-child communication. *Journal of Personality, 68,* 225-252.

[2] Green, S. P., & Pritchard, M. E. (2003). Predictors of body image dissatisfaction in adult men and women. *Social Behavior and Personality, 31(3),* 215-222.

[3] McCabe, M. P., & Ricciardelli, L. A. (2003). Sociocultural influences on body image and body changes among adolescent boys and girls. *The Journal of Social Psychology, 143(1),* 5-26.

[4] Hahn-Smith, A. M., & Smith, J. E. (2001). The positive influence of maternal identification on body image, eating attitudes, and self-esteem of Hispanic and Anglo girls. *International Journal of Eating Disorders, 29,* 429-440.

Under the Clock Tower,
My Father's Wisdom: Teaching Forgiveness

Gregory Roger Janson, Ph.D., CFLE, PCC-S
Associate Professor, Child and Family Studies,
Department of Social & Public Health,
Ohio University, Athens

From the return of the prodigal son to Gandhi's final act of forgiveness towards his assassin as he lay dying, the nature of forgiveness has been the subject of religion, philosophy and psychology. Forgiveness can arise from ethical discrimination: what is right? Or from an affective dimension: our empathy and our ability to experience the pain of others leads us to forgive. Teaching forgiveness can rely on faith or reason, but it is a challenging process since we must somehow help our children to experience forgiving–not just forgiveness–if they are to understand its nature and to make it a living part of themselves. As an observer of my father's life, I witnessed an unusual act of forgiveness, an event that spanned a large portion of his life.

My father died six years ago on a raw March morning after a fifteen-year battle with prostate cancer, a battle he fought with patience, grace and humor–a battle he fought without complaint, as he had lived his life. He was eighty-eight when he died. I was always sure of his love, though he never spoke of it. I was less sure about his thoughts and feelings; those were his own.

There should have been time to understand each other better. We both lived long enough to know each other as men, not just as father and son. But life has a way of intruding. I often wished he were more demonstrative, more emotive, more open. I wished I were more present with him. I often reflected on our relationship with thoughts like these.

I knew my father had been abandoned by his own father at birth. I knew he had left high school during the Great Depression to support his mother, whom he adored. During the Second World War, I knew he served in the Medical Corps, in the First Army field hospital. He was among the first into the concentration camps. His decorations, including a Bronze Star, sat in a bureau drawer for the duration of his life. He never spoke of any of these experiences.

His beloved mother died when he was in Europe. At the end of the war, he returned home, spending six months sitting on a beach in Maryland, staring at the sea. He met my mother at that time. They married and he worked his way through college and law school at St. Johns University in Brooklyn, where my brother and I were born. Six months before he died, he shared with my mother that he had lived in a Catholic orphanage from age two to five. During the first part of the 20th century, that is where devout mothers who were unable to support their children took them until things improved. His mother returned for him.

I know of these things from my mother; my father never spoke of them to me. Knowing them helped to explain to me his reticence, his stoicism, his emotional reserve. As a counselor and a traumatologist, it became easier for me to understand his emotional reserve as generational, as formed by abandonment, and loss, and the horrors of war. He shared none of this with me.

The one story I remember my father sharing with me was about meeting his own father for the first time. His story had a profound impact on me.

My mother, the product of a large and boisterous Greek family, was the emotional antithesis of my father. It was she who called my father's father and asked him to come to New York–without telling my father. She knew that he would have quietly refused. My father was 34 years old and had never seen his father, or wanted to see him. Apparently my mother felt otherwise. My father believed that his father was responsible for his mother's hard life and early death. Yet, I never knew my father to be anything but patient and kind; he never held a grudge and I never saw him angry. I never knew my father to utter a harsh word to my mother, to my brother, or to me.

Out of respect for my mother, he reluctantly agreed to go to Union Station that afternoon. He did not agree to bring my grandfather back.

He told me that during the subway ride to Union Station he stared out the grimy windows, uncertain of what he would do. He had seen pictures of his father, but his father had no way to recognize him, so they were to meet under the clock tower. My father said he could easily walk away, if he chose to.

"I stood on the mezzanine, leaning against the railing. I looked down and saw him standing under that enormous clock. Everyone was moving except him. He was just standing there, all alone. I knew I didn't owe him anything. I just stared for a while, not thinking, and then I realized, it just wouldn't be right to walk away. It wouldn't be right. So I walked down and brought him home to meet you."

This was the heart of his wisdom. Upon writing about forgiveness, the work of Robert Enright describes various qualities of forgiveness: "restraint from pursuing resentment or revenge," "foregoing of resentment or revenge when the wrongdoer's actions deserve it and giving the gifts of mercy, generosity and love when the wrongdoer does not deserve them," and "the overcoming of wrongdoing with good."[1] My father had demonstrated these to me.

Looking back as part of the effort to distill the essence of his life and wisdom into a few words that could be of use to others, I realize that he shared far more that I imagined. Beyond sharing this story with me, he never spoke about forgiveness. Or what "right" was. There were no explanations, no qualifications, no telling me how I should think or feel. He simply lived forgiveness by example. He quietly showed me and let me judge for myself. He did it so respectfully, that I never felt as though he was teaching me.

This was his gift as a "living" teacher: to embody the wisdom he sought to share in a way that enabled me to experience it, to feel it, and to make it my own. I am a different kind of teacher than he was, but I have come to realize that the ultimate foundation of his wisdom was not just his love for me, but his faith in me. That realization enabled me to pass on that love and faith to my own children, and to share with them the wisdom necessary to a good life, well lived. Perhaps that was his greatest gift to me…and to them.

Reference

[1] International Forgiveness Institute. *What is forgiveness*. Retrieved Dec. 9, 2010, from http://www.forgiveness-institute.org/html/about_forgiveness.htm

The Bouquet of Parenting

Clara Gerhardt, Ph.D., CFLE
Professor and Director of International Education,
School of Education and Professional Studies,
Samford University, Birmingham, AL

My mom used to gather small bunches of flowers and dot them all over our home. Not the bold carnations or the confident roses. Her bouquets of wild gatherings consisted of a sprig of heather, a dash of marigold, a little branch that would only reveal its beauty on close inspection. This was my mom's gift: she could find and appreciate beauty in the most ordinary.

My mom held onto life and onto happiness. She wanted to live fully; she did not want to be reminded of the passing of time. When my mother's last year on earth arrived, she changed slowly and almost imperceptibly. A brain tumor was robbing her old self from her. The last time she visited me she again gathered miniature bouquets and sprinkled them in all our favorite places. I did not want to discard them. As they dried up, faded and shriveled, I held onto them, as if I could hold onto my mother.

One sunny morning, after her death, I replaced them with fresh flowers. I looked for the humble varieties. I looked for small forgotten daisies, a curl of jasmine, a yellow bloom posing as a weed, a dark brown prunus leaf. I grouped this unlikely collection of God's Flora together in little vases, and knew that it was right. My mom was no longer with us, but she had given me the skills to live my life fully and constructively. The ability to find and appreciate little flowers anywhere was now within my repertoire.

And so parents give to children. They give them layers of experiences, which become memories, like a watercolor painting, not overworked, but translucent. Layer upon layer, it builds to the depth of a parent-child relationship. Often it feels as if I lost my Mom too early in my life. And then again, when I am reminded how to be the best parent I can be for my own children, it all comes together. Love is never lost. It is given from parent to child in that long chain of little events; the daily hugs, the support, the acceptance. Love grows and love links us; generation-to-generation.

The Marriage Legacy:
Showing Respect in Handling Differences

Charles L. Cole, Ph.D., CFLE
Professor, Marriage and Family Therapy Center,
The University of Louisiana at Monroe,
Calhoun, LA

Hopefully, parents realize that what they model for their children about marriage becomes their child's primary role model for how to create and maintain relationships. If you think about the opportunities we have to teach our children how to respectfully resolve conflicts with our mate, you can see a microcosm of how your child learns to treat others and handle differences when conflicts arise. This is a heavy responsibility, yet it is an awesome opportunity to leave our children a legacy which they will be able to use their entire life.

In this brief essay on the marriage legacy, I will share some key ideas I have learned as a marriage and family therapist and family life educator over the past four decades. I will use illustrations from couples with whom I have worked and cite research that demonstrates how respect is a fundamental legacy which I see parents modeling in how they deal with each other as spouses–behavior that the children see in the day to day life of growing up in the home.

It is common to hear children say "I learned that from Mom and Dad" when you ask them how they learned to treat their playmates, siblings, and others by yelling, getting mad and hitting each other. That is a sad commentary but all too often true. Our children can learn how to disrespect others from watching us (the parents), acting out the drama of conflict before their very eyes. The good news is that, conversely, our children also learn how to respect others by watching their parents interact in a loving manner that conveys respect for each other, even when we disagree and are angry with each other.

In John Gottman's[1,2] research on marriage and parenthood, he reports that what he calls *the four horsemen of the apocalypse* are highly predictive of marital outcomes. The four horsemen are: *criticism, defensiveness, contempt,* and *stonewalling,* things that we should seek to avoid in our relationships. Gottman says, and I have found this to be true in my own clinical work with couples and families, that couples who are highly disrespectful toward each other are less likely to stay together and have more problems parenting their children. Gottman can predict with 94% accuracy which couples are likely to get a divorce within three years just based upon watching them interact for as little as 15 minutes.

It is the *contempt* that is the most devastating in showing a clear disrespect and disregard for the value of the partner. When contempt is present it is hard to see the love behind the ridicule, put-downs and eye rolling that conveys "I not only disagree with you but I think you are a worthless bum." When the contempt is coupled with an emotional distancing and stonewalling response of not even acknowledging your presence by not responding and walking away, it sets in motion a cascade of negative forces that drive the couple further apart, emotionally and physically to the point where little opportunity for repair and reconnection occur. Children can see the parents giving up on each other and walking away or only giving negative messages when they do bother to engage each other. And our children can learn this pattern well and then all too often have difficulty making and maintaining meaningful friendships and loving relationships.

Even when parents separate and divorce they often continue to send the negative messages about the "spouse or ex-spouse" to their children in how they interact with their "ex," since there is a lifetime connection with the children.[3] Occasions like children graduating from high school, getting married, etc. are often a source of tension for the entire family because the "ex" spouses never learned to respectfully work out differences for the sake of the children.

We have seen family gatherings turn into war zones over seating arrangements at weddings. What kind of message does that send to the child on an occasion that should be one of the happiest days of their life? It is common to see the anxiety so high that no one really knows how to handle the situation and the child is literally holding their breath that their parents do not have an "ugly incident in front of everyone." Imagine the tension in the faces when the pictures are taken to capture the event that will be passed down to future generations as they see the scowls and frowns on the faces of their grandparents.

How can respect be maintained and passed down to future generations when all the children have seen is disrespect and maybe even hate? The task is so overwhelming to many families that they simply coexist, never getting over the issues and they simply try to push it under the rug, hoping no one really notices and that the children are not hurt too badly. According to William Pinsoff,[4] the norm of the 21st century is likely to continue to be that the majority of homes will be broken by divorce before the children are reared. At present about half of the couples that marry do not stay married, and the norm is less common for marriages to last for a lifetime than it was up to the final quarter of the 20th century.

For many of these families, help is on the way to learn to move past the struggles and to learn to treat each other with respect even when they disagree. It is still not normal for couples to seek help soon enough to avoid the pains of conflict and disagreements for most. The majority of those that do seek help from trained marriage and family therapists report that they do better after treatment than before. And we now have solid scientific evidence that both marriage enrichment and marriage and family therapy have demonstrated positive benefits compared to control groups receiving no treatment.[5,6]

When either partner becomes aware that they are hurting their children by having their children see them attack each other, it is time for the couple to use this warning sign to slow the process down and stop the cycle of attack and counter attack with their spouse. A simple way to put the brakes on might be to calmly say to your spouse, "Our children are being hurt by us, being so angry and disrespectful of each other. And I want to take responsibility for my part in this and promise you now that I don't want our children to be harmed and I don't want our marriage to be harmed and I don't think you do either. So let's back off for a few minutes and try to calm down."

When couples can purposefully take control of the situation by calming the intensity of the conflict down, they can more effectively communicate what each spouse wants. And each spouse can begin to empathize with their partner and be less likely to feel threatened by the contemptuous messages of "I hate you," that might have slipped out of one's mouth in a moment of anger. Disagreements are normal and all marriages have many disagreements.

It is not the disagreement that hurts the relationship; it is the way the disagreement is handled that makes the difference in sending a message of "I value you and love you" and because I love you I want to let you "know what is bothering me." Many times the intensity of disagreements has little if anything to do with the spouse but rather how we communicate the concern and process the issue by talking about it in either a fair or unfair manner. We want to send a message that we are going to get closer and understand each better by sharing this concern openly in a respectful manner that doesn't hurt either of us. When we choose that strategy for handling our disagreements, we are modeling respect and love for each other and our children are learning how to handle their disagreements in a manner that helps build relationships, not tear them apart.

Parents reading other articles in this book might find writings that inspire them to seek better relationships with all members of their family, including their partner. Another step that could be taken is to attend workshops or retreats which focus on marriage enrichment, a movement that has been developing for about a half a century. One might find out about these programs at their local church, parish, or synagogue, or by contacting representatives of the Association for Couples in Marriage Enrichment.[7]

Concluding Comments

Respect for our mate is vital for both developing a meaningful marriage relationship and for establishing an effective parenting partnership. What we do with our marital partner, or former spouse, becomes images in the blueprints from which our children will draw upon to construct their meaningful relationships. The legacy we pass on to our children about relationships will last them a lifetime and become the fundamental models that they will learn from us on how to treat others.

References

[1] Gottman, J. Gottman, J. M., & Levenson, R.W. (1999). Rebound from marital conflict and divorce prediction. *Family Process, 38,* 287-292.

[2] Gottman, J. M., & Levenson, R. W. (1999). What predicts change in marital interactions over time?: A study of alternative models. *Family Process, 38,* 143-158.

[3] Cole, C.L., & Cole, A.L. (1999). Boundary ambiguities that bind former spouses together after the children leave the home in post-divorce families. *Family Relations, 48,* 271-272.

[4] Pinsoff, W. (2002). The death of "Till death us do part": The transformation of pair bonding in the 20th century. *Family Process 41,* 135-157.

[5] Shadish, W., & Baldwin, S. (2002). Meta-analysis in MFT interventions. In D. Sprenkle (Ed.), *Effectiveness research in marriage and family therapy (pp. 339-370).* Alexandria, VA: The American Association for Marriage and Family Therapy.

[6] Giblin, P., Sprenkle, D., & Sheehan, R. (1985). Enrichment outcome research: A

meta-analysis of premarital, marital and family interventions. *Journal of Marital and Family Therapy 11,* 257-271.

[7] Association for Couples in Marriage Enrichment. (2008). *Educating Couples for Lifelong Relationships.* Look for local and state chapters under the Connect menu. Retrieved October 27, 2010, from www.bettermarriages.org

---

Couple Attachment Moments

Jerica Berge, PhD, LMFT, CFLE
Asst. Professor, Department of Family and
Community Medicine, University of Minnesota
Medical School, Minneapolis

The basic building blocks of intimacy between two people involve being emotionally accessible and responsive to each other, a condition referred to as *attachment.*[1,2,3,4] This term, attachment, is used in reference to the nature of the relationship between a parent and infant, as well as between couples. The level of attachment may vary, being strong to weak, or almost non-existent. Much of the literature relates to aspects of enhancing attachment, or intimacy.

Isn't it ironic that one of the ultimate acts of attachment for couples, conceiving a child (which leads to becoming parents), can decrease a couple's ability to be emotionally accessible and responsive to each other? Research indicates that couples' satisfaction with their relationship declines when they have children.[5] At the very time that parents need emotional accessibility and responsiveness from each other the most, they are both typically too tired and extended to relate to each other in this way.

On the other hand, research also shows that being intentionally responsive and accessible as a couple at important times, like the birth of a new baby, can lead to greater emotional adjustment, attachment and growth for the individuals and the relationship.[5] Thus, when couples exhibit attachment behaviors as parents, they can grow closer from the experience.

Being intentionally emotionally accessible and responsive to each other are essential for parents in order to strengthen their relationship, instead of unintentionally allowing their relationship to falter due to the stresses of parenting. Emotional responsiveness and accessibility do not need to be scheduled events in order for them to occur. In fact, continuous small gestures and efforts add up to create an overall atmosphere of emotional accessibility and responsiveness. For example, when a partner gets home from work and it is clear that he or she has had a tough day, the other partner can simply check-in to let him or her know they are in tune with them. Likewise, when a parent clearly needs a break from interacting with the children, the other partner can pull him or her aside and recognize his or her feelings and then switch off for awhile to allow the other partner to rejuvenate themselves.

Along with the everyday efforts to communicate emotional accessibility and responsiveness, partners need to find moments in which they can spend time together without the children. Because couples have unique lives and schedules, parents will need to be creative in figuring out how they will make alone time happen.

Some examples of how to create couple attachment moments include:

- Having a movie night in the middle of the week after the children are in bed.
- Swapping babysitting monthly with other couples (who have children) to have consistent date nights.
- Going to stores (i.e., Malls, IKEA, etc.) that have in-house free babysitting and going shopping as a couple.
- Reading a book together nightly after the children are in bed.
- Getting up before the children every morning and exercising together. Or get a membership at a gym that has in-house babysitting for free.
- Going on semi-annual or annual vacations together while family members (especially grandparents) watch the children. For instance, one trip to celebrate the wedding anniversary and one 6 months later to celebrate parenting.
- Getting up before the children and having breakfast together.
- Having a nightly cup of hot chocolate/tea/coffee after dinner to check-in about the day while the children play or do homework.
- Meeting for lunch once a week while the children are in school or being watched by a neighbor (with whom you swap babysitting).
- Starting a new hobby together such as woodworking, photography, cooking, home improvement, etc. to do on Saturdays when the children are at friends' houses, sports practice, school events, the babysitter, etc.
- Having quarterly weekend getaways as a couple to refresh (swap babysitting with another couple). These can be relatively cheap by exploring places within your own state.
- Joining a bowling league, or other team sport, together while the children are at home doing homework and/or being babysat.

By combining (1) spontaneous daily efforts to be emotionally accessible and responsive with (2) planned couple attachment moments, parents can feel more close to their partner and can enjoy parenting more fully.

References

[1] Cassidy, J., & Shaver, P. R. (1999). *Handbook of attachment.* NY: Guilford Press.

[2] Johnson, S. M. (2003). Introduction to attachment: A therapist's guide to primary relationships and their renewal. In S.M. Johnson & V. Whiffen (Eds.), *Attachment processes in couple and family therapy* (pp. 103-123). NY: Guilford Press.

[3] Lerner, H. (2001). The dance of connection. NY: HarperCollins Publishers.

[4] Palmer, G. (2006). Couple attachment: Love does have something to do with it. In The American Association for Marriage and Family Therapy (AAMFT), *Family therapy magazine, Vol 5, Num 5* (pp. 21-27). Alexandria, VA: AAMFT Inc.

[5] Feeney, J., Alexander, R., Noller, P., & Hohaus, L. (2003). Attachment insecurity, depression, and the transition to parenthood. *Personal Relationships, 10(4),* 475-493.

The Empty Nest Couple: Thinking Ahead

Dorothea M. Rogers, D. Min., CFLE
Professor of Family Life Education,
Spring Arbor University, Flint, MI

"Where have the years gone?" When a child turns 18 and leaves the nest, parenting has ended. Not so fast–"Once a parent, always a parent." "Parenting is for a lifetime." These are not just phrases. There is truth in each quote. Obviously, as parents, we are interested in our children's lives even when they do leave the nest. In some instances that involvement may be rather extensive, especially when a child experiences a crisis in their life. Moreover, a child may return home to live and bring with them a child of their own. Some children may not leave home until they get married. Occasionally, some grandparents raise their grandchildren. However, for a large number of parents, the transition from having children in the home to having an empty nest is uneventful.

Children may have flown the nest–gone off to college, started a career, or are having families of their own, but...Mom and Dad will continue to be Mom and Dad! With life expectancy expanding in America, parents can find that they are empty nest parents longer than they were full nest parents. Many couples look forward to the empty nest years, but then wonder what they will do with their new-found freedom. Kroll and Hawkins assert that expectations as well as roles change.[1]

   Transition to the empty nest stage can be a time of renewal for a couple, a time to attempt activities that have been put on hold during the childrearing years, and a wonderful time for planning their future. The early stage of the empty nest is a time of transition and exploration where some parents are happy, some parents feel relieved, and other parents are depressed. There always are some feelings of sadness when a child leaves the fold; however, many parents' fare well as they enter into this new life stage. Fittingly, parents can and do have different emotions during this transition.

   Some parents feel elated when their last child leaves home. Many parents experience a week or two of wistful feelings, but also are excited and feel a sense of freedom at the thought of being "just the two of us." "Parents...often feel liberated from the responsibility of childrearing."[1] Some parents also feel relief because gone are the sometimes stressful activities associated with parenting, such as teacher conferences, extracurricular activities, and discipline. Other parents' feel depressed when the last child leaves home. When children leave the home, they sometimes take with them an air of excitement and vitality, which was felt in the house.[3] Additionally, some parents may consider the early empty nest transition to be a fresh start.

   For many couples, the beginning of the empty nest stage may feel like they are in a new marriage! This new transition can be an exciting time as couples move forward, making a fresh commitment to each other, to themselves, and to their marriage.

   Claudia and David Arp (pp.22-24)[2] offer some strategies to help make the most of marriage at the onset of the empty nest stage, suggesting:

- Get some rest–You're exhausted! Take time to regroup yourself.
- Resist filling up your time–Kids' leaving does create a void, but put off filling up time they vacated for a while. Be slow in accepting new responsibilities.
- Make no immediate changes–Change can be stressful–changing jobs or relocating are major changes. While things are changing, you can and will change with them. It is okay to take it slowly–gain perspective first.
- Acknowledge that this is a time of transition–say to each other, "This is a big time of transition for us right now, and its okay." Couples probably will have questions during this time of transition like, "Do I want to go back to school?" "What do I want to be when I grow up?" Or, "What do I want to do with the rest of my life?" By couples' acknowledging that this is a major transition, and by talking about it, couples will be able to manage future changes.
- Don't fear the silence–this new silence may be awkward at first. This silence is typical in the empty nest stage–and that's

okay. You can read a book you've wanted to read for a long time or spend time talking with your spouse. You can remember when you longed for peace and quiet! Enjoy the quiet time right now, and don't worry–just bask.

* Celebrate–you've made it this far. Maybe you don't feel like celebrating. Maybe you are grieving the loss of your child in the home–this is normal. It is important, however, to recognize and accept the fact that you are in this new life stage. Moreover, you can move forward in your relationship with your spouse, your friend, into the future together. Parents who have raised and nurtured children have accomplished a tremendous task!

The empty nest stage is a very real stage where parents may feel differently–some feel happy, some relieved, and yet some depressed. Acceptance of this transition is a positive step. The transition to an empty nest offers couples the opportunity to make fresh commitments to each other, themselves, and their marriage, as they go forward with wonder at what the future holds for them.

References

[1] Kroll, W., & Hawkins, D. (2000). *Prime of your life.* Grand Rapids, MI: Fleming H. Revell.

[2] Arp, D., & Arp, C. (2004). *10 great dates for empty nesters.* Grand Rapids: Zondervan.

Parenting: Today, Tomorrow and Always

Clara Gerhardt, Ph.D., CFLE
Professor and Director of International Education,
School of Education and Professional Studies,
Samford University, Birmingham, AL

Several seasons ago we splurged and a horticultural team transformed our garden into a little Eden. Our intent was simple: "Low maintenance, minimal watering, no cutting, pruning, pampering...we are busy people." The gardener, with the greenest thumb, nodded. He planted the hardiest of hardy, and disciplined the wild forest. Diplomatically, he said that even Eden needs a little TLC, and the benefits of an automated sprinkler system. In our mind, the zero maintenance zone was a patch of white pebbles with a large central boulder. Not a sprig of green in our Zen retreat, no input required if nothing was to grow.

As a very young adult, my notion of parenting was as clear cut as my garden design: call in the professionals, find great day care, put on the automated systems and my life could remain virtually unchanged. After all, I was determined that nothing would upset my career and my self centered life. Raising children, I thought egocentrically, ... is like completing a degree. Several years of intense input, the kids fly into the blue yonder and voila, I am free again. Task complete! Because I wasn't a parent, I missed the essence. I understood nothing. My heart was made of selfish stone and had not yet been remodeled by a child. I had not yet found out that in time I would mortgage my soul for the wellbeing of my children.

Nothing could have truly prepared us for the arrival of our firstborn and the immensity of the emotions precipitated by this small person. Our parental hearts became suspended outside our bodies, held captive by a newborn. Should anything happen to this light of our lives, we would be destroyed. Surely siblings would reduce the emotional investment, half it at least, or spread it evenly. Not so. With more children, the parental vulnerability increased exponentially.

As the kids grew up, we as parents remained fragile, as before. Nothing could safeguard our hearts against the fear of a most catastrophic loss of all–the loss of a child, for which we were thankfully spared. I would have to beseech a team of guardian angels to help us with this enormous task, as supernatural powers were required to shelter, nurture, guide, love and cherish these children to the "safety" of adulthood and beyond.

Again, I missed another hidden message. My work was to last only until they reached the safety of adulthood I thought. Actually, real life had young adults bouncing back into the parental home and challenged young men and women looking for life's dreams and seeking parental advice. Our offspring may be living in adult bodies, but inside part of the child remains asking for parental back up, advice, acknowledgment, praise, comfort, security, love as well as for space, independence, privacy and autonomy. They have special needs, and face challenges that need a parental safety net from day to day. The perception of this magical net, woven of parental love, gives them acrobatic courage to leap, free fall, and trust that in the end they will land safely and unharmed.

As parents we never move out of the danger zone, we are invisibly linked to our children by cords made of heart strings. Our children run their own races, and we are spectators. They fight their own battles, we agonize about the outcome. They take on the bitterness of pain, and we would like to carry the burden for them. They drink from the well of joy, and our cup "runneth" over. They are their own people and we need to let them be.

Back to the garden: an avid gardener once said that what a garden needs most is a shadow. This seemingly makes no sense, gardens need sunshine, and they need water. Then, the realization, the shadow is the one cast by the gardener who daily tends that garden. As the gardener cuts, prunes, shelters, and nurtures, wondrous things begin to happen. Life can be coaxed out of any seed; poppies and sunflowers bloom, berries grow ..., but they do so only in response to careful and appropriate tending of all their needs.

And so it is with our children. There is no maintenance free parenting formula. No television sets, no amusement parks, no expensive gifts can replace the constructive shadow cast by parents tending their children; shadows that cast by parental availability and presence in the garden of life. It is our ongoing love as fathers and as mothers that supports the development of our children. As parents–if by Grace we get it right–we can find the optimal balance of structure and nurturance that will sustain and promote growth. As in plants, this ongoing attention will allow blooms and fruit to appear in many wondrous ways, season by season: through long cold winters and into the gentle awakening of spring, unfolding into the warmth of summer and the maturity of fall. Little by little and ongoing, good parenting is a lifelong task–not just for today or tomorrow, but for always.

Chapter VI

Wisdom for the Early Years: Infants to Young Children

The following two chapters hold a variety of articles for you to read. They are more specific as to the ages of children within families. Hopefully, some will apply to you; perhaps some later on.

Children Develop on Their Own Timetable

Linda R. Cote, Ph.D., CFLE
Assistant Professor, Marymount University, Arlington, VA
&
Marc H. Bornstein
Section Chief, Child and Family Research Section,
Eunice Kennedy Shriver
National Institute of Child Health and Human Development,
NIH, Bethesda, MD

Parents often worry that their child is lagging behind in the "achievement" of one or more developmental milestones. For example, parents frequently express concern that their child is not yet walking like other children of the same age, or is not talking as soon or as well as they would like or expect. Comparing notes with other parents at the neighborhood playground can be a source of stress rather than a source of solace and support, if parents find themselves negatively comparing their child's development to other children's. Today's young adults are more isolated from children than ever before, and many miss out on the opportunity to observe, and engage with, young children until they have a child of their own. Although new parents know more about children's development than those who are not yet parents, parents' knowledge of child development is not always accurate.[1,2]

It is important for parents to recognize that children are individuals, and that each child will develop (physically, emotionally, and intellectually) at his or her own rate. Such variation is called individual differences. Wide individual differences in many aspects of normal development have been well-documented, and these individual differences are particularly notable during the first years of life. For example, with respect to motor development, there is much variability in the ages at which babies first sit, stand, and walk, and differences can be great (a difference of 4 months or more).[3] If we consider children's language development, normally developing 2-year-olds may be able to say just a handful of words, or they may say several hundred words.[4,5] Despite these enormous individual differences, all normally developing children will walk well by the time they are 16 months old and talk (in short sentences, comprehensible to others) by the time they are 3 years old.

It also is important for parents to know that individual differences in children's development (so long as they are within the normal range) do not strictly predict later differences in children's skills and abilities. For example, some children talk in "sentences" (of two or more words) when they are 18 months old, and others do not do this until they are 26 months old; all of these children would be considered to be developing normally. Slowness in learning to talk does not necessarily portend autism or even a quiet child.

As we often tell parents, "be careful what you wish for," when it comes to your child's development. A friend who was worried about her son's slow language development when he was a toddler finds that her now school-aged son talks nonstop. As another example, a child who walks (or runs!) early is not destined to become more graceful on his or her feet, or more likely to become an Olympic athlete than any other child. Parents who wish to accelerate their child's first steps soon find that life with a toddler means reconfiguring some (or all) rooms in the house to accommodate their child's need to explore his/her environment while at the same time keeping their child safe.

Certainly, if parents are concerned that their child's development falls outside the normal range in one or more areas, then they should raise their concerns with a developmental psychologist, certified family life educator, pediatrician, or another professional. Parents might find useful some of the free resources on child development that have been created for parents by the federal government, most of which are available in Spanish and English. For example, the U.S. Department of Health and Human Services offers one-page pamphlets (available on-line), listing normative developmental milestones and signs of problems.[6] These pamphlets highlight important milestones in physical, cognitive, and social development for children at ages 3 months, 7 months, and each year from 1 to 5 years. The U.S. Department of Health and Human Services (in cooperation with the U.S. Departments of Education and Agriculture) also publishes magazines from the White House's "Healthy Start, Grow Smart" initiative that summarize infants' behaviors and needs in a variety of developmental areas for each month for the first year of life and discuss how parents can best foster their infants' healthy development.[7] Parents should be cautioned that the age ranges given are merely averages, noting that differences for any given child may vary from these, as noted in studies we have cited above.

If a professional with expertise in child development is reassuring that a child is developing normally, then by all means, the parent should listen to her or him, and not the other parents at the playground. It is best to remember that each child develops at his or her own rate and that all normally developing children will eventually walk, talk, run, jump, and play. Children's development should not be viewed as a competition, nor should parenting. Ideally, all children will grow up to be happy, healthy, and competent.

References

[1] CIVITAS Initiative, ZERO TO THREE, and BRIO Corporation. (2000). *What grown-ups understand about child development: A national benchmark survey.* Chicago: CIVITAS.

[2] Steenhuysen, J. (2008, May 4). U.S. parents' baby knowledge lacking, study finds. Chicago: Reuters. Available: http://www.reuters.com/article/domesticNews/id USN0230210620080504?feedType=RSS&feedName=domesticNews. Retrieved Dec. 20, 2011.

[3] Frankenburg, W. K., Dodds, J., Archer, P. Shapiro, H., & Bresnick, B. (1992). The Denver II: A major revision and restandardization of the Denver Developmental Screening Tests. *Pediatrics, 89,* 91-97.

[4] Fenson, L., Dale, P. S., Reznick, J. S., Bates, E., Thal, D. J., & Pethick, S. J. (1994). Variability in early communicative development. *Monographs of the Society for Research in Child Development, 59* (5, Serial No. 242).

[5] Bornstein, M. H., Cote, L. R., Maital, S., Painter, K., Park, S., Pascual, L., Pêcheux, M., Ruel, J., Venuti, P., & Vyt, A. (2004). Cross-linguistic analysis of vocabulary in toddlers: Spanish, Dutch, French, Hebrew, Italian, Korean, and English. *Child Development, 75,* 1115-1139.

[6] National Center on Birth Defects and Developmental Disabilities, Center for Disease Control and Prevention, U.S. Department of Health & Human Services. (2007). *Learn the signs. Act early.* Retrieved Dec. 20, 2011, from http://www.cdc.gov/ncbddd/actearly/index.html.

[7] The White House. *Healthy start, grow smart.* Retrieved Jan, 6, 2011, from http://www.whitehouse.gov/firstlady/initiatives/healthystart.html.

Parent-Infant Bonding:
Its Role and Importance

Elizabeth Morgan Russell, Ph.D., CFLE
Clinical Assistant Professor, Family and Consumer
Sciences, Texas State University, San Marcos

"He's such a mama's boy," the young father ruefully said as he watched his 10-month-old son crawl into the next room. We followed the laughing infant into the living room. His father continued, "When his mother is in the room, it's like no one else exists. If I'm holding him and he sees her, he reaches out to her, wriggles to be put down, and crawls over to her. If she doesn't come right over and pick him up, he'll start crying and keep crying until she holds him." As if on cue, the baby's mother walks in the front door with an arm full of groceries, and seeing her, he chortles, drops the toy he has been mouthing, and crawls toward her. His mother smiles down at him, "I'll pick you up as soon as I put the groceries down." She disappears into the kitchen. The baby pauses and his lower lip starts to quiver. He brightens, though, when he hears her voice from the other room calling out, "I'm in here JJ." The now smiling infant crawls eagerly toward the sound of his mother's voice and follows her into the kitchen.

Later in the day, we pick up on our conversation where it had left off, "You're right that JJ has a special bond with his mother. John Bowlby[1] called this special bond between an infant and caregiver an attachment relationship. He theorized, and later a student of his, Mary Ainsworth,[2] demonstrated, that infants are born ready to form social bonds with the adults who spend the most time caring for them. The cries, smiles, and tiny size of infants elicit, when all goes well, loving, nurturing responses from parents or other caregivers. These early, loving interactions have a lifelong impact on the child's development because, according to Bowlby, the infant builds an internal working model, similar to a template, but more flexible, of interpersonal relationships that forms the child's expectations of how others will treat him and how he should treat others. If, in the parlance of Bowlby, the child has a secure attachment with his or her primary caregivers, then the child will anticipate the world is a warm, friendly place and will confidently explore, anticipating the caregiver will come to his or her aid when needed for comfort or safety. You can see that in your son's behavior–he excitedly explores the house, periodically calling out to you or his mother to be sure you are there, or he returns to you and his mother to be held and hugged. He also looks to you and his mother when he is tired, hungry, or hurt. Each and every loving encounter reassures him that the world is a safe and welcoming place, and further reinforces his secure, interpersonal template.

You can also see the impact of early loving, nurturing care– a secure template–on your 3-year-old daughter's interactions with her brother and play with other children. She is loving and empathetic with her little brother. She loves holding him and helping you both care for him. She's worried when he cries. She hugs and loves playing with other children. She has lots of ideas, is adventurous, takes turns with other children, and is assertive, not aggressive in expressing her preferences to the other children. She also comes to you when she is hurt or scared, anticipating that you'll comfort her. According to Sroufe[3] and his associates,[4] both of your children will continue to reap the emotional and social benefits of the loving start you and their mother are providing them throughout their childhood and beyond.

To summarize, infants are born ready to form bonds with the most important people in their lives–their primary caregivers. Although this is usually the mother and father, grandparents, adoptive parents, and foster parents all have the capacity to support the development of a healthy interpersonal template in infants. Loving, responsive, and attentive parents will provide the kinds of social interactions their infant needs to forge a secure template that will later foster healthy social and emotional development. Conversely, infants who forge an insecure template as a result of inattentive, rejecting, and nonresponsive caregiving are at risk for unhealthy social and emotional development. What happens in the early years between infant and caregiver really does matter! So, for now, there is no need to be distressed if your son appears to be "a Mama's Boy." It is a good sign!

References

[1] Bowlby, J. (1969/1982). *Attachment and loss: Vol. 1. Attachment.* NY: Basic Books.

[2] Ainsworth, M.D.S, Blehar, M.C., Waters, E., & Wall, S. (1978). *Patterns of attachment: A psychological study of the strange situation.* Hillsdale NJ: Lawrence Erlbaum.

[3] Sroufe, L.A. (1983). Infant-caregiver attachment and patterns of adaptation in preschoolers: The roots of maladaptation and competence. In M. Perlmutter (Ed.), *Development and policy concerning children with special needs: The Minnesota Symposia on Child Psychology (Vol. 16, pp. 41-83).* Hillsdale, NJ: Erlbaum.

[4] Weinfield, N.S., Sroufe, L.A., & Egeland, B. (2000). Attachment from infancy to early adulthood in a high-risk sample: Continuity, discontinuity, and their correlates. *Child Development, 71(3),* 695-702.

Suggested reading for more information, all retrieved October 27, 2010, from www.aap.org (American Academy of Pediatrics); www.bornlearning.org (Born Learning); www.parenting-ed.org (Center for Effective Parenting); www.zerotothree.org (Zero to Three).

Save As: ...You–My Daughter

My hands
My eyes
My heart
All expanded
To create
The you,
The daughter
That created
Me,
The mother.

The teacher, who
Invited the student,
Created the learner,
Who shaped the teacher
Who learns,
At last,

To Love.

–Marcia Pioppi Galazzi, M.Ed., CFLE
President & Founder, The Family
Schools, Inc., Brewster, MA

The Feeling Child

Sharon M. Ballard, Ph.D., CFCS, CFLE
Associate Professor, Child Development & Family Relations,
East Carolina University,
Greenville

"Big boys don't cry." "Little girls are supposed to be happy." "Don't be sad." Children are often told how they are supposed to feel. Children learn "display rules" very early in life. In other words, they learn where and with whom they can show certain emotions and at what times they are supposed to stuff the emotion deep inside and not let it show. Consequently, children may grow up not knowing how to identify, interpret, and appropriately express their emotions.

More and more attention is being given to the idea of emotional intelligence (EQ). Emotional intelligence (EQ) is the ability to recognize our own feelings and those of others, to motivate ourselves, to control impulses, and to regulate emotions well within ourselves and in our relationships. In his book, *Emotional Intelligence,* Daniel Goleman discussed the important role that emotions play in our lives.[1] Emotions guide our actions; each emotion serves a function in leading us to particular actions. Children who are more skilled with their emotions often experience fewer social problems, fewer behavior problems, and less withdrawal and depression.[1]

There are three basic steps to facilitate young children's emotional development and help them to develop a positive EQ. **First**, help children identify their emotions. Preschoolers often have trouble identifying what they are feeling (sometimes adults do too!). Start with introducing terms when the emotions are present, such as anger, fear, hurt, happiness and sadness and then move to self conscious emotions, such as jealousy and pride as your child gets older.

Second, children need to learn how to interpret their emotions. Children need to know that emotions are never bad. Validate a child's emotion (e.g., "I know you are sad right now. I would be sad too if my friend had to go home"). We are given the ability to experience endless emotions and these emotions should be experienced and not pushed aside.

Third, children need to learn to appropriately express emotions. "I understand that you are angry but it is not okay to hit." Children need to learn outlets for appropriately discharging their emotions. Children may discharge emotions by talking about how they feel, running around the yard (how many of us use exercise as a stress release?), or punching a pillow. For many children, it also might mean crying. Crying tends to make many adults uncomfortable and they try to get children to stop crying, but crying can be an important expression of emotion. The hurt already has occurred and the crying is the release of that hurt. If a child (or anybody for that matter) is not allowed to express or discharge the emotion, it will get hidden inside and eventually it will come out and not always in a positive manner. For example, likely we have all had experiences where something minor happens and we completely lose control. We either start to sob or we yell or use some other mechanism for releasing the strong emotions that have built up. It was not necessarily the minor incident that just occurred that caused the blow-up but all of the incidents and hurts that have been stuffed inside. Pretty soon, there is no more room and it has to come out. If children's emotions are validated and they are allowed to experience and discharge their emotions on a regular basis, that build up is less likely to occur.

Consequently, we should give children permission to feel an emotion and help them to identify and label the emotion. As they are experiencing the emotion, offer to be with them while they do or offer suggestions on discharging the emotion. Sometimes it is scary to have strong emotions and it is comforting to a child to have a trusted adult there. For example, when your daughter realizes that she left a favorite toy at Grandma's house, it will be a loss for her. Rather than trivializing her emotion and asking her to stuff it inside by saying something like "don't be silly, this isn't something to be sad about, forget it and come play," instead, try saying something like "I know that you are sad. I'll call Grandma and have her put it in a safe place until we return and I will sit with you while you are sad and then when you are ready, we can go play." The child that is given permission to feel sad is going to be much more likely to let the sadness go, start playing, and have a happy day, than the child who is told to forget about it and then carries that sadness with them all day.

Like other areas of development, if children are not given the opportunity to develop skill in identifying, interpreting, and expressing emotions, they will not automatically have those skills as adults and will not develop a strong EQ. Because many of us did not have good opportunities to develop these skills as children, we need to examine our own EQ. We will then be more prepared to help our children be successful in their emotional development.

Reference

[1] Goleman, D. (1995). *Emotional intelligence.* NY: Bantam Books.

"As the Twig is bent, so grows the Tree": Making the Early Years Count

Amelia I. Rose, Ph.D., CFLE
Comprehensive Counseling Ministries, Inc.,
West Palm Beach, Florida

"As the twig is bent, so grows the tree," is an old adage grounded in folk wisdom. Sayings such as this have withstood the test of time for one good reason–there is some degree of truth to them. This adage is thought to be of Korean origin, but was widely used in the Caribbean islands by elders in the community, who were thought to have an authority on what constitutes successful child-rearing practices. The prevailing conviction is that a child's character is formed in the early years of life and that his early inappropriate behaviors, if left unchanged, have a lasting impact on his development, thereby shaping his characteristic later in life.

While the majority of child development experts assert the principle of the "window of opportunity,"[1,2] I believe that enough emphasis is not given to the notion that a child's early influences have a determinant effect on character development later in life. Brain development research does imply such a correlation.[3] Unfortunately, despite the wealth of child development studies available over the last two decades, there still seems to be a gap between what the experts say and what parents know or understand about child development and early brain development. As a result, this article will seek to help bridge the gaps between the research and what parents know, especially as it relates to early influences and outcomes later in life.

The first concept I will attempt to help you understand and appreciate more is that you are your children's first and most influential teacher and caregiver, you play a major role in helping them attain their full potential. It is critical for parents to understand this significant principle, as failure to do so can either impede (or enhance) their ability to help their children succeed in life.

The second concept you should understand is the importance of the home in the child's initial academic and social development. When children are born, the home is the first learning environment or "class room" they enter and is therefore their foundation for learning. If parents more fully realize this, they can make a more positive (rather than negative) impact on their children's growth and development, setting the stage for early learning.

Important developments occur during the first five years of a child's life. Parents can capitalize on this critical period and help their children reach their full potential. This does not suggest closure by a certain age, but it does mean that some skills are more difficult to learn after this "window of opportunity" passes.[2]

The old adage, "as the twig is bent; so grows the tree," infers that children are born to grow straight and strong like healthy trees; however, certain conditions can bend the "little twigs" and disrupt that growth process. Unknowingly, some parents contribute to that bending. The following illustrations are intended to help you understand this concept and enhance your parenting skills in the home.

Let us take for example the belief some parents have that responding to their infants in loving and supporting ways can be excessive and can lead to a child being spoiled. These parents could benefit from understanding that infancy is a perfect time for parents to bond with their babies through loving behaviors. In fact, scientists explain that a positive bonding between the parent and child can serve as a model for future intimate relationships and foster a healthy self-esteem.[4] In addition, it was observed that a parent's loving and caring response can enhance the child's cognitive development.

Another example of the gap between research and what parents believe can be noted in the way parents perceive their toddlers' behaviors. Some parents believe that their toddlers are really trying to avenge them when they are "pitching a fit." However, as challenging as these behaviors are, many times when toddlers throw tantrums they are experiencing a conflict between what they want to do versus what they are capable of doing. The reality is that between ages 2-3, children experience a flood of emotions that they are unable to articulate, because they have no reference point based on experience and their language development. This period is therefore an opportune time for parents to begin to teach their children how to appropriately express behaviors which reflect how they feel, especially when they are angry, frustrated, sad or disappointed. An emotion chart[1] depicting various facial expressions can be very helpful; it works for adults and there is no reason why it wouldn't be applicable for children. In fact, it can be used as a game between parents and their children.

Depending on a child's age and language capability, parents can also help children use words to describe their feelings. The emotion chart, "Feeling Faces Poster" or cards, can help to achieve this as well. Children will need language skill to resolve conflicts, which are common during play. If there is a fight, for example, parents can teach the little ones how to express their feelings which are causing the fight. Parents can also encourage children to share and point out that hitting others is not acceptable. Parents should always speak to children about their inappropriate behaviors. You should set boundaries and rules, giving a reason for them as well as the consequence for violating them. This fosters the early development of self control.

Most of all, model the behaviors you want your children to learn. Children are great imitators of behaviors, good or bad. Remember also that the early years are the best time to teach impulse control, because attitudes towards anger are usually formed between the ages of one and three. It is equally important to note that if not appropriately channeled these behaviors may carry over into adulthood.

As suggested in an earlier paragraph, language acquisition is crucial during the first five years of life. Parents can capitalize on this period and lay the foundation for their children's academic success. Every parent should learn that by helping your children master the necessary language skills, along with impulse control, you are giving them the ability to communicate meaningfully with the rest of the world.[6]

It is understandable that not all parents may have the experience desired to perform all of the tasks mentioned in this article nor to the degree they would wish. Yet, whatever you achieve of the above suggestions, your children's development will be enhanced. Recognize that the importance of the early years cannot be underestimated. Nobel Prize winning poet Gabriela Mistral captured this concept profoundly when she said, "Many of the things we need can wait. The child cannot. Right now is the time his bones are being formed, his blood is being made, and his senses are being developed. To him we cannot answer 'tomorrow;' his name is 'today'."[7]

Finally, with the general belief that most parents really want what is best for their children, there is no better recourse but for you to be what you want your children to become and begin early. With this in mind, you can help your children to grow and succeed as you nurture and support them with a solid foundation of learning during the early years in life.

References

[1] Hurlock, Elizabeth B. (1972). *Child development* (5th ed.). NY: McGraw-Hill. NOTE: see discussion under the topic, "teachable moment," attributed to Robert Havighurst.

[2] Smart, M.S., & Smart, R.C. (1983). *Children development and relationships* (4th ed.). NY: Macmillan NOTE: see discussion under the topic, "critical learning period."

[3] Musterd, Fraser, Young, Mary Eming & Dunkelberg, Erika. (February, 2006). Preventing youth behavior through early child development. *Youth Development Notes I,* 1(3) Retrieved Dec. 20, 2010, from http://site resources.worldbank.org/INTECD/Resources/C&YYDNECD.pdf.

[4] Nemours Foundation. (2005). Bonding with your baby. *KidsHealth [for parents].* Retrieved Dec. 20, 2010, from http://www.kidshealth.org/parent/newborn/first_days/bonding.html.

[5] *Feeling Faces Cards.* (2004). Charts are available for view or purchase. Retrieved Dec. 20, 2010, from http://www.feelingfacescards.com/.

[6] Fraiberg, Selma, & Brazelton, Berry. (1996). *The magic years: Understanding and handling the problems of early childhood.* NY: Scribner.

[7] Mistral, Gabriela. Historic quote on the neglect of children. Retrieved Dec. 20, 2010, from http://thinkexist.com/quotes/gabriela_mistral/.

Choosing Quality Child Care

M. Angela Nievar, Ph.D., CFLE
Assistant Professor, Department of Educational Psychology,
University of North Texas, Denton

Many parents have a difficult time finding just the right child care setting for their child. Most mothers are working because they need the income, but they may feel ambivalent about returning to work. Leaving their child may be stressful at first. Placing their child in a quality child care setting can give them reassurance that their child is in a safe and stimulating environment.

Quality child care settings base their practices on research that shows the best ways of teaching young children according to their stage of development.[1] During early childhood, quality child care settings have been shown to enhance children's language skills

throughout the elementary school years.[2] A high quality early childhood program prepares children for success in school, but the majority of preschools in the United States are not good quality.[3]

How do parents find good quality care? Of course, parents
want the best possible situation for their children, but they may not
recognize quality care when they see it. Parents are likely to choose
child care settings that are close to home, within their price range,
and open during the hours that they work. Some child care centers
may do an excellent job of marketing, but a below-average job of
caring for children. Parents may not be aware of quality markers,
such as staff to child ratios. To make it more complicated, the ideal
number of staff to the number of children in care varies according to
the ages and developmental stages of the children. Parents whose
children have serious medical conditions or other special needs may
have an even more difficult time finding a caregiver whom they trust.

One way of finding quality care is to locate a child care setting that has received national accreditation. The National Association for the Education of Young Children (NAEYC) offers an
accreditation program for child care centers that exceeds legal licensing standards in several areas. The accreditation for family child care
homes, administered by the National Family Child Care Association
(NAFCC), requires higher levels of training, safety, and quality than
state licensing authorities.

Although state licensing systems do not guarantee quality,
they do sometimes offer quality rankings or other aids to child care
selection. Some states post licensing violations on a website or make
licensing "report cards" available to the public after inspections. Parents can contact their local resource and referral agency to find out
more information about licensing violations for specific centers or
homes.[4] Every state has different requirements, and many states
simply monitor basic health and safety needs. Yet there are so many
other factors to consider when choosing appropriate child care.

A predictable environment is important to young children's
emotional and cognitive development. If a setting has a high staff
turnover, children are more likely to feel insecure there. Often parents
with young infants prefer a family child care home, which usually
has one or at the most two caregivers. The smaller size and low
turnover in these homes may provide a more stable environment for
infants.

In general, caregivers should be involved with the children.
Experience does not equal quality of care; many parents make the
false assumption that caregivers with more experience must be well
qualified. Staff training is important, however, and caregivers who
are professionally committed to their business with relevant child
care education tend to be more competent. Family child care

providers who are involved in their profession and are operating a child care business out of their homes are more likely to provide quality care than those who view themselves as "babysitters" for one or two children. Similarly, caregivers who are involved in training and education to further their career in early childhood education are more likely to provide quality care than those who are working there temporarily.

The center director should be able to give information about the number of staff members who have received advanced training, such as the Child Development Associate (CDA) credential. Caregivers who have completed CDA training are more likely to be responsive and appropriate when working with children. Trained and qualified caregivers provide early literacy experiences for young children by reading books with them, making lists, and creating activities that give children appropriate opportunities with print. Outdoor experiences, active play, and exercise also should be encouraged. In all cases, parents should be able to drop in at any time unannounced. A quality setting is one where parents feel welcome and their opinions are valued.

To evaluate quality of care, parents should spend a substantial amount of time in a setting. As parents observe a potential setting, they should note if caregivers are talking and playing with the children or mostly talking with other staff members. In some settings, caregivers have unrealistic expectations of young children. Infants do not all sleep or eat at the same time; in infant-toddler settings the staff should be more flexible. Caregivers should not expect toddlers to stand in line or preschoolers to sit still during story time. Knowing children's limits can help staff prevent rather than solve problems. In all cases, an insufficient number of staff leads to a chaotic environment. When parents visit, they should count the number of caregivers and the number of children present. Infants and toddlers should have no more than four infants to one staff member, although three to one is preferred. Ratios increase with children's ages; however, ideal ratios may vary particularly with children who have special needs.

In summary:
- Is the center accredited by NAEYC, or if a home, by NAFCC?
- Are inspection reports available at the center or a state website? Don't hesitate to ask your local resource and referral agency for help.
- Is there evidence of the child care provider(s) having relevant child care education? Do any of them hold the CDA credential?
- Have you spent some time observing the site?
- Does the child/staff ratio seem appropriate? If infant/toddlers, is it 4 to 1 or less?

After parents have made a choice, parents should bring their child to visit before the first day of care. If possible, parents can be involved in their child's preschool or child care. Some centers or child care homes have parent advisory groups or parent nights. Parents then have the opportunity to meet the child's special "friends" and arrange play dates. As a word of caution, older infants who enter care for the first time often experience separation anxiety. A child's crying when parents leave is not a sign that parents have made the wrong choice of a child care caregiver. Bringing a picture of the parent or a favorite toy for the child can help with adjustment. Child care can be a safe and a fun place for infants to grow and develop; caregivers and preschool teachers often develop attachments to their young students and give them another special person who cares about them.

References

[1] National Association for the Education of Young Children. (1999). *Developmentally appropriate practice in early childhood education* Washington, DC: NAEYC.

[2] Belsky, J., Vandell, D. L., Burchinal, M., Clarke-Stewart, K. A., McCartney, K., & Owen, M. T. (2007). Are there long-term effects of early child care? *Child Development, 78,* 681-701.

[3] Espinosa, L. (2002). High-quality preschool: Why we need it and what it looks like. *Preschool Policy Matters,* 1. National Institute for Early Education Research. Retrieved Jan. 2, 2011, from http://nieer.org/resources/policybriefs /1.pdf.

[4] National Association of Child Care Resource and Referral Agencies. (2008). Child Care Aware. See right column for "Your zip code" search. Retrieved Jan. 4, 2011, from http://www.childcareaware.org/en/.

Why Read to Your Child?

Aimee Carmichael, B.A.
Family life education, volunteer with children and families,
Dearborn, MI

When I think of my childhood and recall the times that had the greatest impact on my life, I remember that my parents read to me every day. Many of the details of the books still are fresh in my mind, but what I really remember are the emotions that I experienced during those reading sessions. I felt loved and secure. I am so grateful for the gift my parents gave me. They spent time reading to me.

The benefits of reading to your child have been well documented. What comes to mind immediately is the great impact that reading aloud has on literacy development. Reading to your child has a positive effect on vocabulary and language development and it is the best way parents can support early literacy development. In fact, reading to your child can be far more effective than spending a lot of money on highly publicized videos which have proven to be less effective, as thoroughly reported on in Bronson & Merryman's book, *NurtureShock.*[1] Read their chapter on "Why Hannah Talks and Alyssa Doesn't."

Literacy experts also emphasize additional benefits that can be gained by reading to your child.[2] These benefits apply to the whole family and can enhance family wellness. Spending one-on-one time reading to your child can promote bonding which is necessary to hold families together;[3] can offer a child the opportunity to develop a sense of self;[4] and can help to build family literacy traditions.[5]

When you read to your child, you spend time with your child. When you spend time with your child you create opportunities to bond with your child. In our fast-paced society, we often look for ways to spend time with each other. We plan formal events and recreational activities to promote family relationships. The simplest activities, however, such as reading together, often provide the easiest and best opportunities for families to bond together. Sitting together, giving your child your complete attention, sends the message that he or she is worthy of your attention. All children really want and need to know this. When you devote time to your child, you get to know each other. The time spent may not be extensive, but a set daily time makes it special for both parent and child.

Books can be an avenue by which families can share ideas and have meaningful discussions in a relaxed setting. When parents and children talk about books and characters, children learn to express their feelings leading to healthy emotional development. Books help stimulate conversation, allowing children to get in touch with their own feelings as they respond to the story and characters. Through this process, children are given a chance to develop a sense of self.

Parents can share their own childhood favorites which can help to establish family literacy traditions. This allows generations to make connections with each other. Most parents gain personal satisfaction from passing something down to the next generation. In the process, they can share their own childhood experiences with their children. Often the activities surrounding the reading of books can help to create life-long memories and become family traditions. Growing up, I remember the excitement of the weekly trip to the library, the joy of selecting my favorite books again and again, and the anticipation of having them read to me. The weekly trip to the library has been a tradition in my family for several generations.

Daily reading to your child promotes literacy development and definitely can have a positive effect on family development. It is a very simple and fun way to relax and build strong family ties.

References

[1] Bronson, Po, & Merryman, Ashley. (2009). *NurtureShock: New thinking about children.* NY: Twelve.

[2] Hill-Clark, K. (2005). Families as educators: Supporting literacy development. *Childhood Education: Infancy through Early Adolescence, 82,* 46-47.

[3] Trelease, J. (2006). *The read aloud handbook* (Rev. ed.). NY: Penguin.

[4] Seefeldt, C. (2003). Why read aloud? *Early Childhood Today, 17,* 8-10.

[5] Giles, R., & Wellhousen, K. (2005). Building literacy traditions: A family affair. *Childhood Education: Infancy through Early Adolescence, 81,* 297-299.

Can't We Just Play?

Jean Illsley Clarke, Ph.D., CFLE
Author and parent educator, Minneapolis, MN

"Can we play now?" Clarissa's children begged. Clarissa was perplexed. Why did her children ask to play? They had been playing all day. In the morning they had been at Saturday swim classes, and their mom had spent the entire afternoon playing with them. They had played a competitive math game with flashcards. Clarissa had taught them three games of Taking No For An Answer:[1] Follow Me, Follow You; Traffic Cop; and Red Light, Green Light. They also had gone on a nature walk to see how many different kinds of birds they could spot.

All of that had been fun. At least Clarissa hoped so. Actually, she was getting tired when Mason declared he was bored with birds and Madison whined, "Can we play now?"

"But we have been playing all afternoon," Clarissa snapped, perplexed and slightly irritated; well, more than slightly, when she questioned, "What do you want to play now?"

The children responded, "Just play, Mom. We want to play."

All the "play" they did with Mom was important. It strengthened connections with Mom, and it was good learning time for the children. But adult directed activities need to be balanced with child directed free play, the time children consider to be *real* play.

Mason and Madison needed some time for *real* free play. Time for them to select an activity, engage in it, create their own play scenario (free of adult direction),[2] and bring the activity to closure. This need for free play time spans the childhood years.

Infants need some time to themselves. Babies who are entertained fulltime fail to develop self-comforting skills.

Toddlers must have free time to explore the environment–to touch, drop, taste, wiggle, throw, stack, smell, and listen to a wide variety of safe objects, and yes, people. All are important brain-building activities.

Two-year-olds need free time to practice their newfound physical capabilities, to struggle and to master.

Three to five-year-olds need free play time to explore their own creativity and their relationships with peers, real or imaginary.

School-age children must have free time to develop and test their knowledge of rules. Who makes the rules? Who follows the rules? What happens if you follow them, or break them? A lot of learning happens when two-thirds of a softball game is spent arguing. That can't happen while an adult coach is running the show.

Adolescents need time to explore their relationships, to think about their values, and to dream about their futures.

Free playtime is not time controlled by the TV or game scenarios. It is time controlled by the children themselves and, if they have lost the skill of doing that, adults need to act to alter the children's schedules.[3]

How can free time be provided?

- Allow for time to play out of doors.
- Spend less time with TV, video, games, *and* plugged in earphones.
- Have a limit for lessons, organized sports, clubs, volunteer activities.

Are those activities bad? Not necessarily. Just carve out enough time for free play.

Bergen views the difference between work and play in early childhood programs as a continuum from free play to work.[4] For each of the five types of play or work activity, there is a corresponding type of learning that occurs. On this spectrum, **free play** corresponds to discovery learning, **guided play** (the nature walk) to guided discovery learning, **directed play** (the adult guided Taking No games) to receptive learning, **work disguised as play** (the math flashcards) to rote learning, and **work as drill-repetitive practice**.[4]

How much free playtime does your child need? It varies with the temperament of the child, but we can safely plan for a minimum of half-an-hour to one hour of free playtime every day.

In the overindulgence research studies, many adults who had been overindulged as children complained about having been over-scheduled with not enough free time for themselves as children.[5] We can avoid this for our children by providing the free play time that can benefit them in so many ways.

References

[1] Simons, L. (2000). *Taking "no" for an answer and other skills children need.* Seattle: Parenting Press, Inc.

[2] Jones, E. & Reynolds, G. (1992). *The play's the thing: Teachers' roles in children's play.* Columbia University, NY: Teachers College Press.

[3] Rosenfeld, A., M.D., & Wise, N. (2000). *The over-scheduled child: Avoiding the hyper-parenting trap.* NY: St. Martin's Griffin.

[4] Bergen, D. (1988). Using a schema for play and learning. In D. Bergen (Ed.), *Play as a medium for learning and development* (pp.169-179). Portsmouth, NH: Heinemann Educational Books.

[5] Clarke, J. & Dawson, C., & Bredehoft, D. (2004). *How much is enough? Everything you need to know to steer clear of overindulgence and raise likeable, responsible, and respectful children.* NY: Marlowe& Co. For more information about the Overindulgence Research Studies, see www.over indulgence.info.

Toys for Infants and Toddlers: Learning through Play

M. Angela Nievar, Ph.D., CFLE
Assistant Professor, Department of Educational Psychology,
University of North Texas, Denton

As young children grow and develop, they learn by playing. Toys are an important part of their learning environment. Of course, parents or other caregivers are essential to the learning that occurs through toys. When parents take time to talk and play with their children, they encourage language, physical and emotional development and much more. Early social experiences help children feel loved and enhance their self-worth. In addition to playing with their family members or peers, children often play with toys by themselves. Toys can act as a comforting reminder of the parent's love when the parent is not available. Cuddly toys can help young children feel secure and many children have a favorite blanket or stuffed animal that they use for this purpose.

Various types of toys that stimulate all of the senses–by sight, sound, and texture–are interesting to infants and toddlers. A well-organized collection of toys, appropriate music, and safe places to explore encourage active learning through hands-on experiences.[1] Toys that are just a little bit beyond what children can do on their own may be useful for their growth and development.[2] A useful resource for the selection of toys, for newborns up to 12 year olds, is provided by the National Network for Child Care. By age groups, a guide is provided on what types of toys to choose and to avoid, along with some good questions to ask before purchasing.[3]

Toys can be quite expensive or cost nothing at all. Bright colors and flashy gadgets may be attractive, but parents need to look beneath the surface. Before investing money in toys, parents should ask themselves several questions. Is this toy appropriate for my child's current abilities and developmental level? Even though a toy is labeled age-appropriate, children vary in their interests or level of development. For example, some completely normal and healthy children may not be walking until shortly after their first birthday, whereas other children are ambulatory at nine months, and some children may be more interested in a train set than in construction tools.

Whether children play indoors or out, parents need to be mindful of health and safety issues. Cleanliness is an important issue for all children; however, infants in particular like to put toys in their mouth. Extra vigilance is encouraged to keep children under the age of three safe. For example, it is important to remember that although nontoxic paint is currently used in manufacturing toys (with the exception of occasional recalls of some foreign made toys), antique or hand-me-down toys may contain lead-based paint. Small toys that an infant might swallow or toys with loose pieces may present a choking hazard. Federal toy safety regulations state that toys for children under three should be large enough so that children cannot choke on them, but it is still good to check yourself. If an object fits through a toilet paper tube, it is probably unsafe for infant play. Toys with parts that might be chewed off or broken should not be used with this age group. As always, prevention goes hand in hand with appropriate supervision.

In addition to mandatory regulations, the federal safety commission has established voluntary guidelines for toy manufacturers in cooperation with the Toy Industry Association. Their website has a section for parents with links to safety tips, product recalls, and other toy safety organizations.[4] Labels on toys often give age recommendations and guidelines to encourage safe play. Stringent standards for indoor toys cover battery operated toys, pacifiers, sound levels, and chemical safety, ensuring that toys meeting standards for infant use are safe for infants.

Infant play. When infants are quite young, they begin learning by investigating the world around them. Their first toys are things they can watch. Very young infants like black and white patterns, mirrors, and mobiles. Unbreakable mirrors are delightful toys. Bright colors are attractive to infants, but too many colors and patterns can be over-stimulating. Pictures of human faces also are interesting for infants to watch. Peek-a-boo games with people, puppets, or stuffed animals delight young infants and help them understand spatial relationships. Rattles that make many kinds of sounds or have moving parts are even more interesting for infants to manipulate and enjoy.

As infants begin to gain control of their bodies, they learn by moving their bodies and the things around them. As mentioned earlier, they like to put toys in their mouths. They also enjoy feeling different textures, shapes, and sizes. Toys that allow them to create sounds, such as rattles or musical toys, help them understand cause and effect. Rattles that make many kinds of sounds or have moving parts are even more interesting for infants to manipulate.

Older infants and toddlers play. Soon they begin to order their world by colors, shapes, and sizes. Toys that fit together teach them about physical relationships and help to develop problem-solving skills. Stringing beads, buttons, or spools on string can lead to an understanding of concepts like "in," "out," and "through." Stacking toys also help young children understand spatial arrangements. Shapes that "disappear" into a shape-sorter only to reappear later are fascinating to toddlers and enhance eye-hand coordination. Even at an early age, children can create artwork with water-based markers or finger paints. Pushing and pulling toys, ride-on toys, wagons, and balls help develop large motor skills. Large nontoxic crayons and simple puzzles help develop fine motor skills.

Many toys for infants and toddlers can stimulate intellectual and social skills. Playing with blocks can teach children about mathematical relationships, and building with blocks can encourage pretend play and cooperative skills. Most infants are not ready to share their favorite toy, but they can learn prosocial skills as they interact with their parents, caregiver, or older siblings. Puppets, books, and music give children and parents opportunities for interactive play, language development and expression through dance. As parents select age-appropriate toys for their children, they can encourage children to explore various aspects of their environment and the real world.

Outdoor play. Although safety is important, protecting children too much can interfere with their need to explore their environment. With supervision, even very young children can play safely outdoors. Infants love to be outside and see the world around them. Playing with their regular toys on a blanket spread on the grass is a fun experience. Mobiles or wind chimes hung from a tree branch provide extra entertainment. Infant-sized swings, strollers, and ride-on toys give children the experience of movement while enjoying the sights of nature. Of course, children should wear an appropriate helmet for safety when using riding toys or scooters. Outdoor spaces are great for playing with balls; lightweight beach balls are especially good for teaching toddlers to catch. Drawing with sidewalk chalk allows toddlers and preschoolers to create art on a large scale. Outdoor climbing equipment is wonderful for learning to cooperate with other children, as well as learning to balance, jump, and climb. Small boxes are good for building; large boxes are fun for playing hide-and-seek. Toddlers also like to dig with shovels and mix dirt and water. Small children do need supervision, but they will not learn skills as easily if parents are too overprotective. Realize that some toys and games that are messy can be easily handled out-of-doors, and they encourage the development of creativity in a young child.

Indoor play. When the weather is bad outside, older infants can play with bubbles and water in a protected indoor area. Learning to blow bubbles with a bubble wand develops control of small muscles and teaches toddlers how to solve problems through experimentation. Children's first science lessons may come from playing with bubbles, liquid, and other materials that families have in their own kitchens. For example, cornstarch and different amounts of water mix together to create varying consistencies that fascinate young children. Purchased or homemade clay provides hours of fun at a low cost. Children like to manipulate these mixtures because they have so much control over them. Water play in and of itself can be relaxing, and it teaches children about their physical world.

In conclusion, appropriate toys assist children in all aspects of their development. In the toddler years, toys serve as an aid to enhance imagination and social experience. During the first years of life, toys, books, games and music encourage exploration of the environment and promote learning. Children also develop physical skills as they play ball or draw pictures. In fact, children learn as they play; play is their work. Thus, age-appropriate toys are teaching tools, leading to a happy and healthy future for young children.

References

[1] Piaget, J. (1971). *Biology and knowledge.* Chicago: University of Chicago Press.

[2] Lillard, A. S. (2005). *Montessori: The science behind the genius.* NY: Oxford University Press.

[3] National Network for Child Care. (2002). *Toys and equipment.* Adapted from the work of Lesia Oesterreich. Retrieved Dec. 20, 2010, from www.nncc.org /curriculum/toys.html.

[4] Toy Industry Association. (2007). Retrieved Dec. 20, 2010, from http://www. toyhotline.org.

Chapter VII
Wisdom for Middle Childhood to Teens

Rewards to Encourage:
Spark an Interest in Reading

Mary Bold, Ph.D., CFLE
Department Chair and Professor, Digital Learning
& Teaching American College of Education,
Chicago, IL

In an effort to rear children without bribes, parents may overlook the opportunity to spark an interest with the short term use of an incentive. Besides, we often misuse the term "bribe." A bribe should be understood to mean seeking to get a person, by the use of money or something of value, to do something that is dishonest, unethical, or illegal. The use of rewards or incentives involves seeking to encourage someone to do something that would be desired by or beneficial to them. Many of us work for an incentive, money. Children often engage in summer work for the same incentive.

For limited occasions with specific goals, children can be encouraged to achieve things that will benefit them. For example, a reading habit may need a boost with some children. The need may come at a transition time in reading ability or may arise during a break from school.

Research has long questioned what motivates people (including children) to take on a new task or learn something new. Intrinsic motivation, meaning that the individual acts because of internal rewards, has typically been studied as separate from achievement motivation, but some research suggests these two constructs may be connected.[1] For example, the child who receives recognition for achievement may be stimulated to pursue the next level of achievement or skill, and at that level the reward may be internalized. In general, research tells us that self-determination, or making choices, leads to more creativity.[2] More specific to children's reading, recent research suggests that motivation and reading skill are related, so that an increase in one can spur an increase in the other.[3] Parents' beliefs about their children's reading also can influence how children develop as readers.[4]

To create interest in summer reading for my school-aged children, I announced an ancillary reward system to the local library's program for individual reading. My children had participated in the library program in previous years and the reward of pizza coupons was, by then, routine. To create new interest, I offered hard, cold cash. The bounty was a penny a page. My children made a dash for the thickest books on the library shelves. One hundred pages? No problem: come collect your dollar. Two hundred pages? Impressive; your reward is two dollars. When the novelty wore off, happily the reading habit did not. The money launched the summer's reading and the sheer joy of reading became reward enough.

Our culture has cautioned parents against rewarding children for desired behavior. That caution is appropriate, but sometimes we all need an incentive and the wise parent knows when to use a small reward to spark an interest or initiate a new behavior. The incentive may vary from the planning of a new fun activity to the return to an old family favorite tradition. Some parents worry that children will later ask to be "paid" for doing something else that is asked of them. That kind of a response can easily be turned off by merely saying, with a smile, "Wouldn't it be nice if we all got paid for every little thing we do? Now, please go ahead and do it."

What creative activity or new habit might your child be encouraged to discover by the short term use of an incentive?

References

[1] Puca, R. M., & Schmalt, H-D. (1999). Task enjoyment: A mediator between achievement motives and performance. *Motivation and Emotion, 23*(1), 15-29.

[2] Deci, E. L. (1992) On the nature and functions of motivation theories. *Psychological Science, 3*(3), 167-171.

[3] Morgan, P. L., & Fuchs, D. (2007). Is there a bidirectional relationship between children's reading skills and reading motivation? *Exceptional Children, 73*, 165-183.

[4] Lynch, J., Anderson, J., Anderson, A., & Shapiro, J. (2006). Parents beliefs about young children's literacy development and parents' literacy behaviors. *Reading Psychology, 27*, 1-20.

Taking Candy from Strangers

Mary Bold, Ph.D., CFLE
Department Chair and Professor, Digital Learning & Teaching
American College of Education, Chicago, IL

No greater fear can face a parent than realizing how vulnerable one's child is to predators. We know that children cannot fully understand the threat of a predator or abductor, and so our warnings to "never take candy from strangers" not only are ineffective, they can actually introduce a new concept unintentionally: candy is available from strangers.

I always was confident that I knew the best protection for young children: close supervision. Children cannot be fully taught to protect themselves because an adult who seeks to lure them away or into a behavior can be successful. Adult predators are highly skilled at convincing even the "best trained" children to do something for which parents have warned them. Even though I put my faith in supervision rather than training my children, I knew that they would hear the warning of "never take candy from strangers." The phrase is in our culture and cannot be avoided. My response was simple: I told my children, "If a stranger tells you there's candy for you someplace, you just come straight to me, because I will give you DOUBLE candy." My daughter told me years later that she was grateful for the double candy promise. She remembered it as being something her Mama had in reserve for her. She also recalled that when she was old enough to understand the warnings about strangers and candy, she felt loved–knowing that a parent had given her a strategy for leaving a temptation (which never arose, thank heaven).

This story from my family life highlights the importance of looking past stereotypes about "stranger danger." Actually, my daughter was not among the most vulnerable as a young child and also not among the most vulnerable from strangers. U.S. Department of Justice[1] research corrects these stereotypes: most nonfamily abductions involve youngsters age 12 and older, and the majority of nonfamily abductions are perpetrated by adults who are known to the child. Our stereotype of young children vulnerable to strangers is driven largely by the media stories that we take in. News coverage of abductions and kidnappings is compelling and memorable and the coverage of events surrounding very young children is greater, at least nationally. One stereotype is correct: the majority of abductions occur away from the child's home–on the street, on playgrounds, and in remote areas where there are few witnesses.

As parents consider how best to protect children from threats, including abduction and kidnapping, they can arm themselves with accurate information about the threats themselves as well as professionals' advice about what to do. For example, understanding the higher threat to adolescents can inform parents and school professionals about strategies to teach this age group about self-protection. For all ages of children, safety lessons should focus on how to interpret messages from all the people around them, not just strangers. None of these facts about nonfamily abduction can be called comforting, but the wise parent knows to appreciate that the statistics can be improved because the majority of victims are old enough to learn about self-protection. Our society and media no doubt will continue to emphasize the incorrect stereotypes, but families can act to reduce some of the threats by knowing the facts and guiding children with developmentally appropriate strategies.

Open discussion about personal safety is advised for all ages of children and many of the same concepts apply across the ages, but the language must be appropriate to the child's developmental stage. Emphasis on action, not mottos, is appropriate for all ages. So, rather than warning of "stranger danger," parents should warn of the action of anyone trying to touch the child or lure the child away. The young child can be guided to protect "my own body," emphasizing that the child can come to the parent about anyone trying to touch him or her. Teens may feel they are not likely to be assaulted and therefore react negatively to a parent's warning of vulnerability. A different strategy may be appropriate: using the label "predator" or "criminal" to describe potential threats to teens.

Family rules such as "Travel with a Friend" and "Stay in Touch" are appropriate for all ages, although for the young child, the friend is likely to be a parent. Teens should be asked to share information about where they are going and when they expect to return. Sometimes teens feel invasion of privacy and mistrust are being communicated. The wise parent takes time to present the request in a way that communicates caring, such as, "If I know that your plan is to be home by 11, and you are not here, then I will know that you need help and I can provide it." Parents can also offer teens strategies for checking in with "home base" without drawing attention from peers. For example, a cell phone ring or text message can be sent to the parent without even requiring a conversation. With emphasis on personal safety, a parent's request for a check-in is more likely to be honored.

For other ideas you might want to consider, here are several specific suggestions offered by April Brooks, with the FBI's Crimes Against Children Unit.[2]

- Initially, it is good to set ground rules with your child; an important and basic rule: "You don't go anywhere with anyone unless your parents know about it. The parent needs to know where the child is at all times."
- Establish a code with your child, so that if someone asks your child that they have come to pick them up for Mon or Dad, the child can ask the person what the code is. If not known, immediately and quickly go and tell another person who has authority.
- Abductors will often first try to establish a relationship with a child. Consequently, advise your child that if there is something about a situation that does not feel right, "it probably isn't." Let your parent or a trusted adult know about it.
- Let your child know that adults should not ask them for help. Adults should ask other adults for help, not children. If someone asks a child to help find their dog, or give them directions, the child should know that something is wrong. Do not go with them.

- Other child safety tips can be found at www.fbi.gov on "View Our Kids Page," or at www.missingkids.com, the National Center for Missing & Exploited Children, at their "Know the Rules" link.

A few other useful ideas are provided by Vanessa Rasmussen:[3]
- Instruct children not to answer the door when alone by themselves, or indicate to others on the phone that they are alone.
- Be sure your child know their full name, your address and phone number, and how to call for police assistance.
- Accompany your children for any door-to-door activities such as Halloween or for school fund raising activities.
- Instruct your child not to approach a car unless they know the occupants.
- Teach children "to scream, run away, and tell a trusted adult if anyone attempts to touch or gram them."

Our children are very special to us and we are well advised to alert them to dangers that can be very real for them.

References

[1] Finkelhor, D., Hammer, H., & Sedlak, A. J. (2002, October). Nonfamily abducted children: National estimates and characteristics. National Incidence Studies of Mission Abducted, Runaway, and Thrownaway *Children*. Washington DC: Department of Justice, Office of Juvenile Justice and Delinquency Prevention.

[2] Family Education Network, *Child abduction: What every parent needs to know.* Retrieved Dec. 20, 2010, from http://life.familyeducation.com/stranger-safety/safety/36556.html.

[3] Rasmussen, Vanessa. (2004). *Child abduction.* Retrieved Sept. 26, 2007, from http://www.childfun.com/index.php/providers/general/761-child abduction.html.

Don't Go to Acapulco

Anne C. Chambers, M.Ed, CFLE
Certified School Psychologist, Head of School,
Indian Creek School, Crownsville, Maryland

I was making a speech to parents about expectations of children and party codes or rules. The time came for questions and a mother raised her hand. When I called on her, she said, "Last year, my husband and I went to Acapulco for our anniversary. We couldn't pull our seventeen year old son out of school for a whole week so we left him home. He is an excellent student and a very sensible and responsible boy. When we got home, he was still trying to clean up the house and make repairs because a bunch of kids had showed up and trashed the house. My question is how do you keep your kid from having a party if you are out of town?"

My answer was, "Don't go to Acapulco. Don't go *anywhere* until your kid goes to college." She didn't like the answer. It may sound blunt, however, with rare exceptions, it may be the right advice. Similar experiences of houses being trashed by friends of the teen are not at all uncommon.

Think of it this way. Assume the issue isn't really *your* child's behavior. Your child is a sensible, ethical, responsible, intelligent, moral young man or woman and you know deep in your heart that he or she will not do anything risky or stupid. But you can't be certain about the other kids.

Regarding leaving your child alone at home, another family therapist stated, "I can attest that the issue is one of the most diffi-cult—and wrenching—you'll make as a parent."[1] And mind you, he was merely talking about leaving your teens home alone during the day, while parents work.

Obviously, there are things you can do to decrease the possi-bility for disaster if you have to leave a teenager home alone, but no such attempt can be guaranteed to be successful. One idea is to **have a responsible adult come to the house** and stay with your son or daughter. However, the "adults" most easily found are college-aged older sib-lings, neighbors or friends. They may be too young. They may not have enough assertive experience and personal power to keep things safe, even if they are responsible enough not to party with the teenagers. The same thing goes for other young adults and for a very elderly grandma. Teachers will sometimes house-sit but increasingly they are turning down such jobs because of liability concerns.

Finding someone truly responsible to stay with your teen won't be an easy task. The person you appoint needs to accept a great deal of responsibility and must place his or her interests second for the time involved. Think about the decisions such a person might have to make. Suppose a group of students show up and your son or daughter begs, "Please don't embarrass me by sending them away." Suppose the "house-sitter" *does* send the kids away and your teen gets angry and defies the house-sitter in some way? Then again, what will that person do in the case of a real disaster – a fire, an accidental poisoning, or an alcohol or drug problem? Suppose your young person goes out and just doesn't come back? How soon will the sitter call you? Will he or she call the police?

If your adolescent has fairly young, **active grandparents who have the stamina to hold the line, they might be able to do the job**. It is actually much easier and safer to leave young children with grandpar-ents and friends than it is teens. Nevertheless, relatives speak with more innate authority because they can anticipate your wishes better than a stranger. They also speak with the power of being family members.

You can **send your son or daughter to stay with a friend,** but make certain that you know how much time the friend's parents are actually around. Talk with the other parent ahead of time and be sure there is a common understanding about curfews and rules. You want to know that if your child cooks up some story to escape the surrogate family's supervision he or she isn't going to get away with it. These should be people you know really well or they will feel strange enforcing rules with your son or daughter.

If you must be able to travel during the school year, some might **consider putting their teenager in boarding school,** if they can afford it. Good boarding schools have worked hard to develop systems for constraining, caring for and supervising young people. **Another possibility is summer camp** for the time when you are going to be out of town, if the planned trip happens to fall during the summer. Well designed summer wilderness camps can help your teen to become more responsible while keeping him or her safe and supervised.

The long and short of it is this. Raising children is a tremendous responsibility, which includes a great deal of monitoring. Their birth certificates have no "vacation rights" attached. If you have children between the ages of 13 and 18, anticipate doing all of your traveling *as a family* for these years. Spend lots of time planning that trip to Acapulco, but you might want to put it off until your teen goes away to college.

Reference

[1] Kendrick, Carleton (nd). *Teens home alone.* Retrieved Dec. 20, 2010, from: http://life.familyeducation.com/teen/home-alone/36143.html.

Sex and Tweeners

Diana Stephens, Ph.D., PPSC, CFLE
Assistant Professor, Counseling and Guidance,
California Lutheran University,
Thousand Oaks, CA

Pre-teens have taught me how to talk about sex. They want to talk about it. They can handle the truth. They hear that sex is fun, it's exciting, and it feels good. By ten or eleven they have seen enough of it on television, in movies, and through video-games to know there is something really great about sex. It's also serious business, tricky to navigate, and filled with pitfalls. They are ready to hear far more than parents are comfortable sharing. When it comes to sex education and "tweeners" (that time between childhood and teenager), sooner is better than later. Ongoing conversation is more supportive than school films, parental warnings, and lectures. Healthy sexual development involves the process of building enjoyable conversations and satisfying their curiosities.

The literature confirms that parents are often hesitant and unprepared in talking about sex with their children. They wonder where to start and when to begin ("Parent Survival Kit"[1]). Some very useful resources to turn for guidance are the MissouriFamilies.org, with a useful article by Gonzales[2] and the "Parents' Sex Ed Center."[3]

In today's world, talking about sex is more than a one-time event. The topics of conversation are far more complex than menstrual cycles, wet dreams, and pregnancy. Tweeners are far more advanced in their exposure to sex at younger ages. In our fast-paced world of technology, childhood is becoming shorter. All too often children are ready to learn more and sooner than we parents are prepared to say or to model.

As a parent myself, I am all too familiar with the challenges of sex and children. Long after my own child entered puberty, I developed a weekend workshop for pre-teens and their parents. The topic was adolescent sexual development, and the focus was parent/child communication. This experience quickly taught me that preteens are far more aware than we would like to think. They also are more open to the subject of sex than their parents.

I can still hear the fifth grader in the workshop giving me advice on talking with his parents about sex. It was a morning when I was alone with the tweeners and we were brain-storming about all they already knew about sex. We created a "freedom day" where we could ask any question, share any story, say or write any word we wanted without getting in trouble. I shared some of the words used to talk about sex when I was young. The more we laughed about this together, the more they told me.

After I learned the latest jargon for body parts, kissing, and having sex, I asked the tweeners for suggestions on how I would teach this to their parents later that night. At that moment, a ten year old boy turned to me and said "we can talk about anything in this room and we won't be embarrassed. But when you talk with my parents tonight, go slow and don't laugh, because they aren't ready for this yet." The others giggled and nodded in agreement.

I felt wiser after listening to these tweeners, and I gained a deeper respect for how willing they are to communicate when we adults are ready to listen without judgment. I say, let's lighten up, drop our fear of saying something wrong, and start conversations about sex. Seize the opportunities in daily life to talk about the overt and covert sexual messages when we hear the music, see the billboards, and watch the commercials and movies. I suspect it will ease tension and produce some good laughs.

Give a life-long gift to your child. Put on your boots, fasten your seatbelts, and learn how to create honest, fun-loving conversations about sex. It will guide them for a lifetime.

References

[1] Walsh, D. (2004). *Why do they act that way? A survival guide to the adolescent brain for you and your teen.* NY: Free Press.

[2] Gonzales, J. (2007). *Which type of sex education is right for your teen?* Edited by K. Allen, Director, Center on Adolescent Sexuality, Pregnancy and Parenting. University of Missouri Extension. Retrieved Dec. 20, 2010, from http://www.missourifamilies.org. Follow link to Adults & Children, then Adolescents Features Articles, and scroll down to the article.

[3] *Parents' Sex Ed Center.* Washington DC, with useful links to Topics & Issues and Advocates for Youth, Retrieved March 23, 2007, from http://www.advocates foryouth.org/parents/.

Preparing Daughters for the World of Boys: Wisdom for Fathers

Scott Stanley Hall, Ph.D., CFLE
Associate. Professor, Family Studies,
Ball State University, Muncie, IN

Being the father of three young girls (ranging in age from eight to 11), I often shudder at the thought of boys taunting, flirting with, and perhaps even groping them. I often ponder how I can help prepare my daughters for the world of boys. Having been a boy myself, I can attest that boys are not completely lacking of merit and virtue–but as a father I find myself somewhat prejudiced against the male counterparts to my unsuspecting daughters. Yet, efforts to turn my daughters against boys might only create suspicion toward me, and against other males that likely will be important to them in their near and distant futures. Promoting a positive but cautious perception of boys can be a challenging balance to find.

Research indicates that involved fathers play a critical role in contributing to daughters' healthy psychological and social development, including the promotion of self esteem, social competence, and psychological maturity.[1] Applying Erikson's Theory of Psychosocial Development, scholars have suggested that fathers play an even more important role than mothers in bridging a daughter's family identity and bond to a social identity and connection outside of the family.[2] Part of that identity will be manifested in and shaped by interaction with male peers. In addition, a father is typically the first male figure a daughter loves and admires, and thus he serves as a template for future male-female interactions and relationships.[3] In short, fathers have a unique and valuable opportunity to influence a daughter's self image and how she interacts with the world of boys.

I try to spend one-on-one time with each of my daughters in a variety of formal and informal ways. I have sometimes made it a point during these occasions to mention how my daughters will gradually attract more and more attention from boys and that such attention is not always what it seems. Sometimes the boys just want to be around a cute girl, sometimes they want a kiss or a hug, and sometimes they do want to be a real friend. We talk about knowing and identifying the differences among these motivations. I also try to teach about insisting that girls be treated as people, not objects; that girls should not kiss (or be otherwise physical with) a boy just to keep his attention; and that being smart and a role model for positive behavior are just as, if not more, important than being pretty and fun.

After such a discussion with my seven-year-old daughter, she told me she understood, and then said, "...but I'm still just a kid." She was right, and fathers have to be careful not to say too much too early about this topic in ways that can scare their daughters, or vilify the opposite sex. Boys will be a big part of girls' lives—in one way or another—and creating a deep-seeded suspicion toward them may inhibit healthy relationships with them. However, waiting until puberty to teach these lessons is undoubtedly too late. They need to hear them many times in many different ways so that they internalize the messages. How tragic it is when a naïve young (or old) girl puts up with demeaning treatment and abuse from a boy whom she believes likes or loves her because of the attention he gives her. How tragic it is when girls starve or sexualize themselves to attract meaningless attention from boys who have only selfish interests at heart.

Fathers, take advantages of those teaching moments—while you are alone together, when you watch a television program or movie that includes messages about girls and about relationships, when they ask questions about their classmates, when they ask you about your relationship with their mother—to help your daughter seek appropriate and healthy attention from boys, and to feel confident to stand on her own when she is not the focus of every boy around her. Be sure to mention your daughter's personal attributes that go beyond her pretty eyes and her sweet smile. Well meaning fathers may say too much about how cute their daughters are and not enough about other reasons they value them as people. Mothers can help by encouraging and supporting the daughter's father to be active in this important process, even if he has to endure discomfort that can arise by broaching these subjects.

In summary, fathers of daughters should:

- realize that a warm, accepting father helps a daughter feel confident, important, and worthy of positive male attention;
- explain why boys give attention to girls and how to identify selfish and exploitative motives;
- emphasize that a boy who genuinely cares about a girl will not expect her to abandon her personal or family values and comfort;
- encourage their daughters to value their positive characteristics that have nothing to do with their looks; and,
- convey these messages early and often through words and treatment of their daughters.

These important lessons may come across differently from a father than a mother (not to say she shouldn't be sending or reinforcing them) in that the father has direct experience in the world of boys. Daughters typically yearn for a father's attention and can learn from him on how to feel valued–especially as a girl.[4] Fathers, give your daughter the attention she craves, which she'll seek elsewhere if she doesn't get it from her Dad.

References

[1] Morgan, J. V., Wilcoxon, S. A., & Satcher, J. F. (2003). The father-daughter relationship inventory: A validation study. *Family Therapy, 30,* 77-93.

[2] Snarey, J. (1993). *How fathers care for the next generation: A four-decade study.* Cambridge, MA: Harvard University Press.

[3] Perkins, R. M. (2001). The father-daughter relationship: Familial interactions that impact a daughter's style of life. *College Students Journal, 35,* 616-627.

[4] Hall, S. S., & Tift, J. N. (2007). The daddy-daughter dance: Insights for father-daughter relationships. In S. E. Brotherson, & J. M. White (Eds.), *Why fathers count.* Harriman, TN: Men's Studies Press.

To Know Him is to Love Him[1]

Anne C. Chambers, M.Ed, CFLE
Certified School Psychologist, Head of School,
Indian Creek School, Crownsville, Maryland

Have you ever asked your teenaged daughter "Do you know this boy that asked you out?"

You might get an answer, "Of course I know him. He is in my geometry class."

Case closed, right? Wrong! What you mean by "know" and what your daughter means by "know" are frequently two very different things. And in your daughter's eyes, "knowing" the boy may not be very far from loving him.

Think about what you would expect your daughter to know about a person that she "knows." Is he a nice boy? Does he seem respectful of others' rights? Does he seem to be honest? Does he have actual conversations with your daughter? Does he do well in school? Is he kind? Does he seem to be a risk taker? Does he have his driver's license? Have you heard anything about his driving? Do you think (or have you heard) that he uses alcohol or drugs?

Your daughter, on the other hand, may say she "knows" someone when that person is what an adult would call "an acquaintance." Your daughter knows that he is in her geometry class. She knows he is good looking and there is status attached to going out with him. She knows she is a sophomore and he is a senior. Maybe he tells her that nobody understands him but she is different. Maybe he tells her that his parents are mean to him; that he is in trouble in school or with the police because someone set him up; that his old girlfriend was flirting with other guys so he dumped her. Your daughter will probably believe every word.

She might not think to question why he is taking geometry as a senior. (Maybe she would think his schedule was too full in the previous years.) She will say she "knows" the boy if all he does is say hello to her each day. Frequently, teenaged girls are very flattered if an older boy pays attention to them. A boy who is in the popular crowd is especially attractive to a girl who isn't. By the time she finds out things about him that she knows you wouldn't like, she may already be enamored. She feels she knows him well enough to fall head over heels for him and won't recognize that he is using her to make someone else jealous or, just because he can.

Talk to your teenagers during times when emotions are low and before a specific somebody is in the picture. Both boys and girls can benefit from thinking and talking in advance about the kinds of traits they might look for in friends and in those in whom they have a romantic interest. It is especially difficult to have any influence on your teen after he or she has met someone and started to establish a relationship, so this kind of discussion should go on frequently in small doses when there is nothing riding on the discussion. Lectures are not helpful. Discussions about friends, about what is valuable in a friendship can be triggered by TV shows, even computer games. Drop the subject if it garners a negative reaction and try again another day. Teenagers DO listen to their parents and value their advice as long as it isn't an "in face" kind of exchange.[2] Make sure Dad is involved as well as Mom. Research shows that girls pay a lot of attention to Dad's opinions, especially involving sexual behavior.

Help your teens learn what it means to "know" someone and why it is important to know well anyone with whom he or she will be spending a lot of time.

References

[1] Spector, Phil. (1958). *To Know Him is to Love Him,* a number one hit by his vocal group, The Teddy Bears, in 1958, written when Spector was a high school senior and sung by a sophomore, Annette Kleinbard–from information retrieved Dec. 20, 2010, from: http://www.songfacts.com/detail.php?id =2089. For more on other versions of the song recorded under the title, *To Know You is to Love You,* by Bobby Vinton and by Dolly Parton, Linda Ronstadt and Emmylou Harris, and another version, *To Know Her is to Love Her,* by the Beatles, see Wikipedia, retrieved Dec. 3, 2010 from http://en.wikipedia.org/wiki/To_Know_Him_Is_to_Love_Him.

[2] Faber, A., & Mazlish, E. (2001). *How to talk so kids will listen & listen so kids will talk.* NY: Piccadilly.

Recipe for Raising Helpless Teenagers: Overindulgence

David J. Bredehoft, Ph.D., CFLE
Professor of Psychology and Family Studies,
Concordia University, St. Paul, MN

What parent doesn't want the best for her child? What parent doesn't want to protect his child from the same painful struggles he had to face as a child? What parent doesn't want to make life easier for her son or daughter?

But could this strategy actually backfire? Yes. Goodhearted well-meaning parents sometimes, unknowingly, raise helpless teenagers.[1]

How do we know this? My colleagues and I conducted a study[2] with college students who were overindulged as children; mostly college freshman ages 18-19. We found some startling things. In particular, parents who overindulge were over-loving by giving their children too much attention; ones who didn't require chores or enforce rules, raised teenagers who believe that they are helpless incapable young adults.

When Parents Overindulge

The more parents overindulged their teens as children, the more the teens ascribed to the following self-defeating thoughts:[3]
- *I am incapable of dealing with most of life's problems.*
- *I give up on new things if I am not successful.*

When Parents are Over-loving and Give Too Much Attention

Teens whose parents were over-loving and gave them too much attention when they were growing up, also accept as true the following dysfunctional beliefs:[4]

- *People will not respect me if I do not do well all the time.*
- *It is a sign of weakness if a person asks for help.*
- *It is best to give up on your own interests in order to please other people.*

When Parents Don't Require Chores[5]

The more our sample indicated *that* their parents did not expect them to do chores when they were growing up, the more likely they believed in dysfunctional thinking:

- *There is little point in doing it at all if you cannot do something well.*
- *It probably indicates that he does not like me if someone disagrees with me.*
- *If a person I love doesn't love me I am nothing.*

When Parents Don't Enforce Rules

Finally, the more our college age sample said parents did not enforce rules when they were growing up, the more likely they accepted the following self-defeating thoughts:

- *I soon give up if I am not initially successful when trying to learn something new.*
- *I stop trying if I can't do a job the first time.*
- *I have problems because I cannot get down to work when I should.*

When parents overindulge they unknowingly train their children to become helpless; and, as a result, these overindulged children will have greater difficulty in reaching future vocational, educational, and monetary goals.[6]

It's Never Too Late

Don't give up hope! It is never too late to make adjustments in your parenting. Difficult, but not too late. Focus on one thing at a time and make small changes. When you hit resistance, which you will, be firm and resolved because after all, you want what is best for your children.

Tips for avoiding overindulgence

- Gradually give your teens freedom appropriate for their ages.
- Encourage your teens to solve their own problems. You may wish to coach them in exploring alternatives; however, let the bulk of the thinking and the final decision be theirs.

- Teach your teens to do chores and expect them to complete them, holding them accountable.
- Agree on a set of rules and enforce them.
- Decide which of your rules are negotiable and which are non-negotiable.

References

[1] Clarke, J. I., Dawson, C., & Bredehoft, D. J. (2004). *How much is enough? Everything you need to know to steer clear of overindulgence and raise likeable, responsible, and respectful children –from toddlers to teens.* NY: Marlowe & Co. NOTE: There is more help here about how to avoid overindulging.

[2] Bredehoft, D. J., & Leach, M. K. (2006). *Influence of childhood overindulgence on young adult dispositions – Executive summary: Study 2.* Retrieved January 24, 2007, from the How Much is Enough? web site at http://www.over indulgence.info/Research_Folder/Research.htm.

[3] Weissman, A. N., & Beck, A. T. (1978). Development and validation of the dysfunctional attitude scale: A preliminary investigation. Paper presented at the Annual Meeting of the American Educational Research Association, Toronto, Ontario.

[4] Whisman, M. A., & Friedman, M. A. (1998). Interpersonal problem behaviors associated with dysfunctional attitudes. *Cognitive Therapy & Research, 22(2)*, 149-160.

[5] Rossman, M. (2002). Involving children in household tasks: Is it worth the effort? *ResearchWORKs*, U. of MN, College of Education and Human Development.

[6] Bredehoft, D. J., Mennicke, S. A., Potter, A. M., & Clarke, J. I. (1998). Perceptions attributed by adults to parental overindulgence during childhood. *Journal of Marriage and Family Consumer Sciences Education, 16*, 3-17.

You cannot teach a child to take care of himself
unless you will let him try....He will make mistakes;
and out of these mistakes will come his wisdom.
–Henry Ward Beecher

Know Your Children's Friends

Judi Hirschinger Brenner, BA, CFLE
Administrative Support Coordinator, California
State University, Sacramento

Adolescence can be a trying time for parents. Teenagers tend to seek autonomy while parents strive to maintain a balance between granting freedom and providing needed guidance. Being fully aware of the several dangerous paths children may explore, many parents worry about their children's activities and with whom they associate. It has been recommended that parents benefit from getting acquainted with their children's friends.[1] But, adolescents can be very private, especially while seeking autonomy. Consequently, knowing everything about our children's friends is not likely. Fortunately, there are some things parents can do that can help their children thrive while experiencing adolescence. As parents we can only try to do our best, reassured by research which indicates, although adolescence may be a time of great change, most individuals enter adulthood without lasting negative effects.[2]

Interestingly, I discovered a powerful aid in helping families get through adolescence. Parents may benefit by developing positive relationships with their children's friends. Parents may gain more insight about and appreciation for their own children by taking the time to interact with their children's friends as opportunities arise. Sensing this when my children were young, my children knew that when their friends came over I was going to spend some time with them–getting to know their interests, where they lived, whether or not they had classes with my children, and information about their families. I also discovered how other teenagers can be very interesting people. Getting to know them can be quite rewarding, discovering qualities about them that prompted your own children to befriend them. In addition, it can help build positive relationships between parents, their own children, and their friends. There may come a time when parents have to rely on their relationships with their children's friends, which unexpectedly became necessary for me in my parenting role.

In addition to getting to know my children's friends, I also discovered an unexpected aid with this journey. I had decided when my children were young that I could at least keep track of the names and phone numbers of their friends. The friend may be someone they were going to visit or someone who merely called. So I started a list in our family phone book, recording all information I could possibly gather about any new friend. Caller ID can help make this easier for today's parents. I figured that the list could be useful for many occasions, such as: arranging for a surprise birthday party, checking with other parents about group activities, serving as a communication network in case of an accident involving a group of the friends, etc. The list became useful to me for another purpose, as related below.

My relationship with my children's friends and my list became very crucial when my then 15 year old daughter decided she did not want to come home from a friend's house one evening. At issue was what could be viewed as a minor though essential point. As a parent I was trying to set limits; she, like many adolescents, was seeking autonomy. She needed to come home, so I headed to her friend's house. To my surprise, nobody answered the door. I called from my cell phone, but no answer. Peeking through the windows revealed no sign of a soul, yet I had a strong feeling she was there. My many voice messages of concern and finally threatening to call the Sheriff provoked her to answer her cell phone. She stuck with her decision. In fact, she warned me that she may never come home. After all, she informed me, she could take care of herself. She could even make her own clothes she claimed. The phone call ended, and, baffled, I went home to figure out the next steps. By the time I reached her friend's mother, both girls were missing. As it turned out, they were gone for several days. Even though I felt they would most likely be safe and would soon come home, the unknown was unbearable. To me, my daughter was a runaway, and I could not have felt more helpless.

Back at home, I pulled out my phone list of friends and called every name, asking if they had seen my daughter. Initially, none of them admitted to knowing exactly where she was, but they seemed to think she was with friends, which was slightly comforting. I informed the school that she was missing and I kept close contact with the school's sheriff resource officer. Finally, after two long days of worrying, I got a call from my daughter. I had already planned to be very calm when she called. Somehow I knew she would call–our relationship seemed to be very positive, but obviously there was some tension, perhaps more than I had thought. However, I was a little surprised this time as to how the conversation panned out. She was not calling because she wanted to come home; she was calling because she was running out of clothes and wanted me to bag some up and put them on the porch for her to pick up. Although the sensitive side of me thought of my poor little daughter with dirty clothes, the rational side of me knew I could not support her decision. I expressed how happy I was that she called and that she was safe. However, I explained that I could not give her the clothes, and that I truly wanted her to come home so we could talk and resolve her concerns. She refused.

Finally, I received a call from a friend of hers who knew where the girls were, but I was never to tell who gave me the information. She had apparently tried to talk my daughter into going home, but she too was unsuccessful. She apologized for not calling sooner, but she was conflicted with her loyalty as a friend. I praised her for her strength and true friendship. I am eternally grateful that she knew me well enough to consider me a trustworthy and decent parent. This may never have happened if I had not taken the time to engage with my children's friends. My daughter and her friend were soon picked up by the school officer without much complication.

Our family was fortunate enough to have a positive ending to the story. The mother-daughter relationship, though tested, began to heal. Fortunately, what could have turned out to be devastating was only a minor run-away incident.

My list and friendships with the teenagers had been meaningful and helpful in many ways previously. However, I would like to attribute much of the resolution in the above experience to my list and the positive relationship I had established with my daughter's friend.

I am proud to say that my daughter is now doing superbly. Not only is she doing well emotionally, physically and socially, she was accepted to UC-Berkeley where she is currently in her senior year. She could not be more delightful. I asked her recently why she ran away. She said she did not really "run away," she simply wanted to stay out longer with her friends and didn't like being told what to do. At the time it sure seemed more serious than that to me. It's a good thing adolescence is a lot like childbirth. It can be very painful, but it soon fades into the past.

References

[1] American Psychological Association, APA Online, Public Affairs. (2001). *Protecting children from sexual abuse.* Retrieved February 1, 2008, from http://www.apa.org/releases/sexabuse/protect.html.

[2] Arnett, J. J. (2004). *Adolescence and emerging adulthood: A cultural approach* (2nd ed.). Upper Saddle River, NJ: Prentice Hall.

There are many ways to measure success; not the least of which is the way your child describes you when talking to a friend.
–Unknown

Chapter VIII
Wisdom to be "Read Aloud" Together

The following articles are grouped in this chapter because they sounded like they were meant to be read aloud together, by Mom or Dad with their children. The articles can provide a good opportunity to share and discuss the topics together. For several of them, the latter portion of the article may be directed more to the parent and could be skipped in the "reading aloud together" time.

Courage

SaraKay Smullens,* MSW, CFLE, LCSW, CGP
Philadelphia based clinical social worker, writer and
family life educator

The riddle of belonging is one of the greatest challenges our children will face from early in life on into their adult years. Issues regarding "fitting in" arise in every conceivable sphere: stepping onto a play field with the others kids, yet fearing you may not "measure up"; dealing with a classmate who expects help in cheating on a test; having your date or a friend skilled in bullying to get what he or she wants urge or insist on an unwise choice; experiencing the temptation to receive special favors or treatment others receive through manipulation and distortion. Examples can go on and on. How is an understanding of courage, as a guide to being the best that we can be, involved in these situations?

During my youthful years in the 1950's, my teachers taught that courage was standing up for what is "right." We also were taught that life is fair and that eventually anyone who acted cruelly and without courage would be punished. In this decade the popular kids had the "courage" to know our Country was the greatest, our School a winner, and our music, dance, and fashion choices the only "right" ones.

During my young adult years in the 1960s and 1970s I began to realize that courage and popularity do not go hand-in-hand. I saw that although my teachers had meant very well, they were wrong: life is not fair, cruelty very often goes unchecked, and courage is a very difficult, often lonely state to both achieve in oneself and to decipher in others. I was to learn, to my shock and dismay, that sometimes those who speak out the most charismatically, amassing the strongest following, are but malignant despots and bullies.

The decade of my youth had ignored a prevailing unfairness and injustice and all of the accompanying smoldering rage that would soon explode. As I matured, on the political front I saw that often those who were the most just, speaking the most precious truths, could be ignored. I saw, too, that often their honesty put their lives in jeopardy. And I saw political leaders both break laws and, as in one case, which history has now revealed involved distorted facts, send America's youth to an ill-fated Southeast Asian war.

In the personal sphere, I saw how often people were punished or ostracized by those who did not wish to see, hear or discuss their ideas. I saw parents punish children for ideas with which they did not agree. I saw partners withhold love and humiliate others when things did not go their way. I saw employers demand unethical conduct and torment or make life hard for those whose competence threatened them.

I learned that a well crafted façade, or the appearance of being good and noble, could betray the realities of one's way of treating others and attaining goals, disclosing mind-boggling contradictions. For example, external appearances alone do not reveal a highly educated, articulate, seemingly courageous father who bullies his wife and children; a verbal wife who speaks with seeming courage, but constantly manipulates her husband and children, with no regard for their health or well-being; a charming and intelligent mother who insists that her children live in the shadow of her courageous public persona; a charismatic employer, board chair, or political leader who "rules" through fear and intimidation.

I now know that true courage has absolutely nothing whatsoever to do with the need of my youth: to feel accepted. Nor does it have anything to do with winning popularity contests or achieving power over the lives and choices of others.

Courage cannot develop until an individual has achieved autonomy and is not afraid to stand alone. Such people know their own limitations and do not need power and control over others to compensate for them. It is this life art that brings clarity of thinking and vision. It is this life art that allows courage to stand for and speak for what is worthy.

But how is such a quality to be developed? Dr. Michael Popkin, a leading North American family educator and founder of the Active Parenting programs, investigated the origin of the concept through a linguistic stroke: "For children to gain confidence in themselves and to flourish, they need from their parents an essential quality of parenting–encouragement."[1] Popkin's theoretical basis is that of Individual Psychology, founded by the Viennese physician and sometime member of Freud's inner circle, Alfred Adler. For Adler, all antisocial behaviors stemmed from feelings of discouragement,[2] and this process could begin as early as the second half of the first year. Adler stated that certain types of individuals were especially prone to this discouragement, and the attendant "pathologically heightened feelings of inferiority" (p. 418)[3] including "children who have been robbed of their courage by a strict, unfair upbringing... and pampered children who have never developed courage" (p. 418-419).[3]

The paradox is that as much as courage may require that someone stand alone at the edges of society, it also is motivated by a deep feeling for one's culture and environment. Adler called this personality trait *social interest,* and saw it manifested in such traits as empathy (or feeling the pain or struggle of another), cooperation, and friendliness.[4] While courage may require a constructive self-reliance as a base, it cannot be activated until a person appreciates the art of mutual respect. Courage is seen in those with the ability to truly care about others and understand that sometimes the common good is far more important than any personal aspiration.

We can promote these conditions in our children by fostering feelings of being loved and of loving others in return. In this atmosphere we can encourage them to make their own little, simple choices which grow in complexity as time passes–and to become confident and feel pride in these choices. This growing security will help them become aware of the differences between what is good and honest and what is not. In this way, children learn to recognize those they come into contact with who urge them toward attitudes and behaviors that will not serve them well. They internalize an understanding of the importance of saying "no" to some people and some activities and attitudes in order to say "yes" to life. They develop the confidence that leads to the courage to "stand alone" when necessary, knowing that this choice is the only way to live that is right for them.

* NOTE: *SaraKay Smullens (www.sarakaysmullens.com), a licensed diplomate in clinical social work, is certified as a group psychotherapist, American Group Psychotherapy Association.* SaraKay authored: *Whoever Said Life is Fair?: A Guide to Growing Through Life's Injustices,* a best-seller, and *Setting YourSelf Free: Breaking the Cycle of Emotional Abuse in Family, Friendship, Love and Work.* Her paper, "Achieving an Emotional Sense of Direction," is on her website, and described in greater detail in an article: "The Codification and Treatment of Emotional Abuse in Structured Group Therapy," in the *International Journal of Group Psychotherapy* (January, 2010). Her public papers, documenting a lifetime of community advocacy, are archived at the University of Pennsylvania. Her personal papers are in a special collection at Goucher College.

References

[1] Popkin, M.H. & Albert, L. (1987). *Quality parenting*. NY: Random House.

[2] Eirik, S. (2001). The courage to love: Social interest and sexuo-morphological meaning. *Journal of Individual Psychology, 57(2)*, 158-172.

[3] Adler, A. (1988). The child's inner life and a sense of community. *Journal of Individual Psychology, 44(4)*, 417-423.

[4] Leak, G.K. & Williams, D.E. (1989). Relationship between social interest, alienation, and psychological hardiness. *Journal of Individual Psychology, 45(3)*, 369-375.

Courage is resistance to fear, mastery of fear, not absence of fear.
–Mark Twain

Loyalty in the Family: What It Is and Is Not

SaraKay Smullens, MSW, CFLE, LCSW, CGP, Philadelphia based clinical social worker and family life educator, author of "Whoever Said Life Is Fair? A Guide to Growing Through Life's Injustices" and "Setting YourSelf Free: Breaking the Cycle of Emotional Abuse in Family, Friendship, Love and Work."

Loyalty is a common subject, one relating to expectations of our feelings, attitudes and actions in our workplace, in relationships between friends and family, and in all of our important pursuits. Loyalty in the family is something we tend to take for granted, between parents, as well as by children in expression to their parents.

Yet, loyalty is one of the most misunderstood, misrepresented, and distorted concepts in family living and elsewhere. These ambiguities hold the potential of grave harm, for misguided expectations of loyalty can and are used effectively in emotionally abusive expression in all important relationships.

Ironically, in most cases, those causing harm are unaware of the damage they do. They merely act with the detrimental expectation that they have learned during their formative years. They contend that to be loyal means that family members, employees, citizens should never disagree with the beliefs or decisions of those considered leaders–be they parents, life partners, bosses, or community and political leaders.

Many of us, whether in the family or the work place, have seen how this expectation is imposed and continued through tactics of fear and intimidation. If imposed belief systems are questioned in any way, the result may be rage, punishment, isolation, rejection and/or humiliation. The Jacobson Institute of Ethics, in their Six Pillars of Character, clearly indicates that such behavior results from misunderstood or misused loyalty.[1]

Parenting is the most precious of gifts. Those who do it well understand that parenting is not the expectation, by virtue of loyalty, that agreement with all of our ideas is owed to us by our sons and daughters, merely for bringing them into the world, or for all we have done in caring for them. Although, as Boszormenyi-Nagy and Spark have pointed out, genuine filial (child to parent) loyalty does develop from genuine parental care, this is as a natural and not a coerced result.[2] In many families, the opposite of *loyal* is termed *ungrateful*, an unhappy mixing of separate concepts. As Charles Lutes stated, "Loyalty is something that cannot be bought. Loyalty must be earned. Too many parents try to buy the child's love and fail to give of themselves, and this too often ends in a bitter disillusionment for the parents."[3]

Neither is quality parenting about the expectation that our children should make us happy, fill in our gaps, and bring us pleasure and joy. It is not about our children showing us "loyalty" by affirming our own beliefs, making them their own, and in this way validating our own lives. The job of parents, instead, is to raise children who know how to stand on their own two feet, take care of themselves, and care for and about others. This occurs when parents work hard to understand the importance of the intricate balance of love and limits in the formative years. It occurs when parents understand and work toward their ultimate goal: "letting go." The end goal of quality parenting is to give our sons and daughters permission to live their own lives, make their own decisions, and learn from their own experiences and mistakes.

Good parenting involves the ability to applaud, as Michael Popkin stresses,[4] to encourage our daughters and sons as they journey toward loving others, their own chosen partners and children, even more deeply than they love us. Good parenting necessitates the ability to let others take our place as "the most important ones" in our children's lives. Good parenting also involves the clear expression of family rules, which as Leibig and Green have noted, "are often ambiguous, yet [form] powerful influences on both adaptive and maladaptive behavior" (p. 111).[5]

When these qualities of parenting are accomplished, so is the capacity for loyalty. This means that our children develop the ability to think clearly and disagree even with those who are near and dear to them. It allows the development of the ability to respect another's beliefs, even when they are not one's own.

Loyalty is the ability to show respect and caring, but also to think through another's stated beliefs to see if they are compatible with one's own ethics, morality, and individual need and direction. It also is the ability to assess when another's stated "beliefs" have no authenticity, but are instead a cover for a dictatorial and abusive or needful personality; and hopefully the attendant ability to find the courage to leave such a relationship in order to avoid grave harm.

The capacity to embrace the concept of loyalty to or from another involves an important and hard won ability to be loyal to oneself, abiding by what is felt and believed to be true and correct. Those who achieve this capability can experience loyalty from our children as well as serve as a model for their lives. In this way we both nurture and protect a precious and priceless gift: our children's ability to express and expect loyalty where and when it is appropriate and fitting for them to do so.

References

[1] Josephson Institute of Ethics. (2006). *The six pillars of character.* Los Angeles: Josephson Institute. Retrieved February 13, 2007, from http://www.jose phsoninstitute.org/MED/MED-2sixpillars.htm.

[2] Boszormenyi-Nagy, I. & Spark, G. (1973). *Invisible loyalties.* NY: Brunner/ Mazel.

[3] Lutes, C.F. *Lecture 49: Loyalty in Life.* Retrieved February 13, 2007, from http://www.maharishiphotos.com/lecture49.html.

[4] Popkin, M.A. & Albert, L. (1987). *Quality parenting.* NY: Random House.

[5] Leibig, A. L. & Green, K. (1999). The development of family loyalty and relational ethics in children. *Contemporary Family Therapy, 21(1),* 89-112.

Taking Back Family Meal Times

Donna Raycraft, M.A, CFLE
Executive Director, community agency,
Concord, NH

Most of us are searching for ways to make our families stronger, to give our children a sense that they belong and are important to us, to find time to teach our children values and skills that they will need when they go out into the world as adults. The easiest place to accomplish all of those goals is right under our collective noses, and so often it is being sacrificed in the name of busyness and business and complicated family lives.

Parents' long work days, children's sports schedules, favorite television programs, the telephone, texting, games, and even the search for quiet time have inadvertently made family meal times almost obsolete.

There was a time when families ate together three times a day. They all gathered around the fire in the cave after hunting and gathering; or they gathered around the large table before during and after working in the fields; or they stopped working and schooling when the factory whistle blew. They left work and the places that were stressful and challenging, and they gathered together with people who were safe and supportive. They nourished their bodies at the same time they nourished their souls. When their stomachs registered the need for food, their souls registered the need for a connection to where they belonged and where they were needed and where they were valued. After receiving that nourishment and that connection, they were better able to return to the bush or the field or the factory or the classroom and resume their assignments.

Now our fields are often too far away to journey home at midday, and their demands sometimes don't allow us to gather either at the beginning of the day or the end of the day with our soul-nurturers. Our schools are so busy that students are allowed only 20 minutes to gather their food, find a place to be with their friends, eat their food, and clean up at mid-day.

Our definition of well-rounded children requires that they participate in everything from scouts to gymnastics to debate team to sports. We've filled after school hours with these activities and are now demanding more time for them. The only disposable time left is mealtime.

Developing good conversation skills is vital to being successful in relationships, in school and in the work place. The family mealtime is the best place to learn those skills. Conversation at mealtime leads to more than just developing good communication skills. It also is an opportunity for families to gather together as a group and develop a sense of belonging with each other.

Meal preparation and clean-up can also bring a family closer together. It gives them a daily shared purpose and extra time to chat. Four-year-olds can take great pride in their jobs of clearing dishes from the table. Twelve-year-olds are very capable of meal planning.

To make the best use of our time together, we might want to make it a rule not to fight at the table. Differences of opinion are fine and should even be encouraged. However, arguments and conflict should be given separate time and attention. It is very tempting in our busy lives to use eating time as a place to squeeze in grievances with one another. However, eating time should be pleasant and something to look forward to.

Regular family meal times can help bring order and consistency to each family member's life. Family meals teach children about behavior in a social group. Children can watch parents and older siblings interacting at mealtime. They can have models of effective communications styles and acceptable habits at the table, as long as parents don't have unreasonable expectations of table manners. Children can learn manners much more effectively by watching their elders.

So clear off the table, put the dishes in their places, turn off the television, and nourish your family's souls as well as their bodies.

Note: For further support for the benefit of family mealtime, see: Doherty, William. (2010). *Research on the benefits of family meals.* Retrieved on December 12, 2010, from: http://www.barillaus.com/Pages/Expert-Advice-Detail.aspx?AdviceArticleID=2&AdviceAuthor=Dr.-William-D oherty.

The best things you can give children, next to good
habits, are good memories.
–*Sydney J. Harris*

The Practice Credit Card

Mary Bold, Ph.D., CFLE
Department Chair and Professor, Digital Learning & Teaching,
American College of Education, Chicago, IL

The credit card has become a permanent fixture in U.S. family economics today. Besides providing a convenient means for paying for purchases, the credit card can serve as the first building block of a credit history. The downside is well documented: credit cards can also stimulate high debt. Young adults are especially at risk of generating debt when they turn 18 and find themselves deluged with credit card offers. For many young people, this risk arises on college campuses where students react to marketing pressures without consulting parents or other financial advisors.[1,2]

Credit card debt as well as credit card solicitations present a growing problem in the U.S., especially for young people.[3] Parents can address some behaviors surrounding money management with their children before they finish high school. It is important to discuss with them several features of a credit card such as the importance of paying the balance in full each month to avoid ridiculously high interest charges on unpaid balances, as well as paying on time to avoid stiff late charges, which then have a negative effect on your credit history. Let them know that all of this information gets reported to nationally affiliated credit bureaus, so that this part of one's life is not private, and that you even have to call the company issuing the credit in order to decline their sharing information about you with other companies. Given all of this, the following example shows how parents can learn from their children's own strategies to manage funds wisely.

To prepare my daughter for what would surely be a lifetime of credit card usage, and especially to make her credit-savvy before she left home, I intentionally sought a credit card for her at the tender age of 15. A local department store issued the card in my name and permitted my daughter to carry the card and use it for purchases on her own. We agreed that she would use the card for all of her clothing purchases, which would require considerable planning to last the entire year. The allowance was $50 a month. The rule was that a monthly bill of $50 or less would be paid by Mom. But if the monthly bill was even a penny over $50, the bill would belong to her–to be paid out of her own savings.

With your own children, you might want to vary this plan in terms of an amount that suits your budget and the type of credit card. With a major credit card, an additional one issued to you with your child as an authorized user, you might even budget the entire monthly expenses of your child, and possibly pay that amount on the credit card each month so the child has a credit balance to work from, besides possibly giving them some cash for minor incidentals. Then as my daughter did for clothing, your child could budget their expenses throughout the year, saving funds from one month for use when larger special purchases are planned. Another option, in time, might be to open a checking account for your child along with being an authorized user on one of your credit cards and learn the fuller scope of financial management–whatever makes sense to you.

My credit card plan for my daughter was successful–but not in the way I imagined. She was worried about that one-penny-over-the-limit rule and so developed her own strategy for safety. On the first of every month, she went to the Customer Service desk and used the credit card to purchase a $50 gift certificate. Not only did she never go over the monthly limit, she also found her own way to plan for the year. She stockpiled several of those certificates in order to have more spending power at prime times, such as before the start of the school year. I had a brief moment of feeling outsmarted–but then realized that my daughter has learned the best lesson of all: that she was highly capable of protecting her own credit (by not over-spending by even a penny) and also of budgeting for the long term.

The credit card can serve as a springboard for financial literacy, whereby parents can share crucial information about credit and finances. Use of a card provides the concrete evidence of how budgeting and planning can protect one's finances. Practical concerns like payment due dates and safeguards against loss are obvious with the first use of a card.

Financial literacy is sometimes overlooked in family communication, although many families report that they consider it important and many teens say that they would welcome finance discussions with parents. American teens' spending power rises each year but 75% of teens failed a basic financial literacy survey.[4] Parents can address this need through increased communication, shared budgeting and shopping, and other day-to-day experiences that help make the abstract concepts of finances more concrete for their children.

References

[1] Compton, J. A., & Pfau, M. (2004). Use of inoculation to foster resistance to credit card marketing targeting college students. *Journal of Applied Communication Research, 32,* 343-364.

[2] Stanford, W. E. (1999, March-April). Dealing with student credit card debt. *About Campus, 4(1),* 12-17.

[3] Jump$tart Coalition for Personal Financial Literacy. Retrieved Jan. 11, 2011 from http://www.jumpstart.org.

4 Jump$tart Coalition for Personal Financial Literacy. (1997). *High school seniors lack financial smarts, shows survey.* Retrieved Jan. 11, 2011, from http://www.jumpstart.org/upload/news.cfm?recordid=37.

Blame the Folks

Mary Bold, Ph.D., CFLE
Department Chair and Professor, Digital Learning &
Teaching American College of Education, Chicago, IL

The pressures of social conformity are not limited to the young, but they are sometimes harder to escape for the young. A teenager may not want to go along with the crowd but can have a hard time saying that to the crowd. One suggestion is a good code word, which can be communicated from the child to a parent who won't mind playing "the bad guy."

When my kids called me from a friend's house to ask for permission for an extension or an outing, they knew they could count on me to say, "No." The message was in the greeting. If my teenager said, "Mother, I want to go to the movie tonight" that meant he or she

DIDN'T want to go to the movie and needed me to say, "No, you have to come home." On the other hand, if the greeting was the usual, "Hi, Mom...." I would know that the request was genuine. And I could answer the way I needed to, which was usually OK, but sometimes No.

The pressure to conform has been well documented by research[1] and recent studies suggest that young people strive not only to fit in but also to avoid negative emotions.[2] While parents are sometimes frustrated by the power of their children's peer groups, they also can see that the parent-child relationship is not completely excluded from the peer interactions. The influence of family on peer groups may not be obvious but parents do have some impact.

The wise parent admits that we humans are group-oriented. At all ages! We all conform to society, to our work groups, to our family groups. And we all conform to our social groups. But adults have an easier time of excusing themselves from the group. We get to say, "No, thanks," and not lose a friend. At least at some points in younger years, social groups are not so tolerant and so our children need some support from parents. Will this child never learn to say No to the group? Of course, the child will–but in the meantime, we parents can help out.

References

[1] Asch, S. (1956). Studies of independence and conformity: A minority of one against unanimous majority. *Psychological Monographs, 70,* 1-70.

[2] Lashbrook, J. T. (2000). Fitting in: Exploring the emotional dimension of adolescent peer pressure. *Adolescence, 35,* 747-757.

Incremental Decision Making & the Tipping Point

Anne C. Chambers, M.Ed, CFLE
Certified School Psychologist, Head of School,
Indian Creek School, Crownsville, Maryland

A teenager's ability to make good decisions is usually both uneven and sporadic. That is one of the factors that make parenting a teen so difficult. Just when you are convinced that your logical, sensible teen is thinking in a mature and rational manner, he or she makes some goofy decision that has long-lasting negative consequences.

There is a good reason for this. A teen seldom has much ability to do long term abstract thinking. The logical thinking part of the brain is not fully developed and frequently a teen can't anticipate possibilities. Also, an adolescent doesn't have enough life experience to know all of the possible consequences of a decision.

Teens often make their decisions in small increments. They decide only on the immediate question. They don't think through the whole issue, looking at possible end results. Based on Jean Piaget's theory of cognitive development (our thinking process), many teens haven't achieved the more mature level of what is called the *formal operational stage*, whereby the adult looks at the whole picture, understanding "shades of gray and values."[1] Teaching teens to analyze situations in increments seems to provide a model to recast their own behavior more logically. I call this technique "incremental decision making."

Pick a situation from the news that involved young people and that had a negative outcome. You, the parent, either in discussion with your child or alone, lay out the factors in the order of occurrence. Next, spend some time with your adolescent discussing the situation. Discuss one factor at a time analyzing the decision that was made. "Wonder" what the effect might have been if a different decision was made. You and your son or daughter can together discover the "tipping point"–that point at which it was no longer possible for the situation discussed to have a positive outcome.

Take, for example, a recent college scandal that included drinking and someone dying of alcohol poisoning. You have probably told your child that you hope he or she will have sense enough to avoid such a situation. But the problem is that NO young person sets out to die of alcohol poisoning. Young people think they are invulnerable. As a result, your lectures are ignored because your child doesn't think the lecture applies to him or her.

Instead, avoid lecturing. Talk with your teen about the scandal. Make a list of the events as they occurred. Here is an example.

- John is new at college and doesn't know anyone.
- Someone down the hall invited him to go to a party.
- Once he and his acquaintance get to the party, they find there is lots of drinking going on.
- John has drunk beer but never liquor before. At this party, a couple of young men are pushing mixed drinks on the younger visitors and John takes one.
- John drinks a great deal and ultimately passes out.
- Two boys carry him downstairs and put him on a couch in the corner.
- In the morning, John is dead of alcohol poisoning.

Sit with your teen and discuss the points one by one. At every point until the tipping point, John could have made a different decision.

- **He is new at college.** Instead of waiting for people to come to him, he could have gone out and tried to meet people based on his own interests. He could have found a club of some sort.

He could have gone to his major department and checked the bulletin board for events. It might have been embarrassing but he could have met others who, like himself, have not made any friends. Or, he could have waited and entertained himself until sometime in the future when he could meet more appropriate friends. Had he done any of these things, the incident would not have occurred.

- **Someone invites him to a party.** How well did he know this person? Did he think he was likely to enjoy the party? Suppose he had said "no?" He might have been bored and lonely, but perhaps there was someone else on his dorm floor that was "home alone." Had he refused to go, the incident would not have occurred.
- **Once they get to the party, there is drinking going on.** John could have stayed at the party as he did, or he could have left. If he had left at this point, the situation could have been reversed. Help your teen to realize that everyone makes mistakes but there is often time to rectify the mistake before things go too far.
- **The hosts of the party are pushing mixed drinks on the younger men at the party. John takes one.** He still had choices he could make. He could say he doesn't drink mixed drinks and he would rather have a beer or a coke. He can carry the same drink around pretending to drink, or make that one drink last for the evening. He can pour it in a potted plant. He can decide that he doesn't feel comfortable with the way things are going and pick this time to leave quietly. Any of these decisions might have reversed the outcome. Failure to take action here is the tipping point.
- **John drinks a lot and passes out.** After this, John is not able to make his own decisions and he dies.

Many parents get upset with teenagers and lecture them about the initial decision. "I told you never to go to a wild party where everyone is drinking." The problem is that we can't always teach teenagers not to make that initial mistake. We have to show them that if a mistake is made, they can still salvage the situation by making a better decision at the next stage.

The classic answer to a lecturing parent is, "You just don't understand." There is some truth in that. We forget how badly young people want to belong to the group, and we blast them for doing the wrong things without helping them do the right things. Teaching incremental decision making recognizes that young people sometimes make unwise decisions, but until they reach the "tipping point," there still are ways to prevent a final, negative outcome.

Talk with your teen about where the first "choice" was made and what were the consequences of that choice. Then, talk about the second choice the person made. If the person had made a different choice, was there time to avoid the final disaster? In any one of these issues, there is a final "tipping point" beyond which the results of the whole incident are going to be bad. The trick is to help your teen exercise his or her independence (even if it means an occasional risky decision) while still recognizing the tipping point in time to salvage his or her safety.

Reference

[1] *Theory of cognitive development.* (2007. Retrieved December 15, 2010, from http://en.wikipedia.org/wiki/Theory_of_cognitive_development.

Growing Son to Man

What do I see in
This man in front of me.
Enveloping the boy I knew,
Who suffered, grew
So differently.
And better than I thought.

Assigned to become man,
With no blueprint, or plan.
From confusing messages
Searching paths to manhood
On divergent trails.

Carpenter, boatsman, marksman, cook,
Kind humorist, farmer, friend, philosopher, but
Never sure of what is supposed to be
The outcome of the love he gives to me.

–Marcia Pioppi Galazzi, M.Ed., CFLE
President & Founder, The Family
Schools, Inc., Brewster, MA

Best Gift for Your Children?
Choosing the "Other Parent" Wisely!

Kathy Lettieri, D.Phil., CFLE
National Certified Domestic and Registered Civil
Mediator; President and Consultant, Solution by
Resolution; President and Education Director, AIDS
Education Bureau, Huntsville, AL

When presenting the topic, "What is the Best Gift You Can Give to Your Children?" to a variety of groups, a hidden agenda looms, and interest peaks with the initial answers.[1] Answers vary depending on the group and ages of the audience. Audiences have been youth, teens, parents of the youth and teens, and adults. Adult audiences have included divorced and pre-second marriage adults, potentially step family groups.

On one occasion, a memorable answer was from a five year old girl shouting, "a cell phone." All agreed. Other answers followed: a car at graduation; no, a car at 16; an education; a pet; a birthday party every year; clothes; an iPod–the list was long. Kids were answering as the question was presented–tangible gifts. Eventually a teen answered "love." Parents loving and being able to care for children began to take the lead.

The next question asked was, "Is there one gift that might include all of the intangible things we have listed?" How about: "The best gift you can give to your children is to choose the other parent wisely." The adults in the audience applaud. The kids liked the answer too. We connected.

The third question was, "What is the meaning of choosing the other parent wisely?" As predicted, the youth and teens, youth leaders, and parents in the group answered everything on previous list, often adding something new. The primary responses were love, respect, no hitting, no drugs, no other girl/boy friends, must like kids, stay home with wife/husband, not go out with friends anymore at night, no shouting, keep a job, let me (a girl) have a job, and no drinking. Solid answers to an emotional question!

Fidelity, employment, no drug or alcohol use, and no domestic violence were highest on the list from all audiences, no matter which age group. The important ideals were clear. Solid parenting ideals were vocalized from each group.

In choosing a boyfriend or girlfriend (that potential "other parent") the character of the individual is important. One definition of character is, "intellectual and moral qualities distinguishing one person or group from another."[2] A second definition is, "the way one acts when no one is watching." One wise choice for the woman may be to avoid a boy/man who is a bully: a physical or emotional abuser forcing attention or physical activity upon a female, or cajoling, saying, 'If you love me…" or threaten, "If you don't, I will find someone else who will." Likewise, a wise choice for a boy/man would be to avoid a girl/woman aggressor or one who quickly resorts to pouting or tears to get her way.

Besides considering the above characteristics, boys, too, need to be informed and encouraged to choose a girlfriend, perhaps the potential other parent, wisely. A girl may need or want a way out of the parent's house. Pregnancy along with a plan for marriage is one way. Gut feelings will often announce what is and is not OK; listen and heed.

Since babies can and do sometimes become involved before a marriage, another topic is considered. The content of the speech then includes the following: choosing the other parent wisely has an affect on everything after the first kiss. If infatuation turns into a sexual relationship, even with precautions, a baby is possible. So are sexually transmitted diseases. If the mother is not emotionally mature and the father is not involved, and/or does not have the financial means or family support to help, what happens to the mother and the baby–especially if an STD or HIV/AIDS has been contracted?

A 2006 report counted 75 out of 1000 girls in the United States ages 15 to 19 become pregnant each year (close to one out of every ten).[3] Often grandparents are parenting. Some young parents marry because of pregnancy; others do not. The children of the young parents, married or not married, often never have a stable secure home. Successful young single parent households often prove to be hard, if not impossible, to establish due to emotional and/or financial problems.

Other concerns exist when *the other parent* is not chosen wisely, often leading to very complex family networks. Statistics show 50 percent of first marriages end with divorce.[4] Families splinter. Mothers and fathers remarry, sometimes multiple times, creating stepfamilies and extended stepfamilies. The more children involved, the more difficult is the emotional and financial element of family life. For another failed marriage, the dream of security and comfort may be lost for all, conceivably: parents, children, step parents, step children, biological and step grandparents, aunts, uncles, and cousins. The immediate family as well as the extended family and friends are involved, and each feels the effect of the perceived or real failure.

For a teenager who can easily become a parent, what is the message of wisdom to be gained about parenting from the above statistics? Except in the case of rape, first and foremost, becoming a parent is a choice–by ones activity. The male or female has the choice of not becoming pregnant. Abstaining from sex is the only safe and sure prevention of pregnancy. The use of birth control does not always prevent pregnancy or sexually transmitted diseases. Pregnancy and STDs are the risks for which teens need to be aware, especially realizing that the "sexual partner" may end up being the "other parent" being chosen.

There are things that parents can do to help their child in choosing *the other parent* wisely. Parents can and should encourage, praise, and talk to their child, of any age so as to create, give and establish a positive self-confidence. Also, they can help children become aware of the desirable characteristics described as *the other parent*. Jeffry Larson has written an interesting listing of relationship situations or types of individuals to be avoided for marriage consideration, much of which supports many situations mentioned above.[5]

A useful program on relationship education has been developed by Marline Pearson called Relationship Smarts PLUS,[6] designed for teens to insightfully study the nature of healthy relationships, from the first crush to more serious relationships. It provides teens with the opportunity to explore themselves as well as to recognize desirable characteristics in others and a realistic concept of love. Parents could encourage appropriate service providers in their communities to offer this 13 session program in various settings. The Cooperative Extension faculty at Auburn University conducted a five year evaluation study of the program and has offered the program in Alabama.[7] Parents might contact Cooperative Extension offices (listed in phone books under U.S. Department of Agriculture, USDA) in their states to find out about similar program availability in their area. The Cooperative Extension office also has established at useful national web site which includes access to relevant fact sheets on *"Teens and dating: Tips for parents and professionals," "Teen dating violence: Are you aware?"* and others; the links for these fact sheets are located in the bottom section of the web page.[8]

Parents also must support and *be aware* of where children are and what their activities are—and with whom the children spend time. The internet, telephone, and television, should be monitored by parents, setting controls or limits where helpful. Parents also need to set the example by their own behavior with each other as a couple.

Sometimes parenting is not easy for the parent or child. Children too often accuse parents of being controlling—well, yes, parents need to control, to some extent, because parents have the responsibility to know what is happening in a child's life, to be able to guide them along healthy pathways.

If parents gave children the gift of "how to choose the other parent wisely," a major part of good parenting will have been achieved. Values and skills will have been taught. The life and job of the children as future parents, when ready, will have been made easier. The second generation of parents will then teach the value of parenting wisely, as well as setting the stage of teaching the third generation to parent with strength, and pass along the gift of "choosing the other parent wisely."

References

[1] Lettieri, Kathy. (April, 2006). *What is the best gift you can give to your children?* Unpublished manuscript.

[2] *Webster's II New College Dictionary.* (2001). Boston MA: Houghton Mifflin.

[3] Guttmacher Institute. (2006). *Facts on American teens' sexual and reproductive health.* NY: Author.

[4] Divorse Rate in America. *DivorseRate.* Retrieved Jan. 11, 2011, from http://www.divorcerate.org/.

[5] Larson, Jeffry H. (2005). Whom not to marry! *Family Studies Center, Brigham Young University.* Retrieved Jan. 11, 2011, from www.familycenter.byu.edu/columns.aspx?id=54.

[6] Pearson, Marline. (2004). *Love U2: Relationship Smarts PLUS.* Berkeley, CA: The Dibble Institute. NOTE: Available at www.DibbleInstitute.org.

[7] Adler-Baeder, Francesca, et al. (2005). *Looking towards a healthy marriage: School-based relationships education targeting youth."* Retrieved Jan. 11, 2011, from http://www.extension.iastate.edu/marriage/files/HCHCsummary.pdf.

[8] National Extension Relationship & Marriage Education Network. (2007). *Extension resources: Fact sheets & educational materials.* Retrieved Jan. 11, 2011, from http://www.fcs.uga.edu/ext/pubs/chfd/CHFD-E-42.pdf – or "Google" the network name and "fact sheets."

Chapter IX

Wisdom of the Ages

Robert E. Keim, Ph.D., CFLE Emeritus
Professor Emeritus, Northern Illinois University
Clinton, TN
&
Arminta Lee Jacobson, Ph.D., CFLE
Professor & Director of the Center for Parent Education
and the annual International Conference on Parent Education
and Parenting, University of North Texas, Denton
&
JoAnn D. Engelbrecht, Ph.D., CFLE
Professor, Department of Family Sciences,
Director, Research and Sponsored Programs,
Texas Woman's University, Denton

In this concluding article, we want to share some of the *wisdom* from the past, handed down to us from some of the early pioneers and writers in the field of the family from various disciplines–family science, sociology, psychology, psychiatry, biology, and the medical field. In addition, a brief overview is given of developments over time, which may help parents realize why there are so many theories and programs on parenting. For some parents, in the past, this may have led to confusion or bewilderment. Hopefully, it will be cleared up a little bit here.

Our Historical Roots

While *wisdom* for parents has been around for centuries, from the early Greek philosophers, it appears that the first published handbooks for parents appeared around 1635, as reported by Fein.[1] Later, Jean-Jacques Rousseau was writing in 1773 about the educational process for an ideal citizen, while giving some advice to parents.[2] In 1815 there were informal groups of parents meeting to discuss methods of child rearing, as reported by Ralph Bridgeman.[3] During the 1700 and 1800s, much of the influence on parenting came from religious teachings.

According to Steven Schlossman,[4] formal programs were begun among the Maternal Associations of the early 1800s, first beginning in Portland, Maine, with the goals of "breaking the will" of the child. Among the first known publications dealing with family life were *Mother's Magazine* in 1832 and *Mother's Assistant* in 1841, according to Sunley in the chapter, "Early nineteenth-century American literature on child-rearing."[5]

In the latter decades of the 1800s, the Charity Organization Society(ies) had 92 affiliates in numerous cities which drew attention to the plights of families.[6] In this environment, in 1897 the National Congress of Mothers was formed,[7] which is now the National Parent Teacher Association (PTA). Their goal at the time was to educate parents in "true parent-hood," so as to eliminate the evil resulting from ignorance, indifference, and neglect.[8] A fuller history of the beginning and purposes of the organization was given in 1916 by the president of the organization, Mrs. Frederic Schoff, in an article, "The National Congress of Mothers and Parent-Teacher Association."[9] A detailed history of this period is provided in Schlossman's article, "Before home start: Notes towards a history of parent education in America, 1897-1929."[10]

The U.S. Children's Bureau (now a function of the Department of Health & Human Services' unit, Administration for Children & Families) was founded in 1912 and began publishing *Infant Care* in 1914 to assist parents.[3] The impetus of this and many other activities focusing upon the home and child was spurred by eleven annual Lake Placid Conferences held from 1899 to 1909.[11,12]

Then, in the past century, it seems that an explosion occurred. By 1924, over 75 major organizations were conducting parent education programs, as reported by Orville Brim.[13] Numerous study groups arose in the 1920s sponsored by the National Council of Parent Education, from which emerged the National Congress of Parents and Teachers as overseer of 500 study groups by 1929, noted in Maxine Lewis-Rowley & others' article, "The evolution of education for family life."[14] A detailed view of some of the advice given parents during this period can be found in a book by Steven Mintz & Susan Kellogg, *Domestic revolutions*.[15]

Soon, the more contemporary era began with individuals developing parent education programs. By 1939, Rudolph Dreikurs was actively leading groups with the Adlerian focus in Chicago.[16] Some of the *wisdoms* cited further below also will mention other currently existing parenting programs.

Several recent activities are enhancing the practice of parent education. In 1985, the certification program of family life educators began, being provided by the National Council on Family Relations (NCFR), discussed in the Preface of this book. There are now over 1,500 who are a Certified Family Life Educator (CFLE). Later NCFR began a program to approve academic programs to assist with granting of the CFLE designation, with over 120 approved programs nation-wide.

The National Parenting Education Network (NPEN) was begun in 1995. One of the goals is to provide a means for parent educators to directly communicate with one another through the use of an internet listserv. One can find out more about the organization at www.npen.org.

Classic Books That Have Endured

Interestingly, many of the early books directed to parents have remained as classics though the years and are still being published as subsequent editions or reprints. Here are some of the major ones:

- Benjamin Spock's 1946 book, *Common sense book of baby and child care,*[17] is being published in its eighth edition, now simply called, *Dr. Spock's baby and childcare,*[18] being revised and updated by Dr. Robert Needlman.
- Rudolph Dreikurs wrote a series of books beginning in 1948 with *Coping with children's misbehavior,*[19] followed by *Challenge of parenthood.*[20] Containing his primary thoughts on reasons for children's misbehaviors and the use of natural and logical consequences, his book, *Children: The challenge,* was published in 1964 and has remained in print since then.[21]
- Selma Fraiberg's 1959 book, *The magic years: Understanding and handling the problems of early childhood,*[22] seeks to take the parent into the mind of the child in coping with the early stages of development. It can still be found in print.[23]
- Haim Ginott's 1965 book, *Between parent and child,*[24] which stressed the use of understanding, empathy, sensitivity, compassion, and communication skills, especially involving reflection of feelings with children,[25] was revised and updated in 2003 by Alice Ginott and H. Wallace Goddard and is now available in print.[26]
- Thomas Gordon's 1970 book, *Parent effectiveness training* (P.E.T.),[27] introducing the concepts of "I feel" messages (in contrast to accusatory "You" messages) and the use of "active listening" and the "no-loss" method of problem solving with children, is still in print. Many parenting programs which stress good communication skills utilize principles Gordon presents in this classic.
- Gerald Patterson's 1975 book, *Families: Applications for social learning to family life,*[28] though perhaps less known than most of the above books, presents the behavior management or behavior modification approach. Primarily, it involves parents focusing a child's desirable behaviors and reinforcing them with positive outcomes as a means to encourage the child to repeat the behavior. When used more

intentionally by parents, *charting* (discussed below) is recommended.

When an old person dies, a library is lost.
–*Tommy Swann*

The subject matter of most of these books will be discussed
below in some of the key *wisdoms* which explain the more basic
ideas they convey. When looking at bookstore shelves today, you will
see literally hundreds of other titles from which to choose. It is
reported that the amount of literature focusing upon marriage and
the family from 1900 to 1976 was exploding during the mid and late
1900s, with 25% of all literature on the topic (25,557 items) appear-
ing during the last five years of that period, 1972-1976.[14] There were
3,000 citations alone that appeared on the topic of parent education
in a 30-year period of the late 1900s.[29] In addition, most parenting
programs focusing on emerging theories and concepts were being
developed and offered near the middle to latter part of the 1900s.
Consequently, parents and parent educators have been faced with a
massive array of diverse literature.

Grouping of *Wisdom of the Ages*

It is no easy task for the average person to grasp all of the
writings without some help in seeing these writings organized in
some understandable fashion. There is a helpful way to view these
writings and the *wisdom* that has been passed down to us. They tend
to fall under the following categories:
  1. **Developmental** – viewing changes in infants, children, par-
     ents, and the family over time.
  2. **Social Learning or Behavior Management** – noting methods
     of how children acquire social behaviors.
  3. **Social Order** – viewing how the family is a social system with
     the use of established **rules** to govern it.
  4. **Personality–Character** – viewing the development of "who"
     the child becomes.
  5. **Interactional–Transactional–Ecological** – viewing the actions
     and their effects occurring between family members and
     other social systems.
  6. **Bio-psycho-sociological** – viewing how genetics and biology
     affect individual behavior.
  7. **Eclectic** – looking at parenting issues or problems by use of

several theories or viewpoints, often using themes which have been discussed above in previously mentioned approaches. The eclectic approach often utilizes the ecological or systems framework, with some focusing on specific problem situations.

This framework is primarily based upon those developed over the years for studying the family. Reuben Hill and others suggested in 1957/1960 the need for developing a conceptual framework for family study.[30,31] Directed by Ivan Nye & Felix Berardo, an expansion of the framework was suggested.[32] Building upon the perspectives of Hill and others, the above modeled framework for viewing writing about *parenting* is a modification of one presented earlier by Keim.[33]

Wisdom of the Ages by Categories

The *wisdom* that follows is some of the more classic concepts, from the early writers in the field that relates to parenting, along with a few lesser known concepts, all of which parents might find of interest and beneficial. By no means is this article an attempt to cite all of the wisdom and knowledge that has been developed and passed down to parents and parent educators, nor is it intended to duplicate the theme of some of the earlier articles in this book. In like manner, this is not an attempt to cite the latest research on parenting. The focus here is on key wisdoms; however, throughout will be found some references to contemporary writings on topics being discussed. Also, the last several sections will note current trends in the literature, with suggestions for further exploration and study.

Much has been written throughout the years on most of the following topics. For a more contemporary coverage of the topics, one would need to consult recent reviews, most of which are directed more to the parent educators rather than to parents themselves, such as the 2009 book edited by Bredehoft & Walcheski, *Family life education: Integrating theory and practice.*[34] In addition, there are the numerous reviews and articles in a recent five volume series edited by Marc Bornstein, *Handbook of parenting.*[35]

Some parents also might find it interesting to look through a book designed to be used in a college course for either future parent educators or future parents themselves. One such popular text is by Jerry Bigner, *Parent-child relations: An introduction to parenting.*[36]

SPECIAL NOTE: In the following sections, you will find numerous key points conveying the *wisdom of the ages.* Many of them may be of interest to you, others less so. Nevertheless, it is important that you NOT attempt to read through all of these in one or two readings. There is a lot to digest. As with reading many of the articles in this book, it often is well to read one, think about it and its application to you and your family, and possibly pursue further reading on that topic, before going on to read another article. The same is true with these *wisdoms* below.

1. *Wisdom* from the *Developmental* Approach

The *developmental* approach involves viewing changes in infants, children, parents, and the family over time. The following are some of the prominent *wisdom of the ages* of this approach.

- **Developmental tasks** involve the notion that there are different developmental needs to be fulfilled by children at various stages in their life, involving their physical growth, social life, emotional well-being, and cognitive/thinking development. It is a key concept or *wisdom* underlying this framework.

    The early writing on developmental tasks actually related to the individual child in educational settings, with the 1928 pioneer study by Lawrence Frank.[37] The writings of Robert Havighurst expanded upon the tasks, including development through the life span.[38,39,40]

    Below this are several other *wisdoms* that directly relate to *developmental tasks*.

- **Family life cycle** was the term used when applying notions of *developmental tasks* to the family. The Committee on Dynamics of Family Interaction was an inter-disciplinary group whose co-chairs, Rueben Hill and Evelyn Duvall, gave the committee's report to the 1948 conference of the National Council on Family Relations,[41] which was commented upon by Lawrence Frank in an article of the same year.[42]

    Frank highlighted six stages in the life cycle through which most families move: (1) early marriage and the expectant family, (2) the beginning of child bearing, (3) the preschool family, (4) the family with teen agers, (5) the family as a launching center, and (6) the aging family. Within each stage of the cycle, there are developmental tasks to be performed in meeting the needs of the children as well as the parents and the family itself as a unit or community. And between each stage are transition issues requiring adjustment, which can lead to tensions and frustrations, since the needs of children can change dramatically from one stage to the next. Aspects of these numerous tasks and transition issues are movingly depicted in the chapter, "Family Ritual and the Family Cycle," in James Bossard & Eleanor Boll's 1950 book, *Ritual and family living*.[43]

These stages were refined and expanded upon by Evelyn Duvall in her 1957 book, *Family development*.[44] She cited eight stages through which the family evolves. The stages were: (1) the couple without children; (2) the child-bearing family with the oldest child birth to 30 months old; (3) the family with preschoolers, the oldest child 2-1/2 to 6; (4) the family with school children, the oldest being 6 through 12; (5) the family with teens, the oldest being 13 through 19; (6) the family in the launching stage, with the oldest child gone, to the last child leaving; (7) the "empty nest" with middle aged parents to retirement; and, (8) the aging family, retirement to death of both parents. The limitation of these descriptions of the family life cycle is biased, since they are based on the intact nuclear family, which is only one of many family types. These original conceptions have been applied to more diverse family forms and cultures in the book titled, *Expanded family life cycle: The individual, family, and social perspectives*, edited by McGoldrick, Carter & Garcia-Preto (2010).[45]

- **The teachable moment** is that time when a child is considered ready to learn a task, ready in terms of physical growth (including motor development), as well as emotional, social, and intellectual development. If we seek to have a child learn a task before the *teachable moment*, it may lead to frustration and discouragement, as illustrated by much of the early work of Arnold Gesell who in 1911 established the Clinic for Child Development and later the Gesell Institute of Child Development at Yale University.[46] Much of his work involved working with twins, illustrating this concept. The idea of the *teachable moment* is attributed to Havighurst and discussed more fully by Hurlock.[47]

- **Critical learning period**, which begins with the *teachable moment*, is that period of time within which a child can best learn a task, described more fully by Smart & Smart.[48] The end of the *critical learning period* is that time when, if waiting until then to begin to learn the task, a child may find it difficult if not impossible to adequately learn or master it. This is why having music or language lessons at an early age can be beneficial.

    This principle illustrates the importance regarding the early learning of words and speech patterns by infants. If an infant has any nasal congestion causing a hearing loss, it is important to have it diagnosed quickly to avoid any prolonged hearing impairment which could lead to later speech problems.

- **Bonding (imprinting, attachment)**. Attachment is the emotional bond that a child develops over time with a significant adult. The quality of the attachment is impacted by numerous factors including social interaction, adult sensitivity to the child, and time together. In 1951, John Bowlby initially posited the theory,[49] followed by numerous studies.[50] Through clinical studies, Mary Ainsworth furthered the notion of attachment by assessing patterns of infants' attachment based on caregiver behavior patterns before the age of 18 months.[51] Her early work was conducted with mothers and infants.

   Securely attached infants used their mother as a home base and were at ease in her presence, but became upset when she left, and would go to her when she returned. Avoidant children did not seek proximity to the mother after their mother left, and they seemed to avoid her when she returned as if angered by her behavior. Ambivalent children exhibited a combination of positive and negative reactions to their mother; they showed great distress when she left but on her return, they at the same time sought close contact, yet, hit, and kicked her.[52]

   Infants form secure attachments to any consistent caregiver who is sensitive and responsive in social interactions. These early experiences affect an individual's relationships throughout the rest of life. The importance of the early expression of love and acceptance to an infant is highlighted by this concept, how the infant identifies with the *significant other*, parent, or caregiver, who has most constant or interaction in the early weeks and months of life.

   A contemporary book on this topic which parents likely would find very useful is *Attached at the Heart* by Barbara Nicholson & Lysa Parker.[53]

- **Stages of cognitive development** were the focus of Jean Piaget leading up to the 1960s,[54,55] helping us to realize that children understand and perceive things differently than adults. His primary focus was upon the thinking processes of learning which involve information processing and logical thinking. The stages he described, using his technical terms, are the *sensorimotor*, the *preoperational, concrete operational,* and *formal operational.*

   In the *sensorimotor period,* the child, typically birth to two years, determines most thinking based upon actions that are observed, with the use of some *reasoning* occurring near the end of this period. At that age, they are not able to solve problems or recognize consequences as well as adults.

With children, we parents often get frustrated with them because they don't seem to respond like we think they should. Sometimes we "slip" and expect them to act like an adult would in that situation. At such times, we fail to realize that children's thinking processes and perceptions are not as well developed as ours.

Then, in the *preoperational* stage, typically ages two to seven, the child begins to engage in problem solving, with the use of language and symbols. However, attention is usually focused on only one aspect of a situation. An example of this was illustrated in studies when children were given a choice. They are apt to select a group of candies which *looks* bigger than another group that actually has fewer candies in it.

When a child moves beyond such a response and considers multiple factors in the situation at the same time, thus selecting the group with the most candies, then the child has moved to the *concrete operational* stage, typically by age seven to eleven. At this time the use of logical thinking begins to emerge with the focus more on objects, not abstract ideas. To the frustration of parents, children still tend not to consider the consequences of their behavior unless it is clearly reviewed with them ahead of time.

The *formal operational* stage involves the ability to reason and the consideration of possibilities and consequences, occurring typically around the age of eleven. Even then, however, Piaget concluded that some individuals may never adequately reach this stage.

- **Psychological stages of development** offers some interesting insight into some of the characteristics of children which parents can help to instill in their children. The stages were recognized by Eric Erikson, noting important factors occurring throughout ones life span, noted in his 1950s books, *Childhood and society* and *Identity and the life cycle*.[56,57] Essentially, his message was that one of two opposites tend to develop in a person, resulting from the manner in which we respond to events in our life and how others treat us. During the early years, the following develop: (1) in infancy, the feeling of *trust* of those around them to be caring and loving, vs. *mistrust*; (2) in the toddler years, a sense of having *autonomy*, or control over themselves, with will and determination to explore, vs. *shame and doubt* resulting from scolding and punishment; (3) as a preschooler, the sense of being able to take *initiative*, while developing a feeling of having purpose and courage to do things, vs. *guilt* of not fulfilling expectations of others; (4) in the school age years, having a feeling of *industry*, by completing things with a sense of competence, vs. *inferiority*; and, (5) in the adolescence years, *ego-identity*, having a sense of knowing who one is, establishing oneself with peer groups, vs. experiencing *role confusion*. Then in the later stages: (6) during young adulthood, we should establish *intimacy*, close relationships and love with a partner, vs. *isolation*; (7) in middle adulthood, we need to achieve a sense of *generativity*, contributing to the next generation, vs. *self-absorption*; and, (8) in late adulthood, we should arrive at a point of having *integrity*, accomplishing one's role in life with acceptance, vs. *despair.*

- **Realistic expectations** involves the idea that parents should be realistic in terms of what they expect in their child's behavior, especially in light of what we know about development. Children can become very discouraged if we constantly expect them to perform above the level that is possible or realistic for them. It was interestingly noted by Meyer Nimkoff in Kirkpatrick's study on happiness.[58] Nimkoff observed that our ultimate satisfaction with a child's behavior is a product of what the child does divided by what we *expect* the child to do.

    For the mathematically inclined, the equation looks like this:

    Our satisfaction as a % = % of child's achievement / our expectations as a % (child's achievement divided by expectations, all as a %).

    Thus, if we are always expecting 100%, we likely will be unhappy a lot of the time. The implication here is obvious: if we lower our expectations so that they are more realistic, we will be much happier with our child's performance and, thus, less frustrated with their behavior.

- **Stages of parenthood** are explored by Ellen Galinsky in her 1981 book, *Between generations: The six stages of parenthood*.[59] Many parents have found it to be an interesting book in which parents are portrayed as first beginning to view themselves *as parents* in the *parental image stage*, following on to the *nurturing stage* of the infant, the *authority stage* for toddlers, the *interpretative stage* for the school age, the *inter-*

dependence stage with adolescence, and to the *departure stage* when the child leaves home. A recent 2000 book on this topic with a slightly different slant also might be of interest: *The eight seasons of parenthood: How the stages of parenting constantly reshape our adult identities,* by Barbara Unell & Jerry Wychoff.[60]

It is interesting to keep on the look-out for new books that present findings on developmental issues. One book that will inform you about a number of interesting issues is *NurtureShock* by Po Bronson & Ashley Merryman (2009). These investigative reporters reveal some interesting findings about children and youth. Topics included are: effects of getting less sleep than beneficial, pre-school education, teen rebellion (prominent or not), better ways for acquiring language skills, etc. Probably most parents would find something of interest in the book.

2. *Wisdom* from the *Social Learning* Approach
(Learning social behaviors)

The *social learning or behavior management* approach involves noting methods of how children acquire social behaviors. The following are some of the prominent *wisdom of the ages* of this approach.

- **Taking the role of the other** is a term coined and described in the early 1930s by George Herbert Mead.[61,62] It conveys the notion that children often acquire their own behaviors by observing other people perform them and then repeat them as their own. This illustrates the importance of what we as parents often are cautioned about: that we should be good role models and see that others in our children's lives also are positive role models. Children quickly learn from what they observe.

   As parents, we also hear of the value that play and games can be for children. In Mead's early observation of play and games, he saw how crucial playing and gaming, a term often used, were in the social development of children. The behaviors or the role of others are acted out by children in play, such as mother, doctor, and numerous other symbolized roles. Mead noted that children then move on to gaming, or games. They learn various roles through games, having to abide by rules and interacting in social settings. Through games, children discover *the generalized other,* their impression of social norms and expectations. In this manner, Mead contended that children begin to acquire a sense of self-consciousness.

- **Operant conditioning** is an approach usually used in behavior modification or behavior management programs. It involves a more intentional way of *conditioning* a child's behavior. This approach involves a parent responding to a desired behavior with a positive response or consequence; when an undesired behavior occurs, it should be followed by an aversive response, or a negative response or consequence. Upon using this form of *conditioning* for a short period of time, most children will begin behaving in the desired manner. The child will tend to become self-regulated; that is, the behavior is accepted and owned by the child as his or her behavior. This is discussed more in the next *wisdom.*

- **Charting** is usually recommended to be used when one is serious about using a behavior management approach. It involves a form of keeping track of the behaviors desired and what the child does. Charts are typically designed for a week or two, with boxes for placing check marks when desired behaviors or daily routines are performed. The charts usually are posted prominently, somewhere in the child's bedroom or in the kitchen area. Using charts can help to track progress and provide encouragement. Sometimes "points" are given for achievement and then converted for some favored activity or objects to give to the child. When using rewards of this nature, it is recommended that rewards should be for things the child values and would desire. It is recommended that food should never be used as some form of a reward due to numerous issues related to weight and obesity.

  Often, parents who use charts for a specific behavior find that desired results are achieved in a short time. Consequently, the parent and child may forget to follow up with the chart for keeping track of progress because the focused behavior is no longer a problem. The child has internalized the behavior, making it his or her own intrinsic desire. The charting is just sort of forgotten.

  The early contributors to this approach, *operant conditioning,* were John Watson[63,64] as early as 1919 and then by B.F. Skinner,[65,66] with Albert Bandura later writing a helpful synthesis.[67] Presently, behavior management materials are generally marketed towards the issues of children with special needs, often used in the classroom, or institutional settings.

Books written for parents that cover the key principles are rare and, therefore, tend to be older, such as the still-in-print book, *Families: Applications for social learning to family life* by Gerald Patterson.[28] Another book which is not in-print is *Effective child rearing: The behaviorally aware parent* by William Gosciewski.[68] Both books were written in the mid-1970s. Nevertheless, their methods endure over time. The earlier article titled *Using parent/child contracts* by Alice Davenport deals with this approach.

A more recent book on the topic written by Gail Brewster & others is *The voucher system for home.*[69] Although written especially for parents with children diagnosed with ADD, ADHD, ODD, or autism, it also is intended to help parents who experience typical problems such as talking back, defiance, resistance to doing chores, sibling rivalry, hitting, whining, arguing, outbursts, lying, stealing, being late, etc. The book comes with tear-out vouchers which can be recycled. Another book written by Steven Curtis also has the goal of helping parents with children of special needs, to assess their situation and explore alternative approaches, titled, *Understanding your child's puzzling behavior.*[70]

- **Rewards, not bribes, are used.** Some critics of the behavior management approach suggest that using reinforcers or rewards for achievement is a form of a *bribe*. Behaviorists point to the many areas of life where people most typically perform activities in exchange for some benefit, an exchange, a trade-off, or simply pay. They also point out that bribes are intended to get people to do things which they *should not be doing;* whereas, reinforcements or rewards are seeking to have children do things which they should be doing.

- **"Catch the child doing good"** is a term frequently heard since the 1960s. This idea stresses the benefit of seeking to focus on the desired behaviors of children when they occur and immediately reinforce these behaviors by encouragement or praise. This idea is in contrast to how parents often "catch a child doing bad," which typically results in some punishment or hard feelings by all. Behavior management programs in schools have long stressed the value of having teachers focus on the good behaviors and reinforcing them rather than being obsessed with the bad behaviors. Often children who have been behavior problems for teachers have been turned around by this approach. This focusing on a positive rather than a negative behavior is basically what behaviorists have called a *substitute behavior*, for example, rather than focusing on siblings arguing, reinforce or reward their playing and getting along with each other.

It has long been recognized that using *praise, complements* and *encouragement* can help children achieve the behaviors which parents wish to instill. They especially should be used when *catching a child doing good.*

- **Praise, compliments, and encouragement**, often used by parents, are forms of positive reinforcers related to the *social learning* approach. To help children repeat the desired behaviors we seek, it is helpful for parent to use these positive statements.

- **Cues, prompts, or reminders** are encouraged to be used with children, somewhat as a help for them to remember what is desired or intended. Children don't have the attention span adults have and we can help them to recall what should be done. Also, as with all of these *social learning* approaches, even if frustrated over some behavior, it is very important for parents and caregivers to remind themselves to use a caring and friendly tone of voice when using cues or consequences.

- **Re-directing behavior** can be a way to help avoid some undesired event from happening before it happens as well as be a guidance strategy for parents for children's inappropriate behavior. Parents can strive to focus a child's attention to another activity or interest, away from the source of what could be a possible problem, annoyance, or accident. Re-directing behavior is particularly effective with older infants, toddlers, and preschool-age children. The parent is regulating the child's behavior, but it can develop into internalization and self-regulation by the child.

- **Environmental control** is another approach related to avoiding problems. That is, rearrange things to help prevent accidents, often called "child proofing the area" or simply removing some obvious problem item from being broken. Thomas Gordon discusses this in chapter eight of his *P.E.T* book, under the topic, "changing the environment."[27]

- **"Spit in their soup,"** a weird term, is an old strategy attributed to Alfred Adler,[71] whose primary approach is discussed below. If a parent suspects the real reason for a child's misbehavior and has guessed it correctly, by letting the child know that you understand why they are doing what they are doing, it tends to "take the fun" out of the behavior; and, the child likely will stop doing it. For example, if a child is teasing a brother or sister in order to get even for something, the parent might calmly say in a friendly voice, "You're trying to annoy her because she ..., aren't you?" If correct, the child will almost involuntarily, with a *recognition reflex,* respond with a smile, as if getting caught with his hand in the cookie jar and quit doing it.

An alternate version of this phrase is "don't spit in their soup," noted by Kevin Leman, suggesting that a parent should not add "guilt" into a positive response to a child's request (p. 30).[72] An example of this would be if a child asks if it is alright to go play with a friend, the parent might say, "Yes, but you know how I don't think he is a good influence on you." The point is, if it is alright to go play, don't add the "guilt." If you mean it, why not say, "No, I don't want you playing with her, because ..."

- **Group dating** for children is an activity that some parents may overlook in terms of being a social learning activity. The "jump" from no dating to a single date for a teen or a preteen can be a big leap if there has not been much opportunity for social interaction with the opposite sex. One of the few who has noted this socialization issue is E. E. LeMasters, an investigative sociologist, in his 1957 book, *Modern courtship and marriage.*[73] In viewing the dating process and its stages, LeMasters viewed dating as beginning with *group dating* prior to random or single dating, steady dating, etc.

    Prior to single dating, LeMasters suggested that parents should encourage situations where boys and girls arrive separately at gatherings when no pairing off is expected, such as picnics, home parties, bowling, group movie attending, or school dances. Extracurricular school clubs or activities and religious youth groups serve a similar function. It provides the opportunity for formal social interactions to begin occurring without any lasting commitments. Though all children may not need it, LeMasters observed, for the middle school/junior high school aged youth, *group dating* provides a painless transition from the non-dating one-sexed group activities to the two-sexed dating stage.

- **Bedwetting or nocturnal enuresis** is a concern for many parents and there have been aids to assist them for a long time, though many parents are not aware of them. The condition is often treated using principles of behavior modification. Typically used are "bedwetting alarms" (available at numerous web sites such as: bedwettingstore.com, drii-sleeper.com, bedwetting-alarms.com, wet-stop.com, pottymd.com, etc.).

These alarms along with many other helpful ideas are discussed more fully by Howard J. Bennett, a pediatrician, in his recent book, *Waking up dry: A guide to help children overcome bedwetting.*[74] While there may be medical or emotional issues involved, Bennett noted that most children respond to using the bedwetting/alarm approach. At his web-site (www.wakingupdry.com) there are links to some helpful ideas under "Tips and tricks" and "Bedwetting updates."

- **Antecedent behavior** is a very important notion to consider in regard to much of the above. Some of the behaviorists noted above caution that when seeking to alter some undesired behavior, rather than rushing along with some reinforcement plan, first carefully consider this question: Is there some other event in the child's life that is causing this behavior. For example, continually oversleeping may be caused by not getting to bed early enough. Perhaps more importantly, the ecological approach, discussed farther below, would even suggest that a cause for some undesired behavior may result from some event outside of the home. A simple example might be with a young child having a negative attitude which is affecting behaviors with siblings. A parent may first think it is a sibling problem, but perhaps the child is being bullied by someone at school and carrying the resulting negative feelings home. This suggests that it is important to consider a variety of reasons which might be causing some behavior before deciding what might be the best approach to resolve it.

3. *Wisdom* from the *Social Order* Approach

The *social order* approach involves viewing how the family is a social system with the use of established rules to govern it. The following are some of the prominent *wisdom of the ages* of this approach.

- **Micro-social system** has been used to describe the nature of the family as a social system in itself, much like the larger systems of the political world, as noted by Parsons,[75] Bell & Vogel,[76] and Dreikurs.[20] The point is that the family, as a small social system, also has the need for an economy, a means of governance, a sense of community, and a value system. That especially means setting rules and having some means of gaining acceptance or enforcing them. What does this mean for parents? Rudolf Dreikurs sensed the need for a parenting approach that emphasized aspects of the social order of the family. He contended that if you want your children to live in a democracy, they should be raised in a family reflecting democratic principles, which involve rules and consequences for violation of them.

In line with the idea of community, Dreikurs also suggested that family meetings or councils be held weekly where the children can participate in making family decisions. Some parents may fear that they might be "out voted" on an issue. They should realize that systems of governance often provide the leader with veto powers when felt appropriate—which again should be viewed as fair, yet used with discretion, only when really needed. The following *wisdom of the ages* is key to the approach proposed by Dreikurs.

- **Natural consequences and logical consequences** are two of the primary responses recommended by writers following the tradition of Dreikurs. In seeking to reflect society, it is observed that in many aspects of life, when any of us oppose or violate some natural law, there are *natural consequences.* If we are careless with a fragile object and drop it, it will break; if we are careless with ourselves and fall, we may get hurt. If children come home late, after dinner, they might have to eat cold leftovers, or prepare something for themselves; or, if late getting up for the school bus, walking to school may be the *natural consequence.*

  Logical consequences are planned consequences when some natural consequence doesn't seem to follow or be appropriate. For example, in the case of a toy, if it is used in an unacceptable way, an appropriate natural consequence may not follow; however, it may be put away for awhile, a *logical consequence.*

  Of importance with *logical consequences* is that they should relate to the behavior where possible. This is why writers following this approach tend not to rely too much on "time-outs" or "grounding," since these methods tend not to be a logical consequence, directly related to the misbehavior. Often, parents using "time-outs" use them for most behaviors, even when there may be some very good and more appropriate alternative *logical consequence* that could be used.

If a child recognizes and understands the point which the parent is trying to achieve, the child often can be helpful in arriving at a good logical consequence–such as the use of brain-storming, as strongly urged by both Gordon[27] and Guerney.[77] As implied earlier, consequences should be viewed as fair by the child and used consistently and calmly by the parent.

These principles of *natural* and *logical consequences* are emphasized in two programs which follow the Adlerian approach: Michael Popkin's *Active Parenting* program, as covered in his book, *Active parenting now parent's guide*;[78] and Don Dinkmeyer & Gary McKay's *STEP* program, conveyed in their book, *The parent's handbook: Systematic training for effective parenting.*[79]

All of this is similar to civil laws. If we violate some civil law, there is a *logical consequence* which legislators have established. Dreikurs urged that if children are reared to live in a democracy, such should be established in the home.

- **Responsibility, cooperation, and courage** are important characteristics for all members of the family to possess, as discussed by Dreikurs & Soltz[21] and expanded upon more fully by Popkin in his program, *Active parenting now.*[78] By developing these in children, parents likely will have children who contribute their share to the system and support its rules.

- **Values: See "NOTE" below before References.**

- **Rules and limit setting** are critical elements involved in guiding children in the family, as viewed by Dreikurs. Limit setting was the major topic of an early writing by Louise Guerney.[80] The Guerneys, Louise and Bernard, incorporated an intriguing and effective method of introducing *limit setting* to a child, as utilized in their play therapy program, a non-directive-play parent education program (training workshop, 1979).

  This *limit setting* method, when needed, as instructed by the Guerneys involves the following steps: (1) first inform the child of a rule if a perceived misbehavior occurs (Note: this is assuming that some misbehavior has just happened that you had not been aware of before, but do not want it to be repeated; in contrast, if the child broke a rule that had been previously established, then one would skip this first response, and move on to the next); (2) if the rule is broken a second time, then remind the child of the rule and state the consequence if it happens again, stating what it would be; and, (3) finally, if the rule is broken again, consistently follow-through with the consequence, carrying it out in a calm, matter of fact way with no anger or hostility–a *social learning* experience.. Using this in a home setting, it might be helpful to explain to the child the reason why the behavior is inappropriate.

As parents, we often see our child doing something which we think, "Oops, they should not be allowed to do that." An example of this process might be as follows. A child is playing with a ball and occasionally hits it hard against a window. First, the child would be told, "One of the rules is we can't hit the window with the ball." Of course, you could drop the term "rule" and merely say, "Be careful, we can't hit the window with the ball, it might break it." Then, if it happens a second time, you would say, "Remember, one of the rules is that we can't hit the window with the ball. If it happens again, we'll have to put the ball away for today." Then, if it happens a third time, the child would be told, "Remember, the rule is not to hit the window. We'll now have to put the ball back in the closet for the rest of the day," and have the child put the ball in the closet (or wherever). In the future, if repeated violations occur, the time could be increased for not being able to play with the ball (or whatever toy might be involved).

Naturally, if the misbehavior was of a more serious nature, the process could be speeded up, stating the rule and consequence on the first occasion. For example, saying, "One of the rules is that we can't be hitting our sister like that when playing. If it happens again, you'll have to ... (giving the consequence desired, such as stop playing, or be restricted from some other special outing, etc.)."

This method of warning can be applied in any number of other situations with appropriate consequences. Consistency and carry-through is extremely crucial if the method is to be effective. Speaking of consistency, David Walsh, author for the book, *No: Why kids–of all ages–need to hear it and ways parents can say it*,[81] is the motivation behind the "Say Yes to No" movement. This underscores the importance of limit setting and the benefits which it can instill in children.

- ***Styles of parenting*** refer to the manner in which a parent manages children in terms of control, communication, and nurture. The topic appears to have been first written upon in 1964 by Wesley Becker;[82] however, Diane Baumrind expanded upon the theme, writing to other professionals rather than parents.[83,84,85,86] She describes four styles of parenting: authoritative, authoritarian, permissive (or indulgent, according to Maccoby & Martin[87]), and uninvolved or neglectful. For sake of avoiding repetition describing these four styles, see Kevin Gross' earlier article on this topic in this book, "Parenting with Style." Most parenting books tend to encourage the use of the authoritative style.

4. *Wisdom* from the *Personality-Character* Approach

The *personality-character* approach involves viewing the development of "who" the child becomes. The following are some of the prominent *wisdom of the ages* of this approach.

- *Traits of personality* are what make children and adults different from one another. While not a profound *wisdom* for parents, it is a building block for this area of study, *personality*. Parents are sometimes amazed at how their own children differ so much from one another. This is somewhat explained by *trait theorist* Gordon Allport, an early pioneer of personality theory, who focused upon traits that characterize us. Said to be the first to offer a college course on personality theory,[88] he contended that we all have a few *central traits* that make up our personality, with *cardinal traits* that tend to dominate our personality. Also, there are *secondary traits* which reflect other aspects of a person, such a food preference, and there are *common traits* which are typical, recognized and named in given cultures, such as introverts and extroverts. Allport's 1961 book, *Pattern and growth in personality,* more extensively expanded upon this, including his views of psychological maturity.[89]

  Karen Horney (horn-eye, hornai) suggested a variety of reasons as to why children and adults differ in terms of traits. She observed that the dominant traits depend upon individual gifts (genetics) and psychic substructures, but they also are influenced by external circumstances. These might include different situations which confront a child, early initial interaction patterns with other significant persons, and the satisfaction derived by trial and error. The point being that a child will tend to repeat behaviors that fulfill needs of the situation, repeating those that bring satisfaction, or a sense of safety.[90,91] Consequently, it can be important as with whom an infant or young child interacts on a regular basis–the parents as well as care givers and babysitters. The important factor is whether situations are laden with love and acceptance, or with fear, threats, disapproval, tension, emotional anxiety, or domination. Horney covered much of this topic in her "still in print" classic book, *Our inner conflicts: A constructive theory of neurosis.*[91]

To further explain the differences between children, the more present-time *behavioral genetic theory* has focused upon the genetic aspect of these traits. This topic touches upon the issue that is sometimes debated, *nature vs. nurture*, that is, heredity or environmental influences. Though many of our behaviors are influenced by nurture from parents and others, there is much growing evidence that many of our traits have a genetic root, even including characteristics of our parenting style.[92]

- *Goals of misbehavior,* sometimes referred to as mistaken goals of behavior, is a major theme of followers of Alfred Adler and his notion that each child has a *social interest,* to belong, to love and to be loved.[93,94] If there are occasions of not feeling loved, then a child is apt to respond in what appears to be a misbehavior. As expanded upon by Dreikurs in his classic, *Children: The challenge,*[21] the *discouraged child,* when not feeling a sense of love and acceptance, will tend to respond with misbehaviors either of (1) *seeking attention;* (2) responding with *power or aggression;* (3) seeking *revenge,* getting even; or, (4) *feelings of inadequacy,* and possible withdrawal. This tends to be the explanation for misbehaviors in many of the programs based on the Adlerian model. These goals are often misinterpreted by some writers who suggest that they are the explanation of *all* misbehaviors. However, Alder/Dreikurs made it clear that these misbehaviors pertain to the *discouraged child* and it is the discouraged child who truly needs encouragement.

One can make a long list of other reasons, beyond those of the discouraged child, as to why a child might misbehave (see Appendix C). The reasons could be numerous, including such things as: accidents, anger, anxiety, boredom, confusion or misunderstanding, curiosity, fatigue, fear, frustration, jealousy, mixed message from a parent, modeling other's behavior, peer pressure, and testing limits, etc. Consequently, it is important that parent not too quickly impute negative intent upon all misbehaviors of a child.

Back to the Adlerian view on misbehaviors, Karen Horney gives a helpful understanding of them in her classic book, *Our inner conflicts.*[91] She noted that although we all have some of each tendency, some children (and adults) accent one of the following three behaviors: (1) *moving towards others,* seeking attention, acceptance, and love; (2) *moving against others* (models they have seen in others), being merely assertive, however sometimes becoming aggressive and attempting to control others and the situation; or, (3) *moving away from others,* not finding acceptance and love and, therefore, withdrawing from others where they seek to become self-sufficient and not depend on others who have rejected them. Thus, we see clearer reasons for the importance of expressing love, acceptance, empathy, and understanding to our children. Often, these characteristics as outlined by Horney can readily be observed in some teens and adults.

- **Character development** as a topic was studied well over a century ago by some of the pioneers in the field, including G. Stanley Hall, founder of the American Psychological Association in 1892, who was viewed as the leader of the child study movement with an emphasis on character development.[95] Yet, it was not until 1931 with Gordon Allport's book, *The study of values,*[96] that we find something more insightful for parents. Allport suggested that people have six primary values, expressed as: (1) the *theoretical* person pertaining to *truth;* (2) the *economic* person regarding the usefulness of *things;* (3) the *aesthetic* person regarding *form and harmony;* (4) the *social* person regarding *love of others;* (5) the *political* person related to *power;* and, (6) the *religious* person with a focus upon *unity.* His writing does provide some core character values to build upon. However, there does not appear to have been any attempt to put this material into a more useful format for parents to use.

  For the benefit of parents and others, there now are many books written, often for children, on specific character traits, such as: cooperation, courage, honesty, integrity, justice, kindness, loyalty, patience, responsibility, self-discipline, self-respect, and trustworthiness. The California Department of Education maintains an annotated bibliography of writings on character development.[97] In addition, the Center for Youth Ethics, part of the Josephson Institute, maintains a listing of children's books which focus on character building, involving what they call the six pillars of character: *trustworthiness, respect, responsibility, fairness, caring, and citizenship.*[98]

- **The ordinal position, or the birth order,** of children in the family does tend to influence their development, resulting in different traits between one's own children. This was first observed in 1930 by Adler.[99] According to him, each child in the family will seek to establish his or her own unique place in the family. Eventually, this topic drew further study by others, early ones being Toman[100] and Belmont & Marolla.[101] Kevin Leman has popularized the topic in his writing, *The birth order book,*[102] which parents might find interesting. Adler recognized that the social environment of the child certainly had an effect as well, which Leman expands upon further, including possible effects of spacing of the children, their sex, adoption, and blended families, as well as the effects of physical, emotional, and intellectual differences. Nevertheless, *birth order* often does appear to affect some differences which many parents might see in their children.

- **Self-esteem: See "NOTE" below before References.**

- **Life positions** involve an interesting concept expressed first by Eric Berne in 1962,[103] which he and others have observed in family life. The *life positions* were popularized by Thomas Harris with his book, *I'M OK–YOU'RE OK.*[104] The positions, initially influenced and determined by the responses which parents or primary care givers express to infants, are: (1) *I'm OK–You're OK;* (2) *I'm OK–You're not OK;* (3) *I'm not OK–You're OK;* or, (4) *I'm not OK–You're not OK.* The contention is that a child's initial position is fairly well determined near the end of the first year of life.

Due to the all too typical negative messages parents tend to send to children, Harris contended that during the first year of life, most if not all people begin with the notion of *I'm not OK.* Granted, in the first year, there is the usual cuddling and comforting; however, the negative messages tend to outweigh the positive *strokes* given to infant. It is asserted that for many persons, this position may persist throughout life.

Harris noted that for some children, receiving *strokes* tends to stop after the first year. This may especially occur for children with parents who are cool and somewhat non-expressive, added to the frustrations the parents may feel from the toddler's exploration. From these experiences, some children develop the feeling of *I'm not OK–You're not OK.* Consequently, such a child may become somewhat withdrawn. Unfortunately, other adults who might seek to provide *strokes* to such a child will tend to be rejected as well since the *You're not OK* feeling has become directed to all adults.

The *I'm OK–You're not OK* position is usually acquired by children who are abused, coming to this feeling in their second or third year of life. Harris sensed that such children, when recovering from wounds, come to recognize that by themselves, when alone, they are *OK*, and, in a sense, provide *self-stroking.* Harris noted that many children in this position, as they grow older, eventually tend to strike back, dominating others with their own toughness, which they observed earlier in their own life.

The *I'm OK–You're OK* position is one which children or adults may come to believe after some inward awareness. To achieve this position, they need more information and recognition of how to turn off the effects of negative feelings experienced in childhood, in order for them to assume more of an *Adult ego state–a topic* discussed later below under the *wisdom, transactional analysis.*

Here again, the *life positions* literature provides even more evidence as to the crucial importance for infants and young children to have a loving, caring, compassionate, reasoning, and nurturing environment in which to grow. Without it, some of the outcomes as portrayed by Berne and Harris are tragic.

Numerous books and programs have evolved under the topic of *transactional analysis (TA)*[105] from these notions of Berne and Harris, though Harris' book remains a classic.

5. Wisdom from the *Interactional-Transactional-Ecological* Approach

The *interactional-transactional-ecological* approach involves viewing the actions and their effects occurring between family members and other social systems. The following are some of the prominent *wisdom of the ages* of this approach.

- *"The family as a unit of interacting personalities"* was the title of an article written in 1926 by Ernest W. Burgess.[106] This theme, *a unit of interacting personalities,* has played a dominant place in writings on family and parent/child interactions. Many layers of studies have been built upon this theme to the benefit of families. Topics have covered issues of communication, interaction dynamics, meanings or intentions conveyed, reasoning, cognitive perceptions, and enhancement techniques which contribute to building harmony, respect, and cooperation. An essential notion of this theme is that if one person changes in the system, the entire system will change.

For parents, much focus is upon the parent's role in guiding and influencing the child. However, with this notion of *interacting personalities* another principle comes into play, a *reciprocal affect*: the child also influences/changes the parent by their behavior–it is a two-way street, a bi-directional interaction effect. For example, a parent might "fly off the handle," getting mad with a child; however, the child might respond in such a mature understanding manner that it brings the parent "back down to earth."

Importantly, one parent should recognize the effect she or he can have on the family. Often parents express the concern that they are the only parent willing to take a parent education course or to seek counseling. However, with the dynamics of *interacting personalities,* one person/parent can affect the whole system. If one person in the system changes their behavior, others in the family will have to respond differently as a result. This should encourage parents who feel that they are the only one seeking improvements–they can have a positive effect. Also, we sometimes hear of one member of a family seeking counseling alone, wishing instead to engage in it with a partner or child. Similarly, the advice often given is, "Be assured, if you change your behavior, the others in the family (system) will be forced to change in response to it."

- **The ecological approach** pertaining to the family, while involving interactions within the family, has come to refer also to the *transactions* by or between family members with forces and systems outside of the family, such as the environment in which the family lives. These include the school, community centers, doctor's offices, parents' work settings, and larger institutions of the economy, church, and government. These influences were clearly recognized in 1960 by Hill & Hansen as *transactions* between family members and sub-units or social systems beyond the family. Issues arising from these *transactions* were considered to be *situations,*[31] or the *situational-psychological habitat,*[30] similar to the term *ecology;* that is, a combination of circumstances or factors involving the family and the physical, social, and/or psycho-cultural effects of external forces or systems.

  These *situations* tend to be studied in an attempt to lead to recommendations to benefit the family and its individual members. Such recommendations tend to result from studies involving several different approaches discussed throughout various sections of this article; therefore, they will be discussed more fully in the last approach below, the *eclectic*.

After Hill & Hansen's work, Urie Bronfenbrenner, a psychologist, wrote extensively and in more detail on similar aspects, calling it the *ecological* perspective,[107] derived from the term, *ecology,* a word coined in 1873 by the German zoologist, Ernst Haeckel (Online Etymology Dictionary). Essentially, Bronfenbrenner discussed similar areas, *interactions* between parent and child and siblings as well as *transactions* with other social systems external to the family. The uniqueness of his expanded in-depth analysis was to organize these forces which have an impact upon the child into a logical pattern; for example, how poverty or culture might influence the development of the child.

Bronfenbrenner identified numerous external systems, classified into these levels: (1) moving out from the child to the immediate family and home setting, which was called the *microsystem;* (2) to the *mesosystem,* involving the interaction of two systems, the child and/or the family with care givers, schools, or neighborhood play areas; (3) then to the *exosystem,* involving subsystems which indirectly influence the child, such as the extended family, friends, the neighborhood, community services, school boards, the legal system, and mass media; and (4) the *macrosystem,* other more distant influences involving the cultural customs and social class. A fifth system, the *chronosystem* was added later, to incorporate aspects of time and life transitions of a child that alter the interactions of the subsystems affecting the child.[108] In the edited book, *Parenting: An ecological perspective,* this *ecological system* analysis has been viewed by Okagaki & Luster as providing scholars with a better focus for directing research on the child, parenting, and the family.[109]

In a practical sense, what does this *ecological* view mean for parents? Thomas W. Roberts sought to offer an answer in his book, *A Systems perspective of parenting: The individual, the family, and the social network.*[110] Roberts suggested that a book should be written for parents in which specific parenting issues are discussed using the "systems concepts to parenting" (p.23), or "a new parent-education model" (p. 87). He offers a family portrait of a problem (p. 24ff), analyzing (perhaps with some biases) how different perspectives might handle the situation ineffectively, and then how the *systems* perspective might deal with it. Unfortunately, it appears that such a book has not yet been written.

To the credit of some other approaches, the *systems* or *ecological* perspective is somewhat recognized. As discussed earlier, the behaviorists do recognize that some problems may be caused by *antecedent* factors, which should be considered rather than jumping right into some charting and reinforcement plan. Likewise, in discussions below, the P.E.T approach clearly stresses the need for parents to listen to their children with empathy, which may reveal other unexpected influences causing the child to behave in an undesired manner. The P.E.T approach also encourages the use of the *"no-lose"* method of problem solving, which seeks to explore various causes of a problem, seeking full information that bears on the problem. When carefully considered, these approaches may help parents to recognize that *family problems* may clearly be affected by possible influences which come from outside of the immediate family, involving the *systems* or *ecological* viewpoint.

As inferred above, most studies or ideas generated from the *ecological* perspective focus on specific *situations,* seeking to help parents and/or children deal with the impact upon them from forces outside of the family. Examples would be issues such as work and family, and helping the family to support or assist the school with efforts to educate the child. As noted, they too will be discussed in the last section below, the *eclectic.*

- **Parent/child communication programs** are central in the *interactional* approach for parents. The major program contributor initially was Thomas Gordon with a classic book first published in 1970 called, *Parent effectiveness training.*[27] Concurrently, Bernard Guerney was working on a training manual for educators, published as a book in 1977 called, *Relationship enhancement.*[77] A more contemporary book which covers the topic or parents is by Adele Faber & Elaine Mazlish called, *How to talk so kids will listen & listen so kids will talk.*[111]

One can read a book which contains suggested exercises as a means to improve upon communication skills, such a Gordon's book; however, it can be more effective to take part in a program in which there is group practice along with some feedback on progress. There are national organizations that continue to support the three programs noted above. They can be contacted through their web sites: Thomas Gordon's at www.gordontraining.com, Guerney's at www.nire.org, and Faber and Mazlish's at www.fabermazlish.com.

The following three *wisdoms* are some of the more common ones related to aspects of communication.

• **Active listening** involves listening not only to the words another person is saying but also the feelings and possible veiled meaning behind them. Parents especially are encouraged to use active listening when children are expressing their personal concerns or worries, as well as when involved in what appears to be an argument. Guerney called this *empathic responding,* seeking to pick up on what the child is saying. By doing so, parents might avoid too quickly jumping to some wrong conclusion or not hearing the real message the child is trying to express. If *active listening* is new to someone, it generally does take practice in order to get a feeling of doing it well. Gordon offers some practice exercises in the back of his book to assist parents.

Most of us may think, "Of course, I listen." Yet, when we get in tense situations or arguments, often the other person may not feel that we have really heard or understood them. Poor listening has likely occurred when we hear such things as: "Did you hear what I said?" or "You didn't hear a thing I said." We probably realize that these statements are all too common. They reveal how people often do not listen well. The need is for responses which more closely convey our understanding of what the child is trying to say.

The first century philosopher, Epicetus, adds some insight to this notion of *active listening* when saying: "We have two ears and one mouth so that we can listen twice as much as we speak." If not active listening, we may too quickly respond by giving our own opinion or reaction. In doing this, we often cut off children from more fully explaining themselves or clarifying what they mean. We might wrongly turn the conversation more to our reaction to them than upon what they are trying to say. Gordon called these roadblocks, which might include: orders, warnings, threats, moralizing, advising, lecturing, judging, criticizing, disagreeing, blaming, praising, ridiculing, and questioning.

Roadblock responses can quickly have the effect of shutting our children off from even trying or wanting to talk with us, as we turn conversations away from a child's feelings and concerns and focus upon our lectures or advice. If a parent doesn't helpfully listen to a child, the child may in time seek out someone else who will listen to them. It is a choice that we, as parents, need to recognize.

Another way of explaining what *active listening* involves is the way Carl Rogers, years before Gordon's work, expressed in his 1951 writing, when he encouraged counselors to use *reflective listening.* He described it as verbalizing back to people the key ideas, words, feelings, and thoughts we have heard them say.[112] This is a skill we all use at times but most of us can improve upon it.

Better listening responses convey a clear message of understanding to the child. Granted, it is not always appropriate to respond with *reflective* comments in a lot of normal day-to-day conversations. Yet, when a child is expressing a concern or there is a disagreement, *active listening* is most appropriate. This practice is what "*listening*" training involves. It can help not only when in conflict with someone close to us such as our children, but also when listening to anyone who is upset or bothered, whether a co-worker, customer, or anyone who is frustrated. Often a person or a child merely needs someone who will listen.

The first duty of love is to listen.
– *Paul Tillich*

- "*I" messages* are an aspect of how better to get our point across to someone. It is useful if we are seeking to have a resistant child comply with our wishes or when responding in an argument. Instead of being heavy-handed or accusatory, "*I" messages* are intended to express how we feel about a matter. Instead of telling children that you are upset or mad at them, you let them know *why* you are upset and *how* they can help. For example, "It upsets me when I can't serve breakfast nice and warm for you, and all of us. I really would appreciate it if you'd make a little special effort to be here sooner."

An essential part of the "*I" message* is that we express our feelings about the issue. It has been noted that a person is the world's best expert when it comes to his or her own feelings. A child may argue about our saying, "You SHOULD do this or that." But a child can't deny or argue with your saying, "It UPSETS me when I have to do so and so," or "It HURTS me when someone says to me (or does) ...." or " "It would PLEASE ME if you would help me." Thomas Gordon calls these "*I-messages*," in contrast to "You-messages."

Gordon noted that his conception of the "*I Message*" came from Sidney Jourard and Carl Rogers, both of whom acknowledge the influence of the earlier 1958 writings of the philosopher, Martin Buber, conveyed in his book, *I and thou.*[113] Sidney Jourard in 1964 wrote an insightful book, *The transparent self,*[114] in which he discusses the struggles of fully revealing one's self to another, stressing that for a person to fully know oneself, one should be *transparent;* that is, express the inner feelings of the self. Likewise, Carl Rogers in his 1961 book, *On becoming a person,*[115] discusses the need to recognize and reveal one's own feelings to others, linking self revelation, or *"I" messages,* to Martin Buber's concepts of the *I-Thou* and *I-It.*

The process of using *"I" messages* is a little more complex than *active listening* which was discussed above. In similar vain, Bernard Guerney suggested that such *expressive* messages include the following six steps, not necessarily carried out in this exact order:

(1) *be subjective,* by stating your own views ("I feel..." or "It bothers me when...");

(2) *state your feelings* in terms of emotions you are feeling;

(3) *be specific* in behavioral terms, that is, giving specific instances or examples of the concern, not generalizations, so the other person can better understand what you mean, and not use generalizations, such as, "You always ...(or never) ..."

These three elements could be summarized as Popkin and Dinkmeyer & MacKay do in their programs, by statements such as: "I *feel* [stating the emotion]...*when* [event or concern, not using the word 'you'],...*because* [reason]...;" or, another example: "I'm concerned when...[so and so happens], because ...;" or "I get annoyed because I notice that...[the specific concern]." Translated, one might say, "I'm really upset when I have to pick up clothes and towels all over the bathroom floor when I feel it is not my job to do that."

In addition to these three elements stressed by Gordon, Guerney suggested three additional steps, which seem worthwhile to consider saying.

(4) *Say something good* related to the matter or issue that is of concern, especially if criticism is implied in what you have to say. The purpose of this is to assure the child that you do recognize his past desire or ability to do what you wish. It also can tell the child that you do have a basically good regard for her and really have hope for a positive solution to the issue. The *something good* may involve a compliment on how well a similar thing was done in the past, which acknowledges that the child isn't all bad. Also, if the primary problem discussed involves a strongly emotional issue, it may be better to state the *something good* first, before the first

three steps. The person is apt to feel less hostile or defensive and more willing to listen. An example of this *something good* might be: "I really appreciate how you willingly help me and usually do a very good job. You really make me feel that you want to help. However, when...[the concern], it makes me feel sad. It would make me feel very pleased if you'd...[do so and so, leading into step 5 below]."

(5) Then, *state your desires, suggestion, or request* about how to help solve the issue or problem, and how you'd feel if it is done. Invite his or her ideas, as well. Avoid using shoulds and demands. Keep the door open to other alternatives or ideas. The goal is to maximize the satisfaction for both persons.

When making a request of a child, Marshall Rosenberg interestingly stresses the importance of using positive action verbs, so the child can clearly understand what you want done, and using do's when possible rather than don'ts.[116] A child can more easily comply if we are specific about what we'd like them to do.

(6) The last step of Guerney's is to *convey empathy*, showing how you understand why they might have done what they did; that is, the original action that bothered you. This doesn't mean you necessarily agree with or like what was done, but you understand why it might have been done. You also can let the child know you realize that it may not be easy to do what you want, and how you will appreciate it if they do it. An example might be: "I realize that you have been very busy lately and possibly haven't found much time to do...[what you have wanted him/her to do]; however, it would please me now if you would find the time to do it."

Guerney noted that these six steps don't have to be conveyed or said all in one breath, but it is helpful if they are mentioned eventually as you tell the child about what concerns you. If we express ourselves in this manner, we'll find ourselves talking more calmly or caringly with our child, even though we still may be angry or annoyed. Also, we are more likely to seek solutions to our concerns together if we express ourselves to each other in this manner: (1) being *subjective*; (2) expressing *feelings*; (3) being *specific* about the concern; (4) saying *something good*; (5) stating your *desire or request*; and, (6) conveying *empathy*, or understanding.

If not attempting to convey our concerns in a calm manner such as this, we can easily get into an attacking manner where we get side-tracked from solutions by name calling, accusations, or arguing in circles. Sometimes we need to keep reminding ourselves that our goal is to achieve solutions. By including the last three steps, it can better help us reach our goals, as Marshall Rosenberg suggested in his workshops–we will more likely get others to do what we want by using methods we won't regret later on.

Translating these six steps, one might say: "I know and appreciate how you keep things pretty neat in your bedroom; however, it bothers me when I find your clothes and towels scattered over the bathroom floor when you're done. It seems like I am expected to pick them up. I would appreciate it if you'd put them all where they belong yourself. I know how sometimes you are in a big hurry to go somewhere, but picking up after our self is part of 'living together.'" Lengthy to say all of this? Yes, but it is using a method for which you will not be sorry about later.

For some other helpful suggestions for conveying our feelings better, see Appendix D, "When You Feel Like Yelling, Screaming, or Slamming the Door: Alternatives to Communicate More Effectively."

For most of us, effective listening and expressing ourselves can be improved upon. We are apt to learn better through some form of practice or short-term formal training. It is naive to think that we can simply read this *wisdom* and successfully begin to do all of these things overnight. Certainly, reading books on the topic that have been mentioned above could be helpful.

• **The no-lose method** of problem solving with children is another major theme in Gordon's book, *P.E.T.* Adapting from some of his ideas (p. 237), the problem solving approach involves: (1) understanding the problem, identify and define the conflict; (2) getting more information if possible, possibly asking what happened, not "who did it"; (3) considering alternative solutions, perhaps brainstorming for ideas with the child, keeping the door open to each other's ideas; (4) evaluating alternative solutions by asking what will be achieved by that solution and how the child feels about doing it, as well as ourself–does the solution look like it will solve the problem? Is it fair to all persons? Then, (5) picking the best acceptable solution and trying it out; and, (6) evaluating the outcome after a short while to see if it is working; if not, select anther alternate solution.

If desired goals aren't being achieved, Gordon suggested that we should carefully review all that has been done by examining whether a step has been slighted or ignored and skipped. We also need to ask if we have made the child feel accepted by the manner of our listening or expressing ourselves. If we haven't, perhaps the child isn't being open and honest due to fear or distrust. Again, it is beneficial to keep a calm and friendly mood throughout the discussion.

- **Stupid thinking**, a blunt and hopefully humorous way to put it, is Albert Ellis' term for irrational thinking that either a parent or child may use that creates more problems when trying to resolve a problem. Discussed in his 1957 book, *How to live with a neurotic: At home and work*,[117] Ellis developed an approach called *rational-emotive therapy*, as reported by George Boeree, crediting the influence on his work to the words of the 2nd century philosopher, Marcus Aurelius: "If you are distressed by anything external, the pain is not due to the thing itself but to your own estimate [thinking] of it; and this you have the power to revoke at any moment."[118] Thoughts of a first century philosopher, Epicetus, aptly adds to this: "What concerns me is not the way things are, but rather the way people think things are."

  These thoughts, along with those of Ellis are similar to Aaron Beck's notions about unrealistic negative beliefs about oneself, leading to his book, *Cognitive therapy and emotional disorders*.[119] The goal in dealing with irrational thinking is to help people confront these beliefs when used in reaching conclusions about themselves, about life events, and relationship issues which can lead to poor outcomes.

  Essentially, the approach uses an ABC model. We experience an activating event (A) which we examine, interpret, or otherwise think about what happened. Our perception of these events results in specific beliefs (B) about the event. Then we experience emotional and behavioral consequences (C), our reaction, which is based solely on our belief,[120] not necessarily reality.

  How does this apply to parents and children? William Glasser more recently wrote on this topic to parents in his book, *For parents and teenagers: Dissolving the barrier between you and your teen.*[121] In this book, as somewhat in his earlier one in 1965, *Reality therapy*,[122] Glasser is writing for parents who have teens who are pushing for more freedom. He uses the term *choice therapy* in pointing out how we have *choices* and that it is a false notion to conclude, "She made me do it." A situation does not make us do things; rather, our perception of the situation controls our actions.

When a teenager makes a wrong choice, Glasser seeks to lead parents into understanding how better to deal with such situations, giving numerous case studies in his book. The teen doesn't make the parent ground them; it is a *choice* among others that a parent has.

For parents who favor grounding and find that it isn't working, that is, the same misbehaviors keep occurring, Ellis and Glasser would both agree on a central premise of the cognitive approach: a parent, or person, should realize that *if what you are doing isn't working, don't keep doing it; do something different!* Make a different choice, getting rid of what apparently is some *irrational thinking* being used in reaching decisions. Try to more rationally think through the situation, maybe letting go of cherished beliefs that a certain approach should be used. Coming up with a different solution might be helped by reading Glasser's book, *For parents and teenagers,* or using some of the steps mentioned above in the *no-lose method* of problem solving.

What you believe is true is true in its consequences.
    —*W. I. Thomas*

[Viewed another way: We act as if what we believe is true; that is, we act on our perceptions of what is true, whether they are accurate or not.]

• **Meta-communication** reveals the complexity of our talking, a way of examining *"communication" about "communication."* It involves talking about the nature of what is being said, first expounded upon by George Bateson in 1972.[123] The principle idea here is that often the message sent is not always the message received. Overlying the mere words that we speak are the *intonations* and *volume* of how the words are spoken, the *body language* of those speaking as well as *facial expressions,* the *situation or context* in which the conversation takes place, the *special meaning* that some words may have for one person which differ from the meaning to the other person, and the *power or relationships issues* between the two people speaking.

If there is a crucial misunderstanding, it can be helpful for parents and children to sit down together and talk, *meta-communicate,* about what has been conveyed. Talking about what was said, meant, implied, and intended can be helpful to achieve more effective understanding. This *talking about our talk* can be an interesting exercise for two people. If done calmly, it can be an enlightening and refreshing experience.

Also, implied in the above is the *meta-message,* wherein Bateson contended that with every message, two are sent. One is the words; the other is the meaning intended. They may coincide; yet, they may differ. If they differ, this could introduce a "Catch-22" situation for a child, closely related to the **double-bind** as described by Bateson and others.[124] That is, a child hears two different messages that conflict with each other. It can be frustrating and paralyzing in a sense—the message of the words spoken do not match the tone and feeling by which they are expressed, and the child has no escape from the situation. It could lead to a no-win situation for the child in which acting upon either of the messages will mean that one of the messages will not be fulfilled, with possible punishment following. For example, a child may be told, "It is fine to tell the truth; what really did happen?" The child may know full well from the underlying tone of voice and emotions convey that "all heck" will break loose if he does in fact tell the truth. This situation is expanded on more fully in an earlier article in this book by Jody Johnston Pawel, "Teaching kids to lie? What parents' actions say." Unfortunately, not too much about *meta-communication* has been directly translated into literature for parents.

- **Transactional Analysis** is an interesting way of looking at our communication patterns. Have you ever caught yourself arguing with one of your children and all of a sudden you realize that you sound just like one of them, like another child, as if you are two sisters or brothers arguing with each other? If so, your child likely *hooked* your inner Child. Another example: have you caught yourself hearing one of your children ask you a simple question and, rather than calmly answering, you start talking with a real big bossy tone of voice, telling them, "No, you can NOT do that!"? This time your *Parent* has been hooked. These are two examples of *crossed transactions.*

  Eric Berne, the author of *Games People Play,*[125] proposed that we all have three *ego states,* a system of feelings and behavior patterns. They were expanded upon in a more popular vein by Thomas Harris in his related book, *I'M OK—YOU'RE OK,*[108] discussed in the previous section of this article. The *ego states,* identified by being capitalized, were the

Parent, the *Adult*, and the *Child*, often referred to as P-A-C or PAC. For each person, these three *ego states* are uniquely different, since they are based upon our own individual experiences. When the *Parent, Child,* or *Adult ego states* are being expressed verbally and emotionally by a person, they tend to appear different by virtue of their manner, gestures, words, and tone of voice. As a *Parent*, the voice is apt to sound bossy, as a *Child,* whiney, and as an *Adult,* it is apt to sound more calm, rational, and mature.

Essentially, the *Parent* embraces the *taught concept,* the recorded messages in our memory of the *parent* role, having heard these *Parent* messages from our own parents or other parents, including the emotions felt at the time, the happy occasions as well as the frustrating or sad ones. The *Parent* recordings include the family rules, the dos and don'ts, and the "how to" do things we heard, as well as words of comfort and caring and those of criticism, ordering, or lecturing. Sometimes when these recordings of the *Parent* are expressed by us to our children they may be very fitting and helpful; yet, at times they may be inappropriate and hurtful.

The *Child* involves the *felt concept,* the memories of the inner *Child,* such as seeking strokes or expressions of comfort from others, as well as including feelings of happiness, fear, frustration, or annoyance. The *inner Child* would encompass those feelings, understandings, and reactions to what the child experienced from the messages recorded from their own parents. Harris noted that there is a mixture of feelings in the *Child,* the feeling of the *"I'm not OK" Child* as well as feeling of the creative and playful, happy *Child,* with many fond memories of pleasure and discovery.

The *Adult,* the *thought concept,* is the more mature person living in the here and now, acting with calmness and reasoning, based upon observations, information, impressions, and facts. Harris noted that this *Adult ego state* begins to emerge at about ten months of ago when the child begins to explore and move around under his or her own control; yet, it continues to develop throughout one's life. Eventually, a function of the *Adult* is to examine the content of the *Parent* and the *Child* in order to determine whether their lessons and feelings are accurate and useful. For example, "Don't run into the street!"–yep, it is useful information, as the child observes the family dog being hit by a car; however the fear, anger, or frustration associated with the earlier experience is still there, as a recording. Once understood in terms of the situation where the feelings arose, the *Adult* can choose to ignore those earlier feelings. Another function of the *Adult* is *probability estimation,* anticipating what might happen in the future, so as to plan to avoid foreseen problems. Yet, under stress, Harris points out that the *Adult* may be impaired, allowing for inappropriate emotions to be expressed–from the *Parent* or *Child.*

In the ideal world, it would be nice if we always talked as *Adult* to *Adult.* However, in reality, when talking with a child or another adult, what they say might *hook* into some memory of our *Parent* or *Child,* thus, prompting us to respond with our *Parent* or *Child ego state.* In such cases, the other person may be talking to us as an *Adult* to *Adult,* but rather than responding back as *Adult* to *Adult,* we respond back either as a *Parent* to *Child* or as a *Child* to *Parent,* a *crossed transaction.* When we hear ourselves talking like a *Child* or *Parent,* it is a time to quickly ask ourselves if we have been *hooked* into some pattern of past recording or memory. Then we might apologize to the person and seek to respond more appropriately as an *Adult.*

If some of this sounds familiar, one might find reading Harris' book interesting. Both Berne's and Harris' books are still in print. Also, other books have been written on the topic, including: James', *Born to win;*[126] Steiner's, *Scripts people live: Transactional analysis of life scripts;*[127] Stewart's, *TA today: A new introduction to transactional analysis.*[128] and, a 1970 series by Freed, *T.A. for tots;*[129] *The new T.A. for kids: (and for grown-ups, too);*[130] and, *T.A. for Teens: (and other important people).*[131]

- **The principle of least interest** is an interesting concept. The idea is that the person in a relationship with *the least interest* in maintaining it is in the position to exploit the other person who cares more; or, in disputes, the one with the least interest is in a better bargaining position. While often attributed to Willard Waller who reported it in his textbook, *The family,*[132] Waller did credit Edward A. Ross with the idea, Ross having first mentioned it in 1921, calling it "the law of personal exploration" (p. 191). Ross noted how it was demonstrated in couple relationships as well as between mothers and children. Ross further noted the principle in the study of dating couples, the results of which have been confirmed since in other studies.[133] Brian Jory, who studied aspects of power in families, reported how sometimes parents may exercise control over their children by using threats of sending them to a boarding school, or such, which involves this principle.[133] He further added that trust, loyalty, and personal freedom by family members, all crucial for a supporting and caring family, can be threatened by the misuse of power by parents or children.

This theme, the *principle of least interest,* relates to power structures in families as well, which have been studied widely. Interestingly, Theodore Caplow, in an early 1968 book, *Two against one: Coalitions in triads,* found that mothers have a far greater tendency to join in coalitions, or *coalition power,* with their children rather than their husband, to off-set the power of the father in the family.[135] This was confirmed in a later study of Jory & others.[136] This suggests that families may want to be cautious as to how they unintentionally might be pushing certain members out of the family's circle of intimacy.

This principle has not been directly implemented into parenting programs; however, obviously it is a concept that might benefit parents to recognize and assist their children if caught up in a relationship, dating or friendship, where it may be present.

Related to this *power* issue, French & Raven in 1959 wrote about the various types of power within the family.[137] They noted six: (1) *legitimate power* based on belief systems of the family; (2) *informational power* from knowledge not known to others and used to gain power; (3) *referential power* based on affection and friendship; (4) *coercive power* by the use of physical or psychological power to impose upon or control others; (5) *expert power* based upon knowledge, training, or experience pertaining to some issue the family faces; and, (6) *reward power* due to the ability to provide physical or psychological benefits to others. Added to this complexity, Safilios-Rothschild pointed out that power within the family is significantly influenced by the family's culture and beliefs regarding gender.[138]

It does appear that parenting can be a challenging task, when considering all of the forces at work involving relationships within the family.

- **Family rituals,** perhaps without our realizing it, are among the meaningful ways we transmit our culture and values to our children, as interestingly described by James Bossard and Eleanor Boll whose pioneer study was reported in their 1950 book, *Ritual in family living.*[43] In our family routines, there likely are more rituals carried out than most of us realize. As suggested in the book, they may center upon the following: schooling and homework activities, music or dance lessons, family reading activities, table manners, customs of dress, summer vacation, allowances, religious observances, bathroom activities, caring for the ill, and family work activities.

These numerous rituals can be helpfully categorized into three types, *family celebrations, family traditions,* and *patterned routines,* as suggested by Steven Wolin & Linda Bennett.[139] More recent studies of family rituals and routines support many of the benefits suggested by Bossard & Boll. It is reported that children in homes who practice more family rituals show better performance in school [140,141,142] and are more socially competent.[143]

Besides conveying our culture and values, Bossard & Boll noted how rituals contribute to the social preparation of children: practice in group adjustment, respect individual rights in group living, facilitate household tasks, and stimulate and enhance family relationships, cooperation, and satisfaction. Their findings resulted from the study of about 80 autobiographies spanning most of the preceding 100 years as well as interviews and reports from about 300 families during the 1940s.

For a personal view of a family's experience with rituals, one can read the earlier article in this book by Arminta Jacobson titled, "Nurturing Traditions: Nurturing Family." Further reading on the topic also can be found in William Doherty's book, *The intentional family,*[144] as noted by Jacobson, as well as Barbara Biziou's book, *The joy of family rituals.*[145] Biziou offers numerous suggestions for families to develop their own rituals for specific occasions.

As Bossard & Boll observed, rituals might arise from any aspect of family life, derived largely unconsciously from "a prescribed pattern of social behaviors" in which each family member is expected to participate as part of the group functioning (p. 10). As with rituals in general, they convey "the way a thing is done," with an "element of rigidity" and a "sense of rightness" (p. 16). Calling upon the early work of G. Henke, it was noted that often rituals might emerge from trial and error in dealing with some situation, and rituals may be adjusted or even designed by thought, eventually becoming a "habitual, unconsciously performed pattern of behavior" (pp. 24f).

Early on, Bossard & Boll had focused upon family table talk, the role of guests in the home, and the part played in family life by their pets. While much attention was being given by others to study how society affected the family, they believed that very little study was looking at the family, itself, and how it operated on a day-to- day basis. They contended that stability of the family was an achievement in group living which merited further study, so that certain techniques which contribute to success could be studied, identified, understood, and evaluated in order to be consciously cultivated in family life.

• **Entrapped relationships** is a topic which some parents might find appropriate to discuss with one of their teenagers if they sense it might be a problem. When looking at dating relationships or engagements, we might sometimes wonder why a person doesn't break it off, ending the relationship. Sometimes teens have a problem doing so. This is discussed by Robert O. Blood, Jr., in his 1969 book, *Marriage*,[146] a topic which some parents might find useful to discuss with their teenager. Involved are relationships where the attraction or love that once existed has "died," but the couple does not break up. Blood noted numerous factors that may keep a person from breaking off such relationships, some that can be difficult to act upon for a teenager or young person. It may be helpful to talk over such situations with a daughter or son to help them avoid or get out of such situations.

The following deterrents were observed by Blood: (1) *lethargy* in giving up a known person to search for another, which does involve time and work; (2) *rapport* that one may still feel for the partner, which may involve some positive elements but not enough to wish for it to end in marriage; (3) *physical intimacy* may be involved, which is difficult to terminate due to the gratification it may provide and/or the pain involved in "dropping" the other person; (4) *emotional dependence* in terms of not wanting to hurt the other person or fear that they may not be able to handle the breakup, with Blood noting that a counselor may be more appropriate for the other person than a reluctant partner; (5) *social pressure* which may be felt from friends or families who are used to seeing the couple together; and, (6) *public commitment* resulting from an announced engagement, which would involve embarrassment and the returning of the ring; however, breaking it off may be much easier "now" than later on when ending a marriage by a divorce is much more difficult.

Some other more complex issues could be involved whereby one may allow another person to control them emotionally and, therefore, finds it hard to terminate the relationship. The Hazelden Foundation (www.hazelden.org) has helpful evidence-based programs that that can be offered in the community or school, including one on the topic of dating, *Safe Dates*, which includes abuse issues.

This *entrapped relationships* topic also relates to recent writings about boundaries in relationships. It is important that people maintain their own self identify and some sense of control over their activities. In these regards, Elyce Benham noted numerous factors that could be suggestive of an unhealthy relationship, such as: agreeing when you really disagree; concealing one's true feelings; going along with activities and never stating your preference; not engaging in activities which you really want to do; doing too much for the other person; and, ignoring one's needs.[147] A useful book that explores such issues might be found helpful, written by Charles L. Whitfield, *Boundaries and relationships: Knowing, protecting and enjoying the self*.[148]

Blood, as discussed above, did note that there are some aids to help in dissolving relationships, such as seeing the example of others who do change partners as well as receiving emotional support from friends, family, or a counselor. In expressing the reason for the breakup to a partner, it would be well to recall the suggestions above in the *wisdom* on using *"I" messages*, by expressing how one feels about the relationship rather than casting blame on the other.

- **Emotional nearness** was an intriguing concept noted in a 1961 article by Aaron Rutledge.[149] He was a prominent family professional leader and an early pioneer specializing in pre-marital counseling and wrote a book on the topic in 1966.[150] His conclusions on the nature of intimate relationships could be helpful for teenagers to recognize as they begin establishing meaningful relationships with the opposite or same sex. As adapted by Douglass Brown, Rutledge identified four essential characteristics that should be mutually expressed for there to be true *emotional nearness:* (1) *caring*, (2) *acceptance*, (3) *trust*, and (4) *understanding*.[151] Important aspects of these qualities need to be present for genuine *emotional nearness* to be felt.

  Caring means being concerned for the welfare and continued growth of each other, always valuing the other as a special person, where one feels no doubt about the nature of this *caring*.

  Acceptance involves regarding each other as persons with dignity and worth, having respect not necessarily due to what the other person has done or said; in fact, it may be in spite of what they have done–because there is *unconditional acceptance.* Recognizing the humanness of us all, we realize that there will be faults as well as noble qualities, so we accept some of the bad along with the good. As humorously suggested by another counselor, John Greene, acceptance may involve "liking more about each other than what you dislike" (lecture, 1968, Florida State University).

Trust takes on an important meaning for *emotional nearness.* It is not merely trusting another with possessions or secrets. *Trust* for *emotional nearness* means that you can reveal yourself fully to the other, telling what you have done or thought, without fear of being judged or ridiculed or belittled, either in private or in front of other people. *Emotional nearness* is hard to maintain if this level of *trust* is not present.

Understanding by the other person means that one has the feeling that the person understands you completely, "at least sometimes." Obviously, people are not going to completely understand each other always; however, for some crucial or key issues, there should be genuine attempts to understand one another, even though possibly not agreeing on the matter.

The above qualities, which Rutledge recognized as being important for *emotional nearness* to exist, can be helpful to cultivate and seek to maintain, especially in valued relationships.

- **Take time for fun** is a theme used by both the *Active Parenting* program and the STEP program.[78,79] Following the suggestion of Dreikurs, these programs recommend weekly family meetings, in which each family member takes turns in leading, and open discussion is encouraged. Agenda items, added by anyone during the preceding week, may include: sharing thanks for events of the past week, discussion about some problem, family rules, planning menus for the coming week, discussing upcoming family activities, and any other concerns. Besides these, one of the items is to plan some fun activities for the family, or "taking time for fun." Without intentionally planning such activities, time can easily slip away without having much family fun.

6. Wisdom from the *Bio-Psycho-Sociological* Approach
(Genetics and biology affect behavior)

The *bio-psycho-sociological* approach involves viewing how genetics and biology affect individual behavior. The following are some of the prominent *wisdom of the ages* of this approach.

• **Genes affect behavior,** that is, sometimes nature wins out over nurture. Likely this is not startling news to parents today; however, the extent of it has been debated for years. The genetic influence has long been suspected or even inferred by many early writers, including Gesell, Bowlby, Allport, and Horney, as discussed above. Yes, genetic and biological issues, which are beyond the control of parents, do affect our children's behavior.

　　The early wisdom of the ages did not reveal much solid data about the genetic influences and the effects of biology on the developing child. It now is a rapidly growing and emerging field and is very multi-disciplinary. The fields of psychology, sociology, psychiatry, and physiology, along with various areas of the medical sciences contribute to this knowledge base for parents.

　　Indirectly, these *bio-genetic* influences relate to many of the issues which concern parents in their child's early years of development. Much of this is covered in books regarding early infant and child development. Some of these books have been mentioned earlier.

　　There are pioneers in the field. From the psychological perspective, Donald O. Hebb, writing his 1949 book, *The organization of behavior: a neuropsychological theory,*[152] is considered to be the father of neuropsychology and neural networks,[153] also referred to as biopsychology. Yet, preceding Hebb was the work of Knight Dunlap and his 1914 book, *An outline of psychobiology.*[154]

　　From the sociological viewpoint, an early 1974 writing was by Edward O. Wilson, *Sociobiology: The new synthesis,* and revised recently.[155] Another later book by Anthony Walsh, *Biosociology: An emerging paradigm,*[156] explores the social domain, including influences upon socialization, learning, gender roles and differences, sexuality, deviance, and criminality.

　　Then, from the psychiatric standpoint, Russell Gardner credited Eli Robins, whose career spanned much of the latter 1900s, and his colleagues with integrating psychiatry with medical science, applying the scientific method.[157]

　　Similar to these movements is the more recent emergence of *behavioral genetics* or *bio-genetics*, revealing how many behaviors result from genetic influences. Two books review this area, Rothwell's, *Understanding genetics: A molecular approach,*[158] and Brown's, *Genetics: A molecular approach.*[159] As may appear, these books were written more for the student or professional rather than parents.

Applying genetic factors to parenting, Katherine Karraker & Priscilla Coleman, in their chapter, "The effects of child characteristics on parenting,"[160] noted that there is growing evidence of genetic influences affecting parental behaviors and interactions with their children. They have reviewed studied spanning over forty years. Some have examined *shared genes* between the parent and child in homes with both adoptive and non-adoptive children, observing instances of more favorable treatment for the *shared genes* non-adoptive children.

Also, genetically influenced behaviors of some children have a marked influence upon the parental role, indicated by parents' reactions to children with ADHD (discussed below) by possibly using harsher discipline with them, or by their helping to provide special opportunities for a gifted child. This interestingly reveals that the same parent may use different styles of parenting and discipline with different children in the family–a fact that may at times be appropriate, yet may not be desired. For example, Karraker & Coleman noted that "when parents of difficult children provide warm and stable rearing with appropriate and consistently applied discipline, the child's behavior is likely to become less challenging over time" (p. 158).

They also noted that numerous factors may cause different effects upon the parents, prompting differing reactions to their children, due to things such as: birth order of the children, family size, parental preference for one of their children, similarities between a parent and child's personality or appearances, one child being more effective in gaining parental attention, and possibly influences.

A major portion of their article focuses upon the differing effects due to a child's temperament as well as age, gender, and physical attractiveness. However, **they caution** that most studies on these influences are merely correlational studies–that is, only establishing that there is a relationship between two variables but not necessarily a *cause and effect* relationship. Before too much can be concluded from the effects of these variables, Karraker & Coleman recommended that there is a need for more complex studies involving possible other third-affect variables and even some experimental studies with appropriate controls.

- ***ADHD, attention deficit hyperactivity disorder,*** is not a *wisdom,* as such; however, the topic has been one of concern for many parents. ADHD has long been suspected of having a biological basis. While there was some early thought by Feingold that diet was the contributing cause,[161] newer studies clearly indicate that it is related to a slower development of the brain. Magnetic resonance imaging (MRI) studies of the brain were conducted by the colleagues of the National Institutes of Health and reported in the *Proceedings of the National Academy of Science.*[162] They found that children with ADHD have normal brain development; however, it is delayed by as much as three years in the frontal cortex areas of the brain that supports higher-order executive control functions. This includes functions that can suppress inappropriate actions, assist with focusing attention, and moment-to-moment memory functioning.

One should consult a pediatrician for a proper diagnosis. Current information can be found at numerous websites, including: the National Institute of Mental Health, www.nimh.nih.gov, under "mental health topics;" the Centers for Disease Control and Prevention, www.cdc.gov, using an alphabetical search; and, the American Academy of Pediatrics, www.aap.org, under "health topics."

This *bio-psycho-sociological* approach, though not producing prominent classic *wisdoms,* has a few other topics that might interest some parents. Most such topics could be explored through the web sites noted above under the ADHD discussion. The following are some, though not an exhaustive listing: allergies, autism, Down's syndrome, fetal alcohol syndrome, food additives, and sexual orientation.

Related to the *bio-* approach, this chapter may be of interest to some: "Parenting children with developmental disabilities," by Robert M. Hodapp & Tran M. Ly, in the edited book, *Parenting: An ecological perspective.*[163] While essentially written to professionals, there are numerous resources listed that would be useful for parent support groups.

When nothing seems to help, I go and look at a stonecutter hammering away at his rock, perhaps a hundred times without as much as a crack showing in it. Yet, at the hundred and first blow, it will split in two and I know it was not the blow that did it – but all that had gone before.
– *Jacob Riis, Journalist and Author, 1846-1914)*

---

7. *Wisdom* from the *Eclectic* Approach

The e*lectic* approach involves looking at parenting issues or problems by use of *several theories or viewpoints*, often using themes which have been discussed above in previously mentioned approaches. This often utilizes the ecological or systems approach, with some focusing on specific problem situations. The following are some of the prominent *wisdom of the ages* of this approach, much of which has resulted from research in just the past decade or two.

- **Parenting is influenced by our personality, relationships, and bio-genetic factors.** This is the theme of an article, "Developmental origins of parenting: Personality and relationship factors," by Joan Vondra and others in *Parenting: An ecological perspective.*[164] The authors reviewed studies dealing with several of the approaches discussed above, the *personality*, the *interactional*, and the *bio-psycho-sociological*.

    They found mounting evidence that our parenting style is decidedly influenced by our personality type and the nature of our relationships with others, as well as some bio-physical/genetic influences. These findings suggest that, as parents, different ones of us will likely prefer varying methods of discipline. This factor gives support to the notion that some of the above parenting approaches will appeal to some parents, while another approach may appeal to others. There is no one prescription that fits all of us.

- **Parenting is influenced by our psychological health and maturity.** Vondra and colleagues also found that positive *personality* factors influencing the effectiveness of parenting were: (1) parents with fewer symptoms of depression, or neuroticism; (2) parents who were more outgoing and sociable, or leaning more towards extraversion; (3) those showing agreeableness, leaning more towards compassion rather than antagonism in thoughts, feeling, and actions—that is, being more "softhearted, good-natured, trusting, helpful, forgiving, gullible, and straightforward" in contrast to being more "cynical, rude, suspicious, uncooperative, vengeful, ruthless, irritable, and manipulative"(p. 41); (4) those more open to experiences; and, (5) parents demonstrating conscientiousness (those who were more organized, having higher standards, and striving to achieve his or her goals), in contrast to those who were easy going, somewhat careless, and experiencing more disorder.

    Interestingly, in exploring why these personality traits appear to be linked to parenting, Vondra and others suggested that a key factor may be due to *attribution.* An example of *attribution* was given of a child whining. Parents demonstrating more positive factors noted above would tend to *attribute* the whining to the child being tired, in contrast to linking the whining to the child seeking to manipulate them. These *attributions* may then lead to positive or negative moods and emotions related to the above personality traits.

- **Parenting is influenced by the quality of our relationships.** Vondra and colleagues, referring back to a 1938 study by Lewis Terman on marital happiness, found other studies supporting the evidence that happily married mothers tended to have more positive relationships with others outside of the marriage. And, that parents who had positive relationships with their partner and social support networks also had more positive parenting interactions, observing that they "generally show greater respect for, involvement in, and patience with their children" (p. 48). The marital relationship theme is also explored extensively in the chapter by Frank Fincham & Julie Hall, "Parenting and the marital relationship."[165]
      These findings give support to the value of marital enrichment programs. A frequently heard theme used to promote them is that enhancing the couple relationship will help to foster better family life, including relations with the children.

- **Parenting is influenced by personal social networks** is the topic of a chapter by Moncrieff Cochran and Susan Walker.[166] Their message essentially was that a parent's own parenting skills were enhanced by involvement in social networks, involving friends and kin. Of special note, they reported that when parents are involved in parenting programs they tend to become more involved in social networks, which in turn betters their parenting abilities.

- **Parenting is influenced by parents' jobs and dual careers.** This is the topic explored by Ann Crouter and Susan McHale, in their chapter, "The long arm of the job revisited: Parenting in dual-career families," in *Parenting: An ecological perspective.*[167] They reviewed studies back to the mid-1900s, including the classic study by Mirra Komarovsky, *Blue collar marriage.*[168]
      Of likely interest to many parents, they found that in families with working mothers, there was only slightly less time spent with their children in contrast to mothers who stay

at home. Also, in such situations, fathers tended to become more involved with the children. The authors further noted that studies tend to support the notion that mothers' employment does not increase risk factors for their children.

The authors also found that the type of work experience has an influence upon values parents might emphasize with their children. For example, those working in small establishments may tend to see the value of striving and achievement. Working in a more bureaucratic setting, parents may see the greater importance of interpersonal skills for getting along with others. Findings of Melvin Kohn, the 1977 author of *Class and conformity: A study of values,* were noted, suggesting that middle class workers tend to emphasize independence and initiative in contrast to the working class occupations which tend to stress obedience and conformity.

- ***Parenting, likewise, is influenced by parents' ethnicity and culture.*** The topic is extensively reviewed in the article, "Socioeconomic status, ethnicity, and parenting," by Brigit Leyendecker and others.[169] Upon reviewing numerous studies including Asian, Central American, Latin American, Lebanese, and Mexican immigrant families, they especially focused upon issues related to family values that encourage independence and interdependence and contrasting aspects of various styles of parenting. Many cultures place strong emphasis upon family emotional interdependence, duties and obligations, even in instances where independence outside of the home was taught and valued. It was common among some cultures to practice what might be called permissive indulgence with young preschool children, while later expecting them to be obedient and following a more demanding authoritarian style of parenting.

  While a detailed summary of all such influences would be inappropriate here, we might conclude, as before, that parents from various backgrounds, including different cultures and ethnicities, are apt to find some of the above parenting practices and *wisdoms* more appealing than others.

- ***Most parenting programs today are eclectic.*** Many parenting programs have been mentioned above in other sections of this article, indicating their emphasis of specific major themes. For example, the Active Parenting and the STEP programs were discussed under the *social order* approach due to their emphasis upon maintaining order in the family and the use of consequences when family rules are broken. However, they also were both discussed under the *personality-character* approach, since a major aspect of their underlying theory also deals with different expressions of a child's personality when the child responds to being discouraged, and the need for courage, encouragement and love. Likewise, behavior management programs, while emphasizing *social learning*, also include, as do Active Parenting and STEP, the need for good communication, an *interactional* approach.

The point of these examples is to illustrate that while most programs may emphasize some primary theme, they tend to incorporate several approaches in the final product. When developing a program, many authors, while stressing their own primary concern, recognize the value of other approaches or theories. Consequently, they will include aspects of the other theories into their own program, making the final version *eclectic,* that is, a mixture of theories and approaches. For sake of simplicity, such programs will not be further discussed in this *eclectic* section, since the major themes and theories of parenting programs have been discussed in earlier sections.

Besides the *wisdom* noted above pertaining to the *eclectic* approach, many other topics involve specific family or parenting *situations.* Many topics arise from *ecological* factors–that is, interactions and transactions between family members and multiple social systems outside of the family. For parents, information or support tends to be conveyed either through books, parenting programs, or support groups–which typically include recommended actions to resolve problems or help with improving upon or acquiring new skills. Support groups may be for either parents or children. In addition, many of the issues are approached through community or school related programs, offered directed to children and youth.

The following are some of the more typical topics or issues of the *eclectic* nature that parents may wish to explore further:
- Adoptive and foster parenting
- Bilingual families
- Blended families, step-parenting
- Child bearing
- Death experienced by children
- Delinquency
- Diverse cultures; child rearing issues
- Extended absence of parent
- Fathering issues
- Gay/Lesbian parenting
- The legal system and families

- LGBT issues related to growing up (lesbian, gay, bisexual, and transgender)
- Parenting challenged or exceptional children
- Poverty and families
- Preparation for school
- Runaways
- Sibling rivalry
- Single parenting
- Substance abuse; addiction issues
- Teen pregnancy/parenting
- Toilet training

One might explore the internet for organizations and programs that offer assistance to families on most of the above topics. Several specific resources exist for parents to find more information about many of the above topics. Two internet resources have been developed through the efforts of professionals at the land-grant university Cooperative Extension programs throughout the country. One is the "Children, Youth and Families Education and Research Network" (www.cyfernet.org). It provides research-based information of many topics of interest to parents. In addition, there is the "National Extension Relationship & Marriage Education Network" (www.nermen.org). Both of these can provide helpful information for families.

There are two prominent publishing companies which specialize on parenting topics of diverse subjects: (1) Active Parenting Publishers (www.activeparenting.com), mentioned earlier, founded by Michael Popkin, and (2) Parenting Press (www.parenting press.com)–both of which have numerous books and programs on a wide range of subjects.

Concluding Thoughts

We hope you keep exploring

It is our wish that these *wisdoms* have been useful for you. We encourage you to keep looking and asking whenever questions arise. As mentioned in previous articles, parents should not overlook calling local or regional U.S. Department of Agricultural Extension Service (under U.S. Government or county office listings in phone directories), asking to be connected with a family or child development specialist. In some instances such specialists will be in your local county; otherwise, they may be in a nearby or neighboring county. The specialists may be able to help to find literature on desired topics or help in locating parenting programs in the area. Many state offices of the Extension Service publish booklets that are for residents of the state. Most typically available is literature related to infants and young children.

Also, parents could contact community colleges in the area to see if they offer any parenting programs in their adult or community education outreach. Many colleges and universities have departments dealing with family studies or family science as well as child development. Nationally, there are over 100 colleges offering CFLE (Certified Family Life Educator) preparation, aiding students to become professionally trained to work with families. Faculty at such institutions could be contacted as a resource. In addition, local libraries and neighboring child care-centers may be of help in locating desired resources or programs.

Also, as you do search further, keep in mind the benefit of finding programs that have proven themselves, being *evidence based,* that is, programs that have been found in research studies to be effective. In a recent study, Jennifer Kaminski and others with a unit of the U.S. Dept. of Health and Human Services analyzed 77 programs that were directed to parents with children aged 0 to 7 years, looking for components of programs that were found to be most effective.[170] For this age group, 0 to 7, the following aspects of programs were found most beneficial: the teaching of emotional communication skills, positive parent-child interactions skills, responding consistently to children, and the correct use of time-out, as well as requiring parents to practice with their children during the program.

Hopefully, having read previous articles in this book and the above *wisdom of the ages* with highlights of various programs, you have a more informed knowledge and understanding of program content. While there are many approaches, they flow from different perspectives. They provide different ways to resolve issues of parenting. Consequently, parents may realize that:

- Most theories and programs tend to *complement rather than contradict* one another;
- Parents presently do tend to use a variety of approaches in their own parenting;
- There often are a variety of alternative ways to chose from in dealing with the same problem, and sometimes it is beneficial to explore different options;
- There is no "one fits all" model of parenting; we are different people: different backgrounds, different cultural or ethnic influences, different personalities, different inclinations (as clearly indicated by some of the *wisdoms* noted above). So some of us will be drawn to one approach while others are drawn to another; and,
- The old proverb often makes sense: "There is more than one way to skin a cat."

A related thought might occur to you, which refers to the old Chinese proverb: *"Give a man a fish and you feed him for a day. Teach a man to fish and you feed him for a lifetime."* The literature on parenting often serves a similar purpose–some writings are designed to give you quick answers to specific problems, whereas others will seek to help you develop a new attitude and approach which may benefit you for a lifetime. We hope you have found both here.

NOTE: A person might expect a discussion of *values* and *self-esteem.* They are absent because the literature about *values* and *self-esteem* is extensive, with various viewpoints as well as research questions and issues of methodology. A clarifying discussion would be too lengthy for the purposes of this chapter. Many theorists believe values and self-esteen, in terms of how persons feel about and accept themselves, are acquired through the benefits of wisdom presented throughout this book.

References

[1] Fein, G. (1980). The informed parent. In S. Kilmer (Ed.), *Advances in early education and day care.* (pp. 155-185). Greenwich, CT: JAI.

[2] Rousseau, J.J. (1955). *Emile.* (trans. B. Foxley of 1773 work). NY: Dutton.

[3] Bridgeman, Ralph. P. (1930). Ten years' progress in parent education. *Annals of the American Academy of Political and Social Science, 151,* 32-45.

[4] Schlossman, Steven L. (1983). The formative era in American parent education: Overview and interpretation. In Ron Haskins, (Ed.), *Parent education and public policy: A conference report* (pp. 7-39). NY: Ablex.

[5] Sunley, R. (1955). Early nineteenth-century American literature on child-rearing. In M. Mead & M. Wolfenstein (Eds.), *Children in contemporary cultures* (pp. 150-167). Chicago: University of Chicago.

[6] Charity organization work; Its history and progress during twenty years. (1894, April 27). *New York Times,* p. 6. Retrieved January 16, 2011, from http://query.nytimes.com/mem/archivefree/pdf?_r=1&res=9506E2D61431E033A25754C2A9629C94659ED7CF.

[7] Smith, Camille, Perou, Ruth, & Lesesne, Catherine. (2002). Parent education. In Marc H. Bornstein (Ed.), *Handbook of parenting: Vol. 4. Social condition and applied parenting* (2nd ed., pp. 389-410). Mahwah: NJ: Lawrence Erlbaun.

[8] Old and Sold Antiques Digest. (n.d.). *First National Congress of Mothers.* (Originally published early 1900s). Retrieved January 17, 2011, from http://www.oldandsold.com/articles26/mothers-1.shtml

[9] Schoff, Frederic. (1916). The National Congress of Mothers and Parent-Teacher Association. *The ANNALS of the American Academy of Political and Social Sciences. 67(1).* 139-147.

[10] Schlossman, Steven L. (1976). Before home start: Notes towards a history of parent education in America, 1897-1929. *Harvard Educational Review, 46,* 436-467.

[11] Cox, Bobbie. (n.d.). *A synopsis of the first Lake Placid Conference.* Retrieved July 20, 2008, from http://jschell.myweb.uga.edu/history/event/lakeplacid.htm.

[12] Miles, Joyce Beery. (n.d.). *Ellen Swallow Richards: The Lake Placid Conferences.* College of Consumer & Family Science, Purdue University. Retrieved Jan. 16, 2011, from http://www.cfs.purdue.edu/pages/about/history _Richards_lakeplacid.html.

[13] Brim, Orville G., Jr. (1959). *Education for child rearing.* NY: Russell Sage.

[14] Lewis-Rowley, Maxine, Brasher, Ruth E., Moss, J. Joel, Duncan, Stephen F., & Stiles, Randall J. (1993). The evolution of education for family life. In Margaret E. Arcus, Jay D. Schvaneveldt, & J. Joel Moss (Eds.), *Handbook of family life education: Vol. 1. Foundations of family life education* (pp. 26-50). Newbury Park, CA: Sage.

[15] Mintz, Steven, & Kellogg, Susan. (1989). *Domestic revolutions: A social history of American family life.* NY: Simon & Schuster.

[16] Gamson, Byrna, Hornstein, Hope, & Borden, Barbara L. (1989). Adler-Dreikurs parent study group leadership training. In Marvin M. Fine (Ed.), *The second handbook on parent education: Contemporary perspectives* (pp. 279-302). San Diego, CA: Academic Press.

[17] Spock, Benjamin. (1946). *Common sense book of baby and child care.* NY: Duell, Sloan, & Pierce.

[18] Spock, Benjamin. (2004). *Dr. Spock's baby and childcare* (8th ed., updated and revised by Robert Needlman). NY: Pocket Books.

[19] Dreikurs, Rudolf. (1948). *Coping with children's misbehavior.* NY: Hawthorn.

[20] Dreikurs, Rudolf. (1948). *Challenge of parenthood.* NY: Duell, Sloan, & Pearce.

[21] Dreikurs, Rudolf, & Soltz, VIcki. (1964). *Children: The challenge.* NY: Hawthorn.

[22] Fraiberg, Selma H. (1959). *The magic years.* NY: Charles Scribner's Sons.

[23] Fraiberg, Selma H. (1959). *The magic years: Understanding and handling the problems of early childhood.* NY: Fireside Edition, Simon & Schuster.

[24] Ginott, Haim G. (1965). *Between parent and child.* NY: Macmillan.

[25] Orgel, Authur. (1980). Haim Ginott's approach to parent education. In Marvin M. Fine (Ed.), *Handbook on parent education* (pp. 75-100). NY: Academic Press.

[26] Ginott, Haim G., Ginott, Alice, & Goddard, H. Wallace. (2003). *Between parent and child: The bestselling classic that revolutionized parent-child communication.* NY: Three Rivers Press.

[27] Gordon, Thomas. (2000). *Parent effectiveness training: The proven program for raising responsible children.* NY: Three Rivers Press.

[28] Patterson, Gerald R. (1975). *Families: Applications for social learning to family life.* Champaign, IL: Research Press.

[29] Brock, Gregory W., Oertwein, Mary, & Coufal, Jeanette D. (1993). Parent education: Theory, research, and practice. In Margaret E. Arcus, Jay D. Schvaneveldt, & J. Joel Moss (Eds.), *Handbook of family life education: Vol. 2. The practice of family life education* (pp. 87-114). Newbury Park, CA: Sage.

[30] Hill, Reuben, Katz, Alvin M., & Simpson, Richard L. (1957). An inventory of

research in marriage and family behavior: A statement of objectives and progress. *Marriage and Family Living, 19,* 89-92.

[31] Hill, Reuben, & Hansen, Donald A. (1960). The identification of conceptual frameworks utilized in family study. *Marriage and Family Living, 22,* 299-311.

[32] Nye, F. Ivan, & Berardo, Felix M. (Eds.). (1981). *Emerging conceptual frameworks in family analysis* (Reprint of 1966 book, with a new introduction for the 1980s). NY: Praeger.

[33] Keim, R. E. (1997). *A Conceptual Framework for Child Guidance/Discipline Theories and Programs.* Presented at the Theory Construction and Research Methodology Pre-Conference, National Council on Family Relations, Crystal City, VA. Unpublished manuscript.

[34] Bredehoft, David J. & Walcheski, Michael J. (Eds.). (2009). *Family life education: Integrating theory and practice.* Minneapolis: National Council on Family Relations.

[35] Bornstein, Marc H. (Ed.). (2002). *Handbook of parenting* (2nd ed., Vols. 1-5). Mahwah: NJ: Lawrence Erlbaum Assoc.

[36] Bigner, Jerry, J. (2009). *Parent-child relations: An introduction to parenting.* Upper Saddle River, NJ: Prentice Hall.

[37] Frank, Lawrence K. (1928). The management of teachers. *Am. J. of Sociology, 33,* 705-736.

[38] Havighurst, Robert J. (1948). *Developmental tasks and education.* Chicago: University of Chicago.

[39] Havighurst, Robert J. (1958). *Human development and education.* NY: Longmans, Green.

[40] Havighurst, Robert J. (1972). *Developmental tasks and education* (3rd ed.). NY: David McKay.

[41] Carter, Elizabeth A., & McGoldrich, Monica (Eds.). (1980). *The family life cycle: A framework for family therapy.* NY: Garden Press.

[42] Frank, Lawrence K. (1948). Dynamics of family interaction. *Marriage & Family Living. 10(3),* 52-53.

[43] Bossard, James H., & Boll, Eleanor S. (1950). *Ritual and family living: A contemporary study.* Philadelphia: University of Pennsylvania.

[44] Duvall, Evelyn M. (1957). *Family development.* Philadelphia: Lippincott.

[45] McGoldrick, M., Carter, B., & Garcia-Preto, N. (2010). *Expanded family life cycle: The individual, family, and social perspectives* (4th ed.). Upper Saddle River, NJ: Pearson.

[46] Encyclopedia of Psychology. (2008). Gesell, Arnold (1880-1961). Retrieved July 30, 2008, from http://findarticles.com/p/articles/mi_g2699/is_0001/ai_2 699000150.

[47] Hurlock, Elizabeth B. (1972). *Child development* (5th ed.). NY: McGraw-Hill.

[48] Smart, M.S., & Smart, R.C. (1983). *Children Development and relationships* (4th ed.). NY: Macmillan.

[49] Bowlby, J. (1951). Maternal care and mental health, *Bulletin of the World Health Organization, 3,* 355-534.

[50] Bowlby, John. (1958). The nature of the child's tie to his mother. *International J. Psychoanalysis, 39,* 350-373.

[51] Ainsworth, M. D. S., Blehar, M. C., Waters, E. & Wall, S. (1978). *Patterns of attachment: A psychological study of the strange situation.* Hillsdale, N.J. Erlbaum.

[52] Feldman, R. S. (2000). *Development across the life span* (2nd ed.). Upper Saddle River, NJ: Prentice Hall.

[53] Nicholson, Barbara, & Parker, Lysa. (2009). *Attached at the heart: Eight proven parenting principles for raising concerned and compassionate children.* NY: iUniverse Star.

[54] Piaget, Jean. (1960). *The child's conception of physical causality.* New Jersey, NY: Littlefield, Adams.

[55] Piaget, Jean. (1963). *The origins of intelligence in children.* NY: W.W. Norton.

[56] Erikson, Erik H. (1950). *Childhood and society.* NY: W.W. Norton.

[57] Erikson, Erik H. (1959). *Identity and the life cycle.* NY: W.W. Norton.

[58] Kirkpatrick, Clifford. (1947). *What science says about happiness in marriage.* Minneapolis: Burgess.

[59] Galinsky, Ellen. (1981). *Between generations: The six stages of parenthood.* NY: Times Books.

[60] Unell, Barbara C. & Wyckoff, Jerry L. (2000). The eight stages of parenthood: How the stages of parenting constantly reshape our adult identities. NY: NY Times.

[61] Mead, George H. (1932). *The philosophy of the present.* Chicago: Open Court Publishing.

[62] Mead, George Herbert. (1934). *Mind, self, and society.* Chicago: University of Chicago.

[63] Watson, John B. (1919). *Psychology from the standpoint of a behaviorist.* Philadelphia: Lippincott.

[64] Watson, John B. (1958). *Behaviorism.* Chicago: University of Chicago.

[65] Skinner, B.F. (1953). *Science and human behavior.* NY: Appleton-Century.

[66] Skinner, B.F. (1974). *About behaviorism.* NY: Alfred A. Knopf.

[67] Bandura, Albert. (1969). *Principles of behavior modification.* NY: Holt, Rinehart, & Winston.

[68] Gosciewski, F. William. (1976). *Effective child rearing: The behaviorally aware parent.* NY: Human Science.

[69] Brewster, Gail, Ramsey, Darin, & Chapels, Jessica. (2004). *The voucher system behavior management system for home* (2nd ed.). Richland, WA: Crisara Publishing.

[70] Curtis, Steven E. (2008). *Understanding your child's puzzling behavior: A guide for parents of children with behavioral, social, and learning challenges.* Bainbridge Island, WA: Lifespan Press.

[71] Carlson, John. (2002, April). *Adlerian Brief Couples Therapy.* Paper presented at the First Annual Conference: Sexuality & Intimacy: Conflict, Passion & Power. Las Vegas, NV.

[72] Leman, Kevin. (2002) *Adolescence isn't terminal: It just feels like it.* Wheaton, IL: Tyndale House.

[73] LeMasters, E.E. (1957). *Modern courtship and marriage.* NY: Macmillan.

[74] Bennett, Howard J. (2005). *Waking up dry: A guide to help children overcome bedwetting.* Elk Grove Village, IL: Am. Academy of Pediatrics.

75 Parsons, Talcott. (1959). The social structure of the family. In Ruth N. Anshen (Ed.), *The family: Its function and destiny* (pp. 241-274). NY: Harper.

76 Bell, Norman W., & Vogel, Ezra F. (1960). Toward a framework for functional analysis of family behavior. In Normal W. Bell & Ezra F. Vogel (Eds.), *A modern introduction to the family* (pp. 1-34). NY: Free Press.

77 Guerney, Bernard G., Jr. (1977). *Relationship enhancement.* San Francisco: Jossey-Bass.

78 Popkin, Michael H. (2002). *Active Parenting Now Parent's Guide.* Atlanta, GA: Active Parenting. For other books and programs dealing with different ages, see their web site: www.activeparenting.com.

79 Dinkmeyer, Don, & McKay, Gary D. (1997). *The parent's handbook: Systematic training for effective parenting.* Circle Pines, MN: American Guidance Service. For other program material, see their web site: www.step publishers.com.

80 Guerney, Louise F. (1975). *Parenting: A skills training manual.* State College, PA: Institute for the Development of Emotional and Life Skills.

81 Walsh, David. (2007). *No: Why kids–of all ages–need to hear it and ways parents can say it.* NY: Free Press.

82 Becker, Wesley. (1964). Consequences of different kinds of parental discipline. *Review of Child Development Research, 1,* 169-208.

83 Baumrind, Diane. (1966). Effects of authoritative parental control on child behavior. *Child Development, 37,* 887-907.

84 Baumrind, Diane. (1978). Parental disciplinary patterns and social competence in children. *Youth and Society,* 9, 238-276.

85 Baumrind, Diana. (1991). Parenting styles and adolescent development. In J. Brooks-Gunn, R. Lerner & A.C. Petersen (Eds.), *The encyclopedia on adolescence* (pp. 746-758). NY: Garland.

86 Baumrind, Diane. (1991). The influence of parenting style on adolescent competence and substance use. *J. of Early Adolescence, 11,* 56-95.

87 Maccoby, E., & Martin, J. (1983). Socialization in the context of the family: Parent-child interaction. In E. M. Hetherington (Ed.), P.H. Myssen (Series Ed.), *Handbook of child psychology: Vol. 4. Socialization, personality, and social development* (pp. 1-101). New York: Wiley.

88 Psych Online. (2003). *Personality synopsis.* Retrieved July 30, 2008, from http://allpsych.com/personalitysynopsis/allport.html.

89 Allport, Gordon W. (1961). *Pattern and growth in personality.* NY: Holt, Rinehart, & Winston.

90 Horney, Karen. (1937). *The neurotic personality of our time.* NY: W.W. Norton,

91 Horney, Karen. (1945). *Our inner conflicts: A constructive theory of neurosis.* NY: W. W. Norton.

92 McGuire, Shirley. (2003). The inheritability of parenting. *Parenting: Science & Practice. 3(1).*73-94.

93 Adler, Alfred. (1927). *The practice and theory of individual psychology.* NY: Harcourt, Brace, & World.

94 Adler, Alfred. (1963). *The problem child.* NY: Capricorn Books.

95 Education Encyclopedia. (2000). *G. Stanley Hall (1844–1924).* Retrieved Jan.

16, 2011, from http://education.stateuniversity.com/pages/2026/Hall-G-Stanley-1844-1924.html.

[96] Allport, G. W., Vernon, P. E., & Lindzey, C. (1951). *A study of values* (Rev. ed.). Boston: Houghton-Mifflin.

[97] *California Department of Education. (2008). Annotated bibliography: Books, articles, and research on character education.* Retrieved Jan. 16, 2011, from http://www.cde.ca.gov/ls/yd/ce/bibliography.asp.

[98] Joesphson Institute: Center for Youth Ethics. (2008). *Children's books that build character.* Retrieved Jan. 16, 2011, from http://charactercounts.org/resources/booklist.php.

[99] Alder, Alfred. (1930). *Problems of neurosis.* NY: Cosmopolitan Book.

[100] Toman, V. V. (1959). Family constellation as a basic personality determinant. *J. Individual Psychology, 15,* 199-211.

[101] Belmont, L., & Marolla, A. F. (1973). Birth order, family size, and intelligence. *Science, 182,* 1096-1101.

[102] Leman, Kevin, (2004). *The birth order book: Why you are the way you are.* Grand Rapids, MI: Baker.

[103] Berne, Eric. (1962). Classification of positions. *Transactional Analysis Bulletin, 1,* 23.

[104] Harris, Thomas A. (1969). *I'M OK – YOU'RE OK: A practical guide to transactional analysis.* NY: Harper & Row.

[105] Sirridge, Stephen. (1980). Transactional Analysis: Promoting OK'ness. In Marvin M. Fine (Ed.), *Handbook on parent education* (pp. 123-152). NY: Academic Press.

[106] Burgess, Ernest W. (1926). The family as a unit of interacting personalities. *Family, 7,* 3-9.

[107] Bronfenbrenner, Urie. (1979). *The ecology of human development: Experiments by nature and design.* Cambridge, MA: Harvard University.

[108] Bronfenbrenner, Urie. (1986). Ecology of the family as a context for human development. *Developmental Psychology, 22(6),* 723-742.

[109] Okagaki, Lynn, & Luster, Tom. (2005). Research on parental socialization of child outcomes: Current controversies and future directions. In Tom Luster & Lynn Okagaki (Eds.), *Parenting: An ecological perspective* (2nd ed., pp. 377-401). Mahwah, NJ: Lawrence Erlbaum.

[110] Roberts, Thomas W. (1994). *A Systems perspective of parenting: The individual, the family, and the social network.* Pacific Grove, CA: Brooks/Cole.

[111] Faber, Adele, & Mazlish, Elaine. (1980). *How to talk so kids will listen & listen so kids will talk.* NY: Avon.

[112] Rogers, Carl R. (1951). *Client-centered therapy.* Boston: Houghton Mifflin.

[113] Buber, M. (1958). *I and Thou* (2nd ed., Trans. by Ronald Gregor Smith). NY: Scribner.

[114] Jourard, Sidney M. (1964). *The transparent self.* NJ: Van Nostrand.

[115] Rogers, C.R. (1961). *On becoming a person.* Boston: Houghton Mifflin.

[116] Rosenberg, Marshall B. (1979). *From now on: A model for nonviolent persuasion.* St. Louis: Community Psychological Consultants.

[117] Ellis, Albert. (1957). How to live with a neurotic: At home and at work. NY: Crown.

[118] Boeree, C. George (2006). *Personality Theories: Albert Ellis: 1913-2007.* Retrieved Jan. 16, 2011, from http://webspace.ship.edu/cgboer/ellis.html.

[119] Beck, Aaron T. (1975). *Cognitive therapy and emotional disorders.* NY: International University.

[120] Dryden W., & Neenan M. (2003). *Essential rational emotive behaviour therapy.* NY: Wiley.

[121] Glasser, William. (2003). *For parents and teenagers: Dissolving the barrier between you and your teen.* NY: HarperCollins.

[122] Glasser, William. (1965). *Reality therapy.* NY: Harper & Row.

[123] Bateson, George. (1972). *Steps to an ecology of mind.* NY: Ballantine.

[124] Bateson, George, Jackson, Don D., Haley, Jay, & Weaklund, John. (1956). Towards a theory of schizophrenia. *Behavioral Science, 1,* 251-264.

[125] Berne, Eric. (1967). *Games people play.* NY: Grove.

[126] James, Muriel. (1971). *Born to win.* NY: New American Library.

[127] Steiner, Claude. (1990). Scripts people live: Transactional analysis of life scripts. NY: Grove.

[128] Stewart, Ian, & Jones, Vann. (1991). *TA today: A new introduction to transactional analysis.* Nottingham: Lifespace.

[129] Freed, Alvyn M. (1974). *T.A. for tots* (Rev. ed.). Sacramento: Jalmar.

[130] Freed, Alvyn M., & Freed, Margaret. (1977). *The new T.A. for kids: (and for grown-ups, too)* (3rd rev. ed.). Sacramento: Jalmar.

[131] Freed, Alvyn M. (1976). *T.A. for Teens: (and other important people).* Sacramento: Jalmar.

[132] Waller, Willard, & Hill, Reuben. (1951). *The family: A dynamic interpretation* (Rev. ed.). NY: Holt, Rinehart & Winston.

[133] Sprecher, Susan, & Schmeeckle, Maria. (2006). The principle of least interest: Inequality in emotional involvement in romantic relationships. *J. of Family Issues, 27(9),* 1-26.

[134] Jory, Brian. (2008). *Family relations.* Retrieved Jan. 16, 2011, from http://family.jrank.org/pages/1316/Power.html.

[135] Caplow, Theodore. (1968). *Two against One: Coalitions in Triads.* Englewood Cliffs, NJ: Prentice Hall.

[136] Jory, B., Rainbolt, E., Xia, Y., Karns, J., Freeborn, A., & Greer, C. (1996). Communication patterns and alliances between parents and adolescents during a structured problem solving task. *J. of Adolescence, 19,* 339–346.

[137] French, J., and Raven, B. (1959). The basis of power. In D. Cartwright, (Ed.), *Studies in Social Power.* Ann Arbor: University of Michigan.

[138] Safilios-Rothschild, C. (1967). A comparison of power structure in marital satisfaction in urban Greek and French families. *J. of Marriage and the Family, 29,* 345–352.

[139] Wolin, Steven J., and Bennett, Linda A. (1984). Family rituals. *Family Process, 23,* 401–420.

[140] Brody, G., and Flor, D. L. (1997). Maternal psychological functioning, family processes, and child adjustment in rural, single-parent, African American families. *Developmental Psychology 33,* 1000–1011.

[141] Fiese, Barbara H., Tomcho, Thomas J., Douglas, Michael, Josephs, Kimberly,

Poltrock, Scott, & Baker, Tim. (2002). Review of fifty years of research on naturally occurring family routines and rituals: Cause for celebration? *Journal of Family Psychology, 16(4),* 381-390.

[142] Brody, G., and Flor, D. L. (1997). Maternal psychological functioning, family processes, and child adjustment in rural, single-parent, African American families. *Developmental Psychology, 33,* 1000–1011.

[143] Fiese, Barbara H. (1992). Dimensions of family rituals across two generations: Relation to adolescent identity. *Family Process, 31,* 151–162.

[144] Doherty, W. J. (1997). *The intentional family: How to build family ties in our modern world.* Reading: MA: Addison-Wesley.

[145] Biziou, Barbara. (2000). *The joy of family rituals: Recipes for everyday living.* NY: St. Martin.

[146] Blood, Robert O., Jr. (1969). *Marriage* (2nd ed.). NY: Free Press.

[147] Benham, Elyce. (n.d.). *Boundaries.* YBRT, Inc., retrieved January 1, 2011, from http://www.ybrt.org/bounder.html.

[148] Whitfield, Charles L. (1993). *Boundaries and relationships: Knowing, protecting and enjoying the self.* Deerfield Beach, FL: Health Communications.

[149] Rutledge, Aaron L. (1961). Missing ingredients in marriage–nearness. *Social Science, 36(1),* 53-58.

[150] Rutledge, Aaron. (1966). *Premarital counseling.* Cambridge, MA: Schenkman.

[151] Brown, Douglass. (1967). *Emotional nearness.* Unpublished manuscript, Florida State University.

[152] Hebb, Donald O. (1949). *The organization of behavior: A neuropsychological theory.* NY: John Wiley.

[153] Wikipedia. (2008). *Donald O. Hebb.* Retrieved Jan. 16, 2011, from http://en.wikipedia.org/wiki/Donald_O._Hebb.

[154] Dunlap, Knight. (1914). *An outline of psychobiology.* Baltimore: Johns Hopkins.

[155] Wilson, Edward O. (2000). *Sociobiology: The New Synthesis.* Cambridge, MA: Belknap Press.

[156] Walsh, Anthony. (1995). *Biosociology: An emerging paradigm.* Westport, CT: Praeger.

[157] Gardner, Russell J., Jr. (1997). Sociophysiology as the basic science of psychiatry. *Theoretical Medicine, 18(4),* 335-356.

[158] Rothwell, Norman V. (1993). *Understanding genetics: A molecular approach.* NY: Wiley-Liss.

[159] Brown, Terry. (2005). *Genetics: A molecular approach* (3rd ed.). NY: Taylor & Francis.

[160] Karraker, Katherine, & Coleman, Priscilla K. (2005). The effects of child characteristics on parenting. In Tom Luster & Lynn Okagaki (Eds.), *Parenting: An ecological perspective* (2nd ed., pp. 147-176). Mahwah, NJ: Lawrence Erlbaum.

[161] Feingold, Benjamin F. (1974). *Why your child is hyperactive.* NY: Random House.

[162] National Institute of Mental Health. (Nov. 12, 2007). *Brain matures a few years late in ADHD, but follows normal pattern.* Retrieved Jan. 16, 2011, from

http://www.nimh.nih.gov/science-news/2007/brain-matures-a-few-years-late-in-adhd-but-follows-normal-pattern.shtml.

[163] Hodapp, Robert M. & Ly, Tran M. (2005). Parenting children with developmental disabilities. In Tom Luster & Lynn Okagaki (Eds.), *Parenting: An ecological perspective* (2nd ed., pp. 177-201). Mahwah, NJ: Lawrence Erlbaum.

[164] Vondra, Joan, Sysko, Helen Brittman, & Belsky, Jay. (2005). Developmental origins of parenting: Personality and relationship factors. In Tom Luster & Lynn Okagaki (Eds.), *Parenting: An ecological perspective* (2nd ed., pp. 35-71). Mahwah, NJ: Lawrence Erlbaum.

[165] Finchman, Frank D. & Hall, Julie H. (2005). Parenting and the marital relationship. In Tom Luster & Lynn Okagaki (Eds.), *Parenting: An ecological perspective* (2nd ed., pp. 205-233). Mahwah, NJ: Lawrence Erlbaum.

[166] Cochran, Moncrieff, & Walker, Susan K. (2005). Parenting and the personal social networks. In Tom Luster & Lynn Okagaki (Eds.), *Parenting: An ecological perspective* (2nd ed., pp. 235-273). Mahwah, NJ: Lawrence Erlbaum.

[167] Crouter, Ann C., & McHale, Susan M. (2005). The long arm of the job revisited: Parenting in dual-career families. In Tom Luster & Lynn Okagaki (Eds.), *Parenting: An ecological perspective* (2nd ed., pp. 275-296). Mahwah, NJ: Lawrence Erlbaum.

[168] Komarovsky, Mirra. (1962). *Blue collar marriage.* NY: Random House.

[169] Leyendecker, Brigit, Harwood, Robin L., Comparini, Lisa, & Yalçinkaya, Alev. (2005). Socioeconomic status, ethnicity, and parenting. In Tom Luster & Lynn Okagaki (Eds.), *Parenting: An ecological perspective* (2nd ed., pp. 275-296). Mahwah, NJ: Lawrence Erlbaum.

[170] Kaminski, Jennifer Wyatt, Valle, Linda Anne, Filene, Jill H., & Boyle, Cynthia L. (2009). A meta-analytic review of components associated with parent training program effectiveness. *J. of Abnormal Child Psychology, 36 (4)*, 567-589.

APPENDICES

The following two guidelines are provided for those of you who might have a discussion group in which you are using different articles from the book as a point of focus.

The other items that follow are materials that had been prepared for use in group's misbehaviors, problem solving, and handling emotions. You may find them useful to review. In some case, you might find them helpful with groups who are practicing related topics.

Appendix A

Discussion Guidelines

1. **STAY ON THE TOPIC**: Easy to drift.
   "How does this relate to what we are discussing?"

2. **BECOME INVOLVED IN THE DISCUSSION**:
   If a question or thought, ask or say—
   "What do you think about this?"

3. **SHARE THE TIME**:
   We learn most by sharing time.
   "Maybe we can talk about this in more detail later on."

4. **BE PATIENT—TAKE ONE STEP AT A TIME**:
   More questions than answers?
   Wanting instant change—Attempt one thing at a time.
   "Are you expecting too much of yourself or your child?"

5. **ENCOURAGE EACH OTHER**:
   Become more encouraging by doing it here.
   "How can we encourage _____?"
   "How can _____ encourage his or her child?"

6. **BE RESPONSIBLE FOR YOUR OWN BEHAVIOR**:
   Make constructive comments and actions.
   Basic Principle: Each is responsible for changing own behavior.
   Parents must be willing to change, if they expect child to change.
   "What can you do to change your situation?"

Appendix B

Issues to Raise When Discussing an Article

- **Discuss what you see as the implications of the article.**

- **If you have a discussion leader,** have members of the group share their ideas before the "leader" shares hers or his.

- **Discuss examples of the topic you have seen** illustrated in the lives of other parents and their children.

- **Discuss examples brought out in the article** that you see applying to yourself.

- **How important is this theme or topic** to you as it affects parents and children?

- **Discuss how you have or might consider** following the advice or implications of the article.

- **Discuss important issues** that might arise when you seek to carry out suggestions made.

Ground Rules:

- **Pass, if not wanting to comment.** In the course of discussion, feel totally free not to comment on or answering a question that has been posed. When a person declines, the topic may be something that is too sensitive for them to discuss right now. If a person does come to tears when trying to discuss an issue, don't hurry on to someone else. Pause, let the person know you are there and care for them. Let them collect themself. A person will usually continue talking when able, or else they will indicate for the group to continue without their input. Assure them that you can wait if they need a moment.

- **If you are asked a direct question** from someone, realize that you have the right to answer or not answer it. Also, you have the right to ask that person the same question. The moral: don't ask a question that you are not willing and able to answer.

Appendix C

Various Reasons for Children's "Misbehaving"

- Accidents
- Anger
- Anxiety (tensions in family, etc.
- Attention seeking**
- Boredom
- Conflicting preferences or values–or priority of what is important (not always a right or wrong way to do something)

- Confusion or misunderstanding
- Curiosity
- Experimenting, perhaps unaware of possible consequences
- Fatigue
- Fears
- Frustration
- Inadequate feelings**
- Low regard for self, low self-esteem
- Jealousy
- Mixed messages of parents (one parent giving contradictory messages, or one parent's message to the child conflict with the other parent's message, like a double bind to the child.)
- Modeling influences, of others (possibly or parent or sibling) or from TV watching or Video game playing
- Moodiness, bad moods, emotional problems
- Peer pressure, or from siblings
- Personality related; temperament
- Physical/emotional problems; possibly allergies, etc.
- Power **
- Reinforcements from the past, possibly unintended
- Role identification (possibly names they have been called or identifying with someone else who "misbehaves")
- Revenge** (resentment)
- Testing limits

**   One of the "basic reasons for misbehaviors" of the *discouraged* child according to Rudolph Dreikurs and Alfred Adler: attention seeking, inadequate feelings, power, and revenge. Karen Horney has a very clear description of these four in her classic book, *Our Inner Conflicts* (1945), in print.

Source: Developed by Keim and added to the experiences of parents and college aged adults. From frequent experiences with large groups, it is not at all uncommon to "brain storm" a given topic and arrive at most of the ideas generated by some theorist. Clearly, there are far more reasons for misbehavior than just the classic four as derived from Dreikurs/Adler's early writings.

Appendix D

When You Feel Like Yelling, Screaming, or Slamming the Door: Alternatives–to Communicate More Effectively

Or, "Getting others to do what you want, non-violently, using methods you won't be sorry about later on."
–Marshall Rosenberg

Suggestions by Robert E. Keim, Ph. D., CFLE Emeritus

1. **SEND "I" MESSAGES** (Gordon) rather than "You" this or that. Rather than accusing, express your feelings about an issue, not stating them as proven facts. (We're the world's best authority on how we feel; maybe not on the facts.) Example: "When . . . (so and so) . . . happens, I feel . . . (emotion) . . ., because . . . (reason)."

2. **SAY SOMETHING GOOD** (Guerney) about the other person related to the issue you're concerned about. Think of a goal you want and let the other person know you feel it could happen, such as: "I realize that you usually do remember, and I appreciate it;" OR "When you do remember to take the garbage out, I really appreciate it."

3. **TALK ABOUT THE MATTER DIFFERENTLY**:
   a. Possibly ask yourself: "Am I **focusing on the issue** and not attacking the other person's ego, by name calling or such?"
   b. Talk about what is happening (**meta-communication**); for example, "This is crazy, the way we're talking" OR "Wait! "Wait! We're sounding like two kids arguing!"–then, acknowledge that to each other and begin over.

4. **TAKE "TIME OUT"**: Say, "Let's talk about it later when ...."
   a. Recognize that we **EACH HAVE DIFFERENT THRESHOLDS** or tolerance levels on how long we can carry on an argument.
   b. Then:
      1) REFLECT ON **ALTERNATIVE SOLUTIONS** to satisfy both, remaining open to new ideas which the other person might think of.
      2) POSSIBLY VENTILATE FEELINGS in some way, such

as into a pillow—or jogging, vacuuming, or talking with a friend.

5. WRITE A LETTER (or put a message on tape):
   a. AND THEN TEAR IT UP and throw it away; or rewrite it, OR,
   b. Send it, but LIKELY GO ALONG WITH IT to explain what you meant, if there is any danger of it being misunderstood.

6. LISTEN TO "YOURSELF," to your "self talk."
   a. Listening to your own MORE LOGICAL THINKING, or
   b. Let the MESSAGES OF YOUR "SMALL VOICE" guide you to better reactions than what you are doing.

7. DO SOMETHING UNEXPECTED OR DIFFERENT, by forcing a difference response: (Realize, in some way, what you are now doing is not working; do something different.)
   a. STOP AND hug the other person; or hold hands while talking. ACKNOWLEDGE THAT YOU CAN POSSIBLY UNDERSTAND why they did as they did (we do things for reasons; all are not bad).
   b. SAY, "I'M SORRY," when it fits, expressing genuine feelings. FORGIVE THE OTHER PERSON, without putting him/her down.
   c. DO SOMETHING FUN with the other person.
   d. TRY "SITTING DOWN" TO TALK, or change the atmosphere in some way.
   e. ROLE REVERSE, try taking the other person's position, discovering his or her feelings by taking the other side of the argument.
   f. USE HUMOR, trying to SEE THE RIDICULOUSNESS in things, laughing with each other, not at each other.
   g. THINK BEFORE SPEAKING, of how to speak more caringly, or such.

8. LISTEN TO WHAT THE OTHER PERSON IS SAYING, really listening:
   a. Ask yourself, "Am I really letting her/him know I hear what s/he says, feels, and means?" Do I convey in a friendly or caring manner that I understand, possibly reflecting key ideas or words that have been said?
   b. KEEP SILENT UNTIL the other finishes, then respond reflectively on what you heard being said—see if you heard it correctly.

Maybe even ask:"I'd really like to know how you think I could improve things between you and me. Please tell me." Listen then and merely say, "Thank you; I'll consider those things," and do consider them in a way that maybe you haven't before.

Subject Index

AUTHOR INDEX

CPSIA information can be obtained
at www.ICGtesting.com
Printed in the USA
FSHW011146230520
70390FS